Russian Negotiating Behavior

CONTINUITY AND TRANSITION

Jerrold L. Schecter

United States Institute of Peace Press
Washington, D.C.

The views expressed in this book are those of the author alone. They do not necessarily reflect views of the United States Institute of Peace.

United States Institute of Peace
1550 M Street NW
Washington, DC 20005

First published 1998

Printed in the United States of America

The paper used in this publication meets the minimum requirements of American National Standard for Information Sciences—Permanence of Paper for Printed Library Materials, ANSI Z39.48-1984.

Library of Congress Cataloging-in-Publication Data
Schecter, Jerrold L.
    Russian negotiating behavior : continuity and transition / Jerrold L. Schecter.
       p. cm.
    Includes bibliographical references and index.
    ISBN 1-878379-78-X (pbk. : alk. paper)
    1. Russia (Federation)—Foreign relations. 2. Negotiation. 3. Negotiation in business—Russia (Federation) I. Title.
JZ1616.S34 1998
302.3'5'0947—dc21   98-9998
                                                CIP

Contents

Foreword

For anyone planning to travel to Russia for business—be it the business of finance and industry or of politics and diplomacy—this book deserves to be among the first things packed. Pragmatic and forthright throughout, Jerrold Schecter dissects the characteristic Russian approach to negotiation, laying out the stages through which negotiations typically will pass, assessing the tactics that one's Russian counterparts will likely deploy, and offering advice on how one should respond. Furthermore, this nuts-and-bolts analysis is set squarely within the broad framework of Russian history, culture, and enduring values and norms. Schecter's objective is to give the reader a sense of the cultural context within which Russian negotiators operate, and thus of how to avoid misjudgments and misunderstandings in order to reach mutually beneficial agreements. These qualities make *Russian Negotiating Behavior* an indispensable primer for those new to the Russian negotiating game as well as a valuable reference for veterans.

These same qualities also help to make this book an appropriate volume with which to launch the Institute's series of country-focused studies on cross-cultural negotiation. Several years ago, the Institute committed itself to explore the field of cross-cultural negotiating behavior, an understanding of which is clearly essential to strengthening propects for resolving international disputes by political, rather than military, means. The objective of our cross-cultural negotiating project is to illuminate the apparent inscrutability of distant and unfamiliar cultures, to remove the mysteries and enigmas of outlook and behavior that can confound American—or other foreign—interlocutors, thus clearing the way for more productive negotiating encounters.

In addition to Russia, other countries that are a focus for this effort now include China, North Korea, Japan, and Germany. Together with subsequent studies of other countries that play important roles on the world stage but often seem culturally bewildering to their would-be negotiating partners, these volumes will be used by the Institute in training programs in the theory and the practice of negotiating across cultural divides.

The kind of cross-cultural insight the Institute will provide to government, academic, and nongovernmental constituencies requires, of course, authors who are intimately familiar with their subjects. Jerrold Schecter fits the bill. A Russian-language speaker, Schecter began his firsthand acquaintance with Russia in 1968 when he became *Time-Life's* bureau chief in Moscow. During his two-year residency, he traveled extensively in the Soviet Union, making the sort of contacts that ultimately enabled him to play an instrumental role in acquiring Nikita Khrushchev's memoirs. After working as White House correspondent and diplomatic editor for *Time* magazine, Schecter entered government service and, during the Carter administration, participated in negotiations with the Soviets as a member of the National Security Council staff. He has since visited Russia frequently, and in the early 1990s was a founding editor of a joint venture between the Hearst Corporation and *Izvestia* to launch a U.S.-Russian newspaper.

For this book, Schecter has drawn on a wealth of academic studies and ambassadorial memoirs to produce an analysis that not only explores the historical and cultural roots of Russian negotiating behavior but also captures the current negotiating trends in a country that, since the dissolution of the Soviet Union, has witnessed remarkable political, economic, and social dynamism and dislocation. The end of the Soviet empire also has given Schecter access to unique and uniquely well-placed sources—namely, former Soviet diplomats who, in interviews with the author, have provided an insider's perspective on how the Soviet foreign ministry managed negotiations with the United States. This behind-the-scenes information has been complemented by numerous interviews with important players on the American side of the negotiating table.

Schecter's study underscores the endurance of negotiating patterns across decades and across political regimes. Culture changes only slowly, and so the patterns of thought and behavior that culture shapes are likewise resistant to swift transformation. After pinpointing the origins and nature of key Russian cultural traits, Jerry Schecter shows how those traits have endured beyond the tsarist and the Soviet eras. He demonstrates the marked degree of continuity from the Soviet period to the present, and the persistence in today's Russian Federation government of negotiating expectations, strategies, and tactics that were ingrained into the apparatchiks of the Soviet regime. That said, however, he sees a generational process of change now beginning, a process powered by a younger generation of Russians in business and diplomacy who are eager to engage the outside world and are able to do so without the heavy ideological and bureaucratic encumbrances of the Soviet era.

Russian Negotiating Behavior is, in short, an analytically fluent and eminently practical guide to what Western negotiators can expect from their contemporary Russian counterparts. As such, it serves not only as a valuable resource for government officials and private entrepreneurs alike, but also as a fine introduction to the series of country-focused studies in cross-cultural negotiation that will be forthcoming from the United States Institute of Peace.

Richard H. Solomon, President
United States Institute of Peace

Acknowledgments

I would like to thank Richard Solomon and Steve R. Pieczenik for their encouragement and critical suggestions on how to approach the dynamics of the negotiating process. Their hands-on experience as crisis managers and negotiators was helpful in filtering and distilling the impact of cultural influences on the negotiating process. Nigel Quinney's careful reading of the manuscript and his editorial suggestions were of great help, as were Natalie Melnyczuk's diligent research efforts. Joseph Klaits, Sally Blair, and their colleagues at the United States Institute of Peace were genial, supportive, and unfailingly cooperative. Leona Schecter and Barnet Schecter read the manuscript and made helpful editorial suggestions, as did Kate Schecter, who updated changes in Russian society from her own research. The final responsibility is, of course, my own.

Russian Negotiating Behavior

Introduction

The Empire's New Clothes

Negotiating for an apartment in Moscow, for oil-drilling rights, or for strategic arms reductions, Americans are faced across the table by a distinct Russian style. It is a style rooted in Russia's complex history, in which violence and authoritarianism have coexisted with scientific sophistication and Russia's yearning to be accepted as an equal by the West. Those who look to the tsarist and Soviet past will more clearly see the Russian future. The rigid networks of Russian life and present-day bureaucratic disorder make dealing with Russians a high-risk adventure. It is an adventure, however, with great potential rewards. Thus far in the short history of Western negotiations with the Russian Federation the rewards have included a reduction in the threat of nuclear war. The future may bring oil to international markets from the frozen tundra of Siberia and the Caspian Sea. Engagement between East and West may also bring Russia into a new era of peace and democracy.

In 1995 Richard H. Solomon, president of the United States Institute of Peace, suggested I apply my experience as a longtime student of the Soviet Union and Russia—first as a journalist, then as a government official, and later as a historian—to a study of Russian negotiating behavior. This work is part of a broader United States Institute of Peace project on cross-cultural negotiating behavior that will examine differing attitudes and responses to such concepts as the rule of law, compromise, consensus, and timing, and their impact on the course and outcome of negotiations. The work aims to draw cultural comparisons that will provide insight into negotiating behavior and thus make negotiating encounters more productive by reducing misunderstandings. We also hope to provide U.S. negotiators with a clearer sense of what they can and cannot expect from their Russian partners during this unstable period while Russia makes the transition from Soviet communism to a market economy with new and still fragile democratic institutions.

I began my study with an extensive review of the literature—much of it generated during the Cold War, when the West sought to fathom the depths of Soviet character and motivation. I searched for analyses that would expand, illuminate, or disagree with what I knew about Russia from my own experiences in Moscow since 1968. Historians, sociologists, and political scientists who have sought to clarify and define Russian cultural identity have affirmed the durability of its inheritance through the period of Soviet rule. There is minimal disagreement between their scholarly work and memoirs of the Cold War period by American diplomats and negotiators.

These perspectives were illuminated by extensive interviews with a unique and only recently available source: former Soviet diplomats and negotiators. From their side of the story a revealing portrait of Soviet and postcommunist negotiating behavior emerged for the first time. These interviews with Russians would have been impossible under the conditions of Soviet rule. As Paul Nitze noted in his foreword to a recent study of Soviet arms control negotiations, "This information would have been as closely guarded as the capabilities of the weapons themselves."[1] Survivors of the Soviet period freely offered trenchant comparisons of negotiating maneuvers under the Soviet Union and the bureaucratic breakdown since 1991.

Interviews with senior U.S. government officials, ambassadors, diplomats, trade negotiators, and business people offered rich insights into the exasperation and occasional exhilaration of negotiating with Russians both before and after the fall of communism. My personal experiences in Moscow—from 1968 to 1970 as *Time* magazine's Moscow bureau chief, during the glasnost and perestroika days of 1987, and from 1990 to 1994 when I was a founding editor of *We/Mbl,* a joint-venture Russian-English–language newspaper of the Hearst Corporation and *Izvestia* newspaper—provided hands-on verification of changing conditions since the fall of the Soviet Union.

The last rites of the Soviet Union were intoned in the December 1991 declarations of independence issued by its fifteen successor states.

Marxism-Leninism no longer holds sway. The Kremlin can no longer dictate its will over the peoples of the former empire. Even within the Russian Federation, central authority has been severely weakened by the institutional breakdown that accompanied the dissolution of the Communist Party. The chaotic political and economic environment that has since developed leaves in doubt the transformation from dictatorship to democracy.

Yet when it comes to negotiating with Russians, how much has really changed? Do Western diplomats, politicians, and entrepreneurs need to adapt themselves to a new and profoundly different set of beliefs, aims, and strategies on the Russian side of the negotiating table? Or is there a core of continuity that draws its identity from a distinct and consistent national experience?

These questions lie at the heart of this study of Russian negotiating behavior. When we describe and analyze how Russians conduct negotiations, the theme of continuity and change inevitably predominates. The strand of continuity emerges when we locate those enduring traits of Russian identity, behavior, and culture that characterize the Russian negotiator no less today than they did during the Soviet and the pre-revolutionary eras. Yet, while Russian negotiating behavior draws on a heritage that Russians would be hard-pressed to reject even if they wished to do so, there is also a legacy of a more dynamic kind, one that can be disowned or outmoded in part or whole by political and attitudinal shifts. Although our focus is on post-Soviet Russia, the marked degree of continuity with the past means that we need to extend our study to the experience of Soviet-American negotiations since World War II, particularly since the 1960s.

The official whose career was established under communist rule remains psychologically confined by Soviet-era approaches and attitudes, no matter how much the official might wish to adapt. Moreover, the Soviet legacy reflects and reinforces traits that have for centuries characterized a distinctly Russian outlook: mistrust and jealousy of the outside world; ambivalence toward the West reflecting a sense of moral superiority and material inferiority; deep-seated insecurity and—its antidote—willing acceptance of an all-controlling leader; respect for power and certainty of goals; distaste for compromise and readiness to threaten the use of force. The historic record of foreign invasions colored the policy of tsars and Soviet leaders alike, and it still influences Moscow's calculations. The Russians defended their motherland from outside invaders, sought outlets for trade, and maintained control over a vast empire threatened by hostile neighbors on all sides. They saw themselves as the victims of foreign penetration and domination—the oppressed, not the aggressors.

Beginning with George Kennan's influential "Long Telegram" of 1946, American analysts and negotiators came to display an astute appreciation of the maneuvers and machinations to be expected from the Soviet side of the negotiating table. Armed with their own accumulating experience and with the insights of an expanding squadron of Sovietologists, U.S. negotiators were able to engage the Soviet Union effectively on a broad range of issues.[2] The long process of U.S.-Soviet negotiating exchanges helped discourage unfriendly action. In his classic 1964 study, *How Nations Negotiate,* Fred Iklé makes the point that "a history of past negotiations establishes a *habit* of communicating, which may induce governments to keep in touch during emergencies. Such a habit is well ingrained between Moscow and Washington but lacking between Peking and Washington."[3] That habit helped keep forty years of Cold War rivalry and confrontation between the United States and the Soviet Union from bursting into flames.

Certainly, Americans fooled themselves with misperceptions of the Soviet side, not the least of which was the tendency to project American values onto Soviet leaders and to misconstrue the Soviets' real intentions.[4] Henry Kissinger has sharply remarked: "The theme that the incumbent in the Kremlin was in his heart of hearts a peaceful moderate in need of help in overcoming his intransigent colleagues was to remain a constant of American discussions ever after [the Yalta conference in 1945], regardless of the Soviet leader. Indeed, these assessments survived even in the post-communist period when they were applied first to Mikhail Gorbachev, and then to Boris Yeltsin."[5] In the extended debate over NATO expansion, a key argument against enlargement was that it would undermine the democratic Yeltsin and encourage nationalist extremists.

Now that the Cold War is behind us, to what extent can we rely on assessments of Russian negotiating behavior culled from the experience of bargaining with Brezhnev and Gromyko, or Gorbachev and

Shevardnadze, who like Stalin is a Georgian, not a Great Russian? Today, the United States is trying to replace confrontation with new rules for cooperation in a market-based, internationally interdependent system. Dealing with the Russians has become more demanding because the former Soviet Union is in the midst of a wrenching transition from a centrally planned, command economy to a market economy. American negotiators are faced with the challenge of dealing with a fallen superpower that demands equality at the bargaining table. It is necessary to develop a sophistication about how the Russians operate that will bridge the gap between our former adversaries and ourselves and make it possible to communicate both ways: their needs to us and our needs to them. Negotiations managed in this manner—unlike the adversarial negotiations of the early Cold War years—focus on consensus building and partnership in solving problems rather than on a zero-sum, I-win–you-lose confrontation. The United States and the Russian Federation continue to negotiate nuclear arms control (destroying missile silos and removing nuclear warheads); they have added new negotiations to conduct commercial business and develop major projects to produce oil and gas. Winner-take-all is being replaced by win-win, where both sides benefit from mutually achieved solutions.

No longer are capitalism and socialism world-dividing enemies. Convergence, the 1968 vision of Nobel Prize–winner Andrei Sakharov, in which East and West would take the best from each other's systems, has been overtaken by new realities. The balance for Russia's future has tilted away from socialism and toward developing a market economy whose characteristics are still unfolding. Which Russia is real? The one with a precarious ruble, with *mafiya* rule replacing governance, and with secessionist war in Chechnya a foretaste of yet greater internal violence and disarray? Or the Russia of a rising middle class with the beginnings of new legal, judicial, financial, and law enforcement institutions?

With the fall of the Soviet Union in 1991, the centralized sources of political control—the Politburo, the Central Committee, and the Communist Party apparatus—have disintegrated and left a power vacuum that has not yet been filled by the new presidential decision-making system. Once dependable and rigid, the institutions of political control in Russia are now fluid, shifting, and constantly surprising. In the transition from centralized party control to a market economy, new activators have come into play. Where once ideology ruled, now a revived Russian nationalism, money, and "practical interest" (in the form of jobs or regional development) are the rationales motivating negotiating behavior. The Soviet legacy still exercises a significant influence on Russian negotiators, although the younger generation of Russians is beginning to display an un-Soviet-like appetite for risk and flexibility.

Because there is no longer top-down control in Russia, decisions are harder to enforce, contracts less certain to be carried out. One of the most marked changes from the Soviet era is the growing possibility of nonfulfillment and nondelivery of commitments that seem to be made in good faith. The old rules, in which the Ministry of Foreign Affairs reflected unitary political authority and internal bureaucratic discipline, no longer prevail. Today, it is every ministry for itself. After a draft is initialed by the Ministry of Foreign Affairs, American negotiators have to make their own deals with the other ministries involved.

Russia remains a colossus without effective rule of law. It lacks a functioning legal system with judges and courts whose rulings are enforced on property rights and civil rights. There is a criminal code, but laws for bankruptcy, the sale of securities, real estate, banking, taxes, the environment, and personal property remain unwritten or unenforceable in Russian courts. President Mikhail Gorbachev tried and failed to create a legal framework for the Soviet Union, and his successors are still facing the challenge.

This study aims to provide a guide to the characteristic patterns of contemporary Russian negotiating behavior derived from the twin inheritances of national culture and Soviet ideology. Our goal is to provide a road map and guide to the constants of Russian negotiating style and to show how the behavioral patterns and institutional practices of the Russian Federation depart from those of the Soviet Union during the Cold War years.

Chapter 1 examines the enduring impact on negotiating behavior of Russian identity and the Soviet legacy. Traits and behavioral patterns born of Russia's history, geography, and cultural traditions have long shaped how Russians perceive the outside world. Historians have pointed out that centuries of commercial, cultural, and religious isolation have fostered a sense of inferiority and envy while encouraging an inward-looking mentality suspicious of outside influences; centuries of invasion have engendered an obsession with security and an aggressive attitude toward other countries. The tradition of despotic rule, extending from the Tatar invaders of the thirteenth century through tsarist control to Soviet totalitarianism and beyond, has profoundly affected attitudes toward power and authority. Some historians point to child-rearing practices and the role of the Orthodox Church as key determinants of Russian psychology. Whatever its origin, we can discern the corpus of a distinctly Russian outlook in reviewing the experiences of Western diplomats with Soviet officials. Obviously, such characteristics are not identically manifested in all Russians, but Russians do have traits in common. They demonstrate a recognizable style that Western negotiators can readily identify and would be unwise to ignore.

These traits were evident in the behavior that characterized negotiations by Soviet-era officials. Stalin was a Georgian and Khrushchev was a Ukrainian, but the question of nationality was not an issue within the leadership, where loyalty to communist dogma unified behavior and transcended most cultural variants. Mother Russia and the Russian people were the focus of Soviet strength; cultural diversity was subordinated to communist ideology as defined from the ruling center. The classic example was Stalin's victory speech in the Kremlin in 1945 commemorating the end of World War II. Stalin was careful to thank only the Russian people for their contribution to winning the war, ignoring the other nationalities.[6]

The Soviets injected new elements into the Russian negotiating style. The second part of chapter 1 demonstrates that Marxist-Leninist ideology and the political calculus of the Bolsheviks greatly influenced the way in which Soviet negotiators operated. First described by sociologist Nathan Leites in 1951,[7] the Bolshevik Code established a set of rules according to which dominance and control, perseverance, shiftiness, flexibility, and opportunism were the keys to effective political conduct. With dialectical materialism influencing both strategic and tactical decisions, Soviet negotiators were animated by a readiness to attack. They believed in the constancy and the historical necessity of conflict. In the service of Bolshevism they were ready to employ violence and falsify reality. They were motivated by a sense of moral superiority coupled with a desire for recognition as a world power. They respected power and certainty of goals. They were subservient to the concept and the person of the *vozhd*, the all-controlling leader.

After 1985, with Mikhail Gorbachev in power and his "new thinking" reshaping Soviet priorities and practices, several of these traits were modified. In his attempts to reform the Soviet system, Gorbachev underestimated the inertial hold of the Bolshevik Code. Torn between wanting to reform the Bolshevik system and wanting to become part of the Western economic order, Gorbachev allowed his pragmatism to come to the fore. He pushed aside Soviet ideological considerations for a more cooperative and flexible approach to negotiations. However, although Gorbachev and his foreign minister Eduard Shevardnadze represented a departure from the Soviet tradition, that departure has proved to be temporary. With the coming to power of Boris Yeltsin, the tradition has been substantially revived; the psychological conditioning, behavior patterns, and personal style of those raised under the Bolshevik Code continue to dominate Russian negotiating culture. Soviet-trained diplomats and bureaucrats adhere to top-down decision making, a system that lacks adequate provisions for consensus building and the checks and balances of a legal system. The result is most often a shifting and unpredictable negotiating environment, compounded by the peculiarly chaotic circumstances that prevail within today's Russian Federation.

Chapter 2 assesses the effects of contemporary political uncertainty and institutional breakdown on Russian negotiating behavior. Russian nationalism has replaced Marxism-Leninism as an ideological driving force in foreign policy decision making. Whereas the dictates of Marxism-Leninism were defined by a small, disciplined leadership group, Russian nationalism is a volatile, protean force that competing political factions interpret, encourage, and exploit in their own ways. The fierce domestic struggle among them to become the popular champion of nationalism helps explain the remarkable and unpredictable twists and turns in Russian foreign policy. It explains Russia's constantly shifting position on NATO expansion. The absence of decision-making institutions has left a vacuum yet to be filled. Russian negotiators are limited to dealing with specific practical issues. The failure to delegate individual and institutional responsibility leads to gridlock in negotiations, while neglect of executive coordination and control has resulted in ministries making their own foreign policy.

Amid such chaos, however, the twin inheritances of Russian identity and the Bolshevik legacy still exert a potent psychological influence over the Russian people and their leaders. In some ways Russia's changed circumstances have only accentuated preexisting traits. Resentment of the West has been exacerbated by the acute sense of wounded pride inflicted by Russia's loss of its superpower status. The desire to keep up with the West in material terms, coupled with the difficulties of adjusting to Western-style capitalistic market forces and nascent democratic processes, has made Russians yet again wary of being put in a vulnerable, dependent, and inferior position. Yeltsin's decision in 1994 to crush the Chechen rebels rather than negotiate with them reflected fear of further disintegration of Russia and echoed past Russian responses during challenges to Moscow's authority.

Despite Russia's changed circumstances, the Russian negotiating process is still governed by the Bolshevik Code. Chapter 3 describes the various stages in a Russian negotiation: the cautious phase of pre-positioning during which Russian negotiators weigh up and seek to cultivate relationships with their counterparts; carefully scripted, aggressive opening moves designed to force out the other side's position while concealing the distance Russia is prepared to move toward accommodation; the prolonged probing in the midgame, during which Russian negotiators look to exert pressure on and divide the opposing delegation and prevail with their own position; the typically sudden endgame, when side issues are swiftly settled once Moscow believes negotiations on the central subject have yielded the best result attainable under the circumstances.

At each stage the Russian negotiator, who enters with prepared instructions, a predetermined fallback position, and an abiding fear of Moscow's displeasure, enjoys only limited freedom of maneuver. Unexpected proposals from the other side must be referred back to Moscow, where domestic political considerations can exert a powerful influence over diplomatic calculations.

Chapter 3 also examines the tactics typically favored by Russian negotiators, among them: stalling and repeating opening positions; failing to respond to questions so as to create uncertainty; wearing down opponents through intransigence; exploiting entertainment and protocol in order to consolidate their position; operating on the basis

of hidden agendas; treating compromise as a form of bartering; apply-
ing pressure through threats, verbal abuse, and shifting deadlines;
manipulating the press; and operating through back-channel diplomacy. These stages and tactics are illustrated with examples drawn
from both the Soviet and the post-Soviet eras.

The utility of money has been added as an incentive to reach agreement on arms control, trade, and ecological issues. Money has replaced ideology as a rationale for behavior, and who has it and who
doesn't have it influences action and response. The U.S. government
and American corporations are deeply involved with supporting and
investing in the future of Russia, and this American commitment of
funds has changed the nature of negotiations on many levels.

Chapter 4 offers guidelines for specific counterstrategies and coun-
tertactics. The chapter looks at past negotiations and the advice of former and current senior negotiators, bridging past and present Soviet
and Russian behavior and suggesting how to exploit it successfully. A
keen awareness of both the similarities and the differences between
Soviet and Russian Federation negotiating processes is crucial for Western negotiators. No less important is an understanding of which coun-
tertactics and counterstrategies are likely to prove most effective in
dealing with Russian negotiators. Condescending to the Russians, feeling sorry for them, and demonstrating superiority are tactics guaran-
teed to create stalemate or defeat. Listening hard, precisely defining
the issues to be negotiated, and determining the bottom-line needs of
the Russians that can be met within the context of our own carefully
defined goals are critical to success. By assessing both mistakes made
and victories won by Western diplomats and politicians in bargaining
with their Russian counterparts, negotiators can formulate effective
responses.

Chapter 5 surveys the problems of doing business in contemporary
Russia and former Soviet republics. This chapter discusses the difference
between political and commercial negotiations and the importance of
generational changes: the influence of the Bolshevik Code lingers in
senior government officials but is lost on the younger generation.
Although the influence of Russian culture remains strong, changes in
the form of doing business are creating new values that promise adap-
tation to Western market behavior and institutions. The creation of

these institutions—reliable banking, predictable and nonconfiscatory taxation, and business law—remains inchoate, and rule of law is a vision, not a reality, in Russia.

The negotiating behavior pattern described in formal diplomatic situations applies to nongovernmental negotiations by international entities such as the World Bank and the European Bank for Reconstruction and Development, and to the business sphere.

Corporate business negotiations, large scale or small, in the end rely on the creation of a market economy structure. A *mafiya*-ruled marketplace where disagreements are settled by assassination—six hundred bankers and business people have been killed since the fall of the Soviet Union, according to Moscow estimates—cannot function in the world economy because investment capital will not flow into Russia. Experienced business people and young entrepreneurs will find chapter 5 helpful in understanding the context, contradictions, corruption, and realities of doing business in Russia.

The concluding chapter summarizes the competing challenges of continuity and transition in Russian negotiating behavior: class struggle and the Bolshevik Code versus a market economy governed by democratic institutions and legal norms. The drag of the top-down command economy, the Soviet legacy, is under attack from the new business culture grafted onto the old socialist system. The "black economy" undercuts the legal economy and creates a trading mentality dominated by the flight of capital, not domestic investment in new industries. The struggle for democracy and responsive government is still overshadowed by the lingering strength of the Bolshevik mentality and behavior patterns, but change is possible. The chapter provides diplomats and entrepreneurs with a series of negotiating rules of thumb.

Figuring out what makes the Russians tick in their unique manner is a source of endless fascination and practical necessity. The negotiating process between Russians and Americans reveals useful pointers for those with patience, self-assurance, and the ability to listen. For those who know their goals clearly, and pursue them while remaining firm, pleasant, and patient, negotiating can bring both intellectual and material rewards.

▪ 1 ▪

Inheritance

Russian Identity and the
Soviet Legacy

With their strategies and proposals, negotiators bring to the table a set of beliefs, instincts, and expectations that grow out of their political culture. The national characteristics of U.S. diplomats developed over two centuries of political independence reflect an openness that contrasts sharply with old-world tradition. Russian negotiators are shaped by the formalism of the tsarist court and the ideological zeal of the Bolshevik revolution. The heritage of an old professional bureaucracy creates exacting demands for loyalty and conformity. The more rigid the political culture, the more control it exerts over its individual representatives. Like the Soviets before them, the Russians bring proposals precisely formulated in Moscow that demand strict discipline and observance by their negotiators. Americans think of themselves as more flexible and inventive, but in fact their positions are also carefully crafted through an arduous interagency testing and bargaining process.

The differences in style and culture reflect the national experience and the core beliefs of negotiators. For centuries, Russians have negotiated burdened by a besieged mentality that perceives the opposing side to be an enemy—whether of the imperial state or of the revolution or of the Russian nation—and expects a zero-sum outcome from the negotiating encounter. U.S. negotiators stress pragmatic solutions; they bring litigating skills to the table, willing to split the difference for a win-win agreement in which both sides achieve enough of their goals to feel successful.

Centuries of a turbulent, violent history have left indelible marks on the Russian psyche, deeply coloring attitudes toward individual and national survival in a hostile, hierarchical environment. These characteristically Russian reflexes and beliefs were reinforced by Soviet political culture. The Soviets created a Marxist-Leninist behavioral code that retained key ingredients of Russian national character. There is a duality in the Russian personality: on one side is the spiritual, generous, nature-loving Russian; on the other is the cynical, cruel Russian who distrusts his neighbor and betrays friendship for survival and personal gain. The deprivation and brutality of peasant life and the terror of the purges have left to generations of Russians a legacy of fear and suspicion. Fear creates a yearning for the firm authoritarian hand of the Slavophile past, a preference for the familiarity of totalitarianism over the risks of change and an uncertain future.

Boris Yeltsin's reelection in 1996 revealed Russia to be a society divided. Those Russians still fighting against the Western-oriented technological future cherish the images of a third Rome led by the Russian Orthodox Church, a communist utopia, or a Russian variation of a military-controlled market economy modeled on Pinochet's Chile.

In the recent past Soviet negotiators looked on their U.S. counterparts as naive because the Americans did not appear to understand that international concerns were secondary to the Soviet Union's primary agenda, which was to maintain mastery over its empire. We dealt with the Soviet Union as a unitary power controlling all the fifteen republics. Now we have to cope with the aspirations of all the fifteen newly independent states and their more than one hundred different nationalities, all struggling against revived Russian nationalism. The rival powers on the Russian borders, China, Iran, and Turkey, all compete for cultural dominance, and the flow of natural resources has created new pressures and new realities.

The Soviet Union has dissolved, but changes in national character usually proceed at glacial speed, and Russian national identity has yet to adjust to the country's new circumstances. The chaos of the first half of the 1990s has only accentuated several preexisting traits. The rigidity and the content of Soviet behavior continue to mold the outlook and the actions of those officials who grew up in the Soviet system. To understand the underlying forces that drive contemporary Russian negotiating behavior, we need to examine the twofold inheritance bequeathed to Russian Federation negotiators: prerevolutionary Russian culture and the Soviet legacy (especially that set of rules for Soviet political conduct known as the Bolshevik Code).

RUSSIAN NATIONAL CHARACTER:
NATIONAL IDENTITY AND SELF-IDENTITY

Most Russians see themselves as open, fun-loving, frontier people and believe themselves to be very much like Americans. In diplomatic encounters, they play to this shared stereotype, harking back to Soviet-American cooperation in World War II and the victorious linking of American and Soviet forces at the Elbe River in Germany in 1945. *Rodina*, the word for homeland, is feminine, and Mother Russia is the symbol of the nation. In this motherland, women are strong, hardworking, nurturing, long-suffering, and the true heroes of Russia.[1] Love of the motherland and patriotism have long dominated Russian character.

Yet the true Russian character is more complex. The strong feminine side of Russian national identity coexists uneasily with a masculine component. In her 1988 study, *Mother Russia*, Johanna Hubbs argued that Russian peasants' conception of the maternal land served as a contrast and challenge to the despotic and military order of the tsars, who, like the government, the nation, and the state, were seen as "Father": "The turn to the land as mother emerged against a background of social and psychological dislocation produced by the then tsar-mandated modernization of an agrarian society." Today, as in the days of the tsars, whereas "male identity is perceived as precarious . . . woman is regarded as the essence of stability, of life, of growth, of *lichnost*, individuality itself. She is whole, while man is neurotic, torn."[2] In the 1996 presidential election campaign, ultranationalist politician Vladimir Zhirinovsky appealed for votes by linking himself to Russian women as the soul of Mother Russia.[3]

Writing some thirty-six years before Hubbs, the British psychiatrist Henry V. Dicks likewise discerned a tension between two halves of the Russian character. Indeed, according to Dicks, the outstanding trait of the Russian personality is its contradictoriness—its ambivalence. "On one side is the omnivorousness, the tendency to rush at things and to 'swallow them whole,' the need for quick and full gratification, the spells of manic omnipotence, the anarchic demand for abolition of all bounds and limitations. On the other side is the melancholy closeness and suspicion, the anxious and sullen submissiveness, the moral masochism and grudging idealization of a strong and arbitrary authority which is thought of as the only safeguard against the excesses of Russian nature. Authority, thus, if it is to be *authority*, must be hard, deprivational, arbitrary and capricious; if the *vlast* [power] were weak, nobody would obey it."[4]

Whether or not one subscribes to Hubbs's fashionable gendered approach or follows Dicks's psychohistorical tack, the fact remains that Russian national identity comprises a complex set of sometimes contradictory impulses and attitudes. The origins of this complexity owe much to geography and history, both of which have weighed heavily on Russian consciousness.

The Tatar invasion of Muscovy in the thirteenth century cut the Muscovites off from the rest of the world for two hundred fifty years. "The bloody mire of Mongol [Tatar] slavery . . . ," wrote Karl Marx, "forms the cradle of Muscovy, and modern Russia is but a metamorphosis of Muscovy."[5] The Russian sense of a special role, a third Rome, a superpower with a mission, is often traced to the Mongol connection. "Russia is European on the surface, but deep inside it is Asian, and our link between Europe and Asia is the Russian soul. Russia's mission is to unite Europe and Asia," explained a Russian intellectual to American diplomat Yale Richmond.[6] With the fall of Constantinople to the Turks in 1453, Russia's commercial, cultural, and religious isolation was further accentuated, hindering its development for centuries.[7]

Byzantine and Mongol rule served as models for Russia. Russia's vast geographic expanse evolved into a state ruled from its center and organized along paramilitary lines. Service to the state became a duty for both nobles and peasants. Historian Ronald Hingley traced the roots of Russian authoritarianism to the imposition of the Tatar yoke in 1240, after which a Russian prince or princeling was compelled to journey to Tatar headquarters at Saray on the lower Volga to make obeisance to the Khan and to undergo various humiliations before receiving, if he found favor, a patent to rule. "The system," noted Hingley, "put a premium on extreme sycophancy toward the Khan, combined with extreme treachery toward competing princelings—a process of natural selection which only the most cunning, ambitious and obsequious could hope to survive."

"In the end," commented Hingley, "it was the princes of Moscow who revealed the greatest tenacity in ingratiating themselves with their masters and betraying their fellows. . . . Muscovite Grand Princes continued to rule on principles absorbed from the Tatars: arbitrary despotic violence and the total absence of concern for the welfare of the subject."[8]

In the fifteenth century the autocratic Moscow princes conquered Novgorod, the competing commercial city-state that carried on extensive trade with Northern Europe. Novgorod was a republic whose princes were elected and had to swear to uphold charters that strictly circumscribed their powers. In his searching assessment "Russia's Past, Russia's Future," historian Richard Pipes lamented the fall of Novgorod, which "closely resembled the self-governing communes of medieval Europe which contributed so much to the evolution of liberty and rule of law in the West." "Still," Pipes added, "although Novgorod did not survive into the modern era, its very existence demonstrates that Russians are not constitutionally averse to Westernization."[9]

The authoritarian tradition was significantly strengthened in the sixteenth century, when serfdom was established. According to sociologist Dinko Tomasic, serfdom served and bound together the interests of the church, the state, and the landlord. Each of these three forces benefited from a system that not only bolstered the power of the village elders but also fostered in the village dominance-submission relationships, absolute power with dependence, blind obedience, and self-abnegation.[10]

Russian preoccupations with authority, power, and submission evolved as responses not only to the nature of rule within the country but also to the constant threat of invasion from outside. In America the broad expanse of the western frontier was a symbol of opportunity, growth, and freedom for pioneers; the Russian steppes, in sharp contrast, were undefended avenues for threat, invasion, and terror. American settlers conquered the native tribes inhabiting the American frontier in bloody wars and reaped rich rewards of natural resources and economic development. The Russians were subject for centuries to invasions from the east and from the west—the Napoleonic Wars, the Russo-Japanese

War, World War I, the postrevolution allied intervention on behalf of the Whites in the civil war, and the German invasion of World War II.

The "painful experience of centuries of invasion has affected the Russian psyche, resulting in an obsession with security, which in turn induces an extreme habit of secrecy regarding defense matters and a belligerent attitude toward foreign countries," noted Leon Sloss and M. Scott Davis.[11] They cited Richard Pipes's observation that "early Moscow had to establish its sovereignty by conquering territory and incorporating it into Russia, while Western states were being built by their monarchies' suppression of the feudal nobility and church." Pipes argued that the Soviets, like the tsars before them, "consider the status of lands and peoples presently under their control entirely beyond discussion."[12]

With the omnipresent threat of foreign attack, Russians have historically relied on government for security, not for justice. Rule in precommunist Russia was by imperial decree, and the tsar's will was not subject to law. "Soviet leaders continued this tradition of being above the law," noted Yale Richmond.[13] "Not surprisingly, Russians discount the law's ability to provide the truth and justice they seek. More important than the legalisms of the law has been the consensus of the community," explained John J. Maresca, deputy chief of the U.S. delegation to the Conference on Security and Cooperation in Europe negotiations in Helsinki and Geneva. "In Russia, endless exceptions to the law are allowed which permit almost any outcome sought by the courts and the state."[14]

Explaining the neglect for law and legal institutions, Roberto Calasso has written that "in Russia, law is an imported article. Like all exotic curiosities, it stirs the imagination and attracts devotees. But the background to which it is applied is hostile to it. Two possibilities thus present themselves: either law is immediately expelled, because it strives to corrupt the genuine prosperity of the country; or else it is assimilated, but in such a way as to forever be held in contempt."[15]

The struggle to establish and legitimize national authority in Russia has been an unending process that began with the tsars and continues to the present day. By its nature, revolution casts doubt on legitimacy and demands that the usurpers prove their right to govern and their ability to gain international acceptance. All Soviet leaders from Lenin onward pursued this quest for legitimacy. None, however, accomplished the task. The communists' right to rule was never mandated by elections or popular choice: until Russia's free election of 1991, democratic governance was experienced only once, in 1917, during the brief period between the February Revolution and the October Revolution. Soviet parliamentary institutions, such as the Supreme Soviet, had no autonomous power and were in reality no more than organized extensions of the leader's authority. There were no institutions for transition and change, only the designs of the leader exercised through the Communist Party and the secret police. From tsarist Russia through to the end of the Soviet Union, authoritarianism has been the rule in Russian governance. "The result," Richmond wrote, "has been a usually submissive citizenry (at least until 1990), accustomed to—indeed expecting—direction from above, being told what to do and what to think."[16]

In February 1946, attempting to analyze the sources of Soviet foreign policy and to suggest how to deal with the Russians, George Kennan, then a political officer in the American embassy in Moscow, wrote his now famous "Long Telegram." Kennan argued that Soviet foreign policy was a combination of communist ideology and tsarist quest for empire:

At [the] bottom of [the] Kremlin's neurotic view of affairs is [a] traditional and instinctive Russian sense of insecurity. Originally, this was insecurity of a peaceful, agricultural people trying to live on vast exposed plains in [the] neighborhood of fierce nomadic peoples. To this was added, as Russia came into contact with [the] economically advanced West, fear of more competent, more powerful, more highly organized societies in that area. But this latter type of insecurity was one which afflicted Russian rulers rather than Russian people; for Russian rulers have invariably sensed that their rule was relatively archaic in form, fragile and artificial in its psychological foundation, unable to stand comparison or contact with political systems of Western countries. For this reason they have always feared foreign penetration, feared direct contact between [the] Western world and their own, feared what would happen if Russia learned [the] truth about [the] world without or if foreigners learned [the] truth about [the] world within. And they have learned to seek security only in patient but deadly struggle for total destruction of rival power, never in compacts and compromises with it.[17]

Other analysts have accounted for the origins of Russian character by referring to psychological influences such as swaddling at birth—wrapping an infant in strips of cloth to immobilize its arms and legs.

This custom, by severely constraining movement, has been said to engender a mixture of passivity and rage.[18] The Orthodox Church, by offering confession and absolution, has been said both to induce and to make tolerable the greatest psychological stresses.[19]

Former U.S. diplomat Raymond F. Smith, in a book published in 1989, commented, "While each of these theories is fascinating in itself, their importance for understanding the Soviet negotiating style is that they converge around the same point. Whether because of the Tatar influence, the influence of peasant society, the practice of swaddling infants, or for some other reason, Russians are acutely conscious of hierarchical issues in a relationship, and their expectations of behavior differ dramatically depending on how they see those issues in any given relationship."

The role of authority, the avoidance of risk, and the necessity for control are vital to understanding Russian negotiating behavior. They provide the context, the background, and the circumstances within which the specific issues on the table are negotiated, whether between two bargainers at an open market in Moscow or Russian and American diplomats in Geneva. Societies differ in the degree to which they consider the context of transactions important. Drawing on his experience negotiating with the Soviet Union, Smith observed that whereas Americans emphasize content and slight context, guarding emotions but sharing facts, the Soviets do the opposite. Americans focus on the words, Soviets on the pauses. Smith explained:

> We Americans tend to be low-context people. We focus on the substantive issues, on what is being said: "Just the facts ma'am." The Soviets are considerably higher-context. Issues involving authority, risk, and control, and how they affect the relationship among the negotiating parties, are so important to them that it may be difficult for them to get to the subjects on the agenda until those issues are resolved. In fact, though perhaps not on a conscious level, those often are the real issues to a Soviet negotiator. Americans, impelled by democratic impulses, are disdainful of form, downplay its importance, and seek to divorce it from substance. To a Soviet, form and substance are inextricably linked.[20]

Former *New York Times* Moscow correspondent Hedrick Smith arrived at a similar conclusion. "For Russians," commented Smith, "the instinctive question is: 'who is stronger and who weaker' . . . any relation becomes a test of strength." Smith drew on a number of experiences from his time in Moscow to illustrate the point. "If a person bumps into someone or has an accident, he is ready to stand up for himself," a young professional woman told him. "But if he finds out the other one is some official, say, from the District Party Committee, the next moment he is bowing and fawning and trying to avoid trouble. . . . Put a Russian in charge of a little plot of ground or a doorway somewhere . . . and he will use his meager authority over that spot to make life hard for others."[21]

Richard Pipes noted that despite the best hopes, Russia has neither embarked on a slow but irreversible course of Westernization nor been transformed into a democratic market-oriented society. In reality, Pipes observed, "Russia has ended up with a nondescript regime that is unable to provide its people either with the prosperity and freedom of capitalist democracy or with the rudimentary social security of mature Communism." The change from Soviet rule has hardly altered Russia's political culture. As Pipes pointed out, "Until Russians become aware of what they have to change in their own culture, it is unlikely to become a 'normal' society, a condition to which most of them aspire."[22]

THE SOVIET LEGACY

The same preoccupations that shape Russian psychology—the yearning for security, legitimacy, status, authority, and power—also featured prominently in the political culture of the Soviet Union. The philosophical basis was Marxism, a doctrine developed by a German much more concerned with the tides of history in the West than in the East. But Marxism, as interpreted and applied by Lenin and Stalin, inevitably brought to bear the concerns and approaches peculiar to the historical and cultural tradition of their own country. Pipes noted, "Yet while it is true that Marxist *theory* was imported from the West, it is no less true that Marxism in *practice,* as a system of government, acquired in Russia a uniquely despotic character. In Western countries, Marxism . . . evolved into the democratic welfare state. In Russia . . . it produced totalitarianism."[23]

In his landmark studies on the modus operandi of the Soviet elite— *The Operational Code of the Politburo,* published in 1951, and *A Study of*

Bolshevism, published in 1953—sociologist Nathan Leites synthesized Russian classical literature with the ideological tracts of Marx, Lenin, and Stalin to describe and define the rules that governed Soviet political conduct.[24] Leites's definition of the Bolshevik Code remains a framework for analyzing the behavioral style of the Russian negotiating elite.

According to Leites, the Bolshevik Code denied the rule of law, defined truth as the voice of the party's Central Committee, and elevated the doctrine of the means justifying the ends to new levels of cynicism and violence. Leites argued that the Bolshevik self-image formed before the 1917 October Revolution did not change when the Bolsheviks took power. Soviet leaders "have continued to see themselves in the same position as they were in relation to the tsarist government, i.e., out of power and in a dangerous position."[25]

Leites defined the following as key elements of the Bolshevik Code:

- Politics is a war.
- Push to the limit (in any political encounter, such as a negotiation).
- Pressure creates opportunities.
- It pays to be rude (to one's counterpart or adversary). Rudeness intimidates and forces an adversary to seek acceptance by compromising.
- Do not yield to provocations from one's adversary.
- Avoid the danger of allowing personal feelings to intrude into matters of policy ("the party line"). The party leadership knows best.
- More force is better than less force. Annihilating the enemy and starting anew is better than trying to convert a class enemy.
- Enemies cannot be persuaded to accept the Bolshevik position by rational means.
- All politics is a life-and-death struggle of who will dominate whom. Thus, who-whom *(kto-kogo)*—the destruction of the enemy—is necessary not only for victory but also for the survival of the party. The "interests" of the party and the enemy are so incompatible that their coexistence is unstable.[26]

Leites's seminal works have been heavily analyzed. A major retrospective study by Elizabeth Wirth Marvick, published in 1977, emphasized

Leites's use of psychoanalytic theory and method in tracing the origins of elite political doctrines: "As a Freudian, [Leites] sees these group norms originating in the experience of individuals from early childhood. As a social scientist, he sees this experience patterned by group culture, as it is transmitted to members from generation to generation. Political behavior is shaped by such regularities of experience."[27] Leites, noted Marvick, "suggests that Russian culture burdens the typical individual with strong feelings of guilt. . . . He demonstrates how the old Russian culture resolved guilt in a variety of ways, some of them exalting and humane. The typical Soviet solution, however, has been to project guilt onto others, defined as enemies of the Party, and to convert one's own latent fears of being overwhelmed by destructive forces into a systematic, ever more ruthless and violent eradication of opposition—real or imagined."[28]

The preoccupation with overwhelming destructive passion was transformed into the Bolshevik doctrine of "who-whom" (*kto-kogo*), which postulates that the only alternative to being annihilated by one's enemies is to eliminate them first. In *A Study of Bolshevism*, Leites traced the motivation "for an ever-mounting scale of violence" back to this doctrine.[29] If the party does not use violence against its enemies, it opens itself to violence from them[30]—it is a lesser mistake to use too much violence than too little.[31] Marvick contended that "the history of Bolshevism shows what seems to be a high incidence of more or less sincere imputations to enemies of acts or intents of one's own, coupled with denials of such acts and intents in one's own case."[32] Stalin's purges offer ample testimony to the doctrine's practice. The doctrine of who-whom continued to exert great influence on the behavior of Stalin's Soviet heirs, although mass terrorism was replaced with selective repression.

In post-Soviet Russia, policy decisions still betray the who-whom mind-set, as evidenced in Moscow's response to Chechen separatism. First, the Federal Counterintelligence Service tried to overthrow the Chechen leader, General Dzhokar M. Dudayev, through what appeared to be an internal coup d'état but in fact was a political maneuver organized by Moscow and heavily supported by Russian troops. Then, when the Russian troops were caught and exposed by Dudayev's men, President Yeltsin refused to negotiate with Dudayev. Instead, Yeltsin accepted the arguments of his military advisers and his defense minister Pavel

Grachev that an overwhelming application of force would easily settle problems in Chechnya in a matter of days. The massive military assault launched on Grozny in December 1994 resulted in heavy civilian casualties, but failed to overwhelm Dudayev or to end the war.

As both Russians and Marxist-Leninists, the Soviet leaders found that the logic of the who-whom doctrine fit perfectly within their broader worldview. Centuries of invasion from both east and west engendered fear and distrust of the outside world; better by far to strike first against one's external and internal enemies than to wait for their inevitable onslaught. For the Soviets, the greatest external threat was posed by the implacable hostility of the capitalist world. This belief was a bedrock element of Soviet consciousness. Despite his alliance with the West in World War II, Stalin assumed the "imperialist" countries were implacably dangerous and untrustworthy enemies with whom there could be no stable accommodation or reconciliation.

From this perspective, Western efforts to work with Stalin to pursue shared objectives, such as defeat of the Nazis, were especially suspect. Stalin feared the enticing appeal of Western professions of interest in reaching accommodation with the USSR. Fred Iklé noted in *How Nations Negotiate*, "Of all the tricks of which Stalin's ally adversaries were capable, none was more insidious than their repeated declarations of warmest friendship. They could not possibly be sincere."[33] In the spring of 1944 Stalin told Tito's emissary Milovan Djilas: "Perhaps you think that just because we are the allies of the English that we have forgotten who they are and who Churchill is. They find nothing sweeter than to trick their allies. During the First World War they constantly tricked the Russians and the French. And Churchill? Churchill is the kind who, if you don't watch him, will slip a kopeck out of your pocket. Yes, a kopeck out of your pocket! By God, a kopeck out of your pocket! And Roosevelt? Roosevelt is not like that. He dips in his hand only for bigger coins. But Churchill? Churchill—even for a kopeck."[34]

Khrushchev spoke of peaceful coexistence, but reserved the right of the Soviet Union to support wars of "national liberation" against imperialists in Africa, Asia, and Latin America. Political scientist Kalevi J. Holsti has noted that during the Brezhnev years "it became an article of faith that less belligerent policies by the leading imperialist states could be explained by the growth of Soviet military power. . . . Détente was the fruit of nuclear weapons and Soviet military strength, not a change of heart among the leaders of the capitalist world. A particularly favorable correlation of forces made peace and détente possible, not an alteration in the nature of imperialism."[35]

Victor Israelyan, a leading Soviet arms control negotiator during the 1980s, recalled that "unfortunately, the negotiations were based on mistrust. You didn't trust us and we didn't trust you. Our styles were different. We would seek an agreement in general and if you agreed that both of us were seeking peace we would take it as a big victory. Even if it was self-evident we'd say, 'Let's fix it in a communiqué.' This was a game based on mistrust."[36]

The obsessive concern with foreign threats that lay at the heart of the Soviet worldview was also ideological. The Soviets viewed history through the lens of dialectical materialism—a concept that evolved from the work of the German philosopher Georg Wilhelm Friedrich Hegel (1770–1831), who posited that every entity or thesis generates its own opposite, with which it clashes. Out of this encounter a synthesis is created, which then repeats the pattern by generating another antithesis. For the Soviet Marxists, all change was thus the product of a constant conflict between opposites arising from the internal contradictions inherent in all events, ideas, and movements.

Under the Leninist notion of "democratic centralism," the significance of constant change and the definition of objective reality were determined by the top communist leadership and then fed to the masses. Holsti observed:

> Westerners commonly regard conflict as a form of *deviant* behavior. Marxist thought about conflict is almost exactly the opposite. Rather than a deviation from the norm of social intercourse, conflict is an inherent condition of all relationships between different kinds of social formations, international ones being no exception. Conflict is the motor of history, the source of human and social progress. Soviet foreign policy constantly contends with conflict not just because the interests of the great powers may clash, but more importantly, because socialism, a higher form of economic organization, and its leaders must confront the forces of reaction. . . . Diplomatic conflict is a positive indicator that the two antagonistic forms of socioeconomic organization are performing the historical roles assigned to them in scientific Marxist-Leninist thought.[37]

In the postcommunist world the influence of dialectical materialism is evident in the negotiating style of President Boris Yeltsin and high-ranking officials under him—notably, former foreign minister Andrei Kozyrev and his successor, Evgeni Primakov. Their definition of objective reality is based on political pressures generated by extreme nationalism. These officials are forced to constantly struggle for power in a society without strong law enforcement and viable political institutions. This behavioral pattern of accepting, then rejecting, of agreeing, then demanding more, is an ingrained response based on long years of operating in a political culture organized around notions of democratic centralism and justified by the ideological construct of dialectical materialism. This erratic conflictive pattern is considered normal and thus legitimate and justifiable. In her classic study of Soviet behavior, *Soviet Attitudes toward Authority,* anthropologist Margaret Mead noted: "The typical Soviet figure of speech is to unmask in one gesture; one position, that of friend, is replaced by a diametrically opposite one, that of enemy. . . . In Soviet expectation the closer the relationship and the greater the trust, the greater the danger, the more possible a betrayal, and the greater the need for suspicion."[38]

In *An Inquiry into Soviet Mentality,* Gerhardt Niemeyer and John S. Rehstar stated that the Russians are highly incalculable, idiosyncratic, and even unpredictable in their unpredictability. "While they seek to collect information and learn from experience, their idea of reality is so distorted by their millennial vision, and their dialectic reasoning so involved and often contrived, that it is impossible to compare their instrumental reasoning with any reasoning familiar to westerners."[39]

On a less cosmic level, dialectical materialism, the philosophical foundation for Marxist-Leninist thought, allows for any change of tactics or backing away from commitment to suit the needs of the moment. During the talks in Geneva in 1977 on SALT II (the second Strategic Arms Limitation Treaty), General Rowny complained to his counterpart, General Trusov, that the Soviet argument was illogical and contradictory. "Don't waste your time trying to understand it," Trusov said. "It's a matter of dialectical materialism." He then provided Rowny an example: A factory worker went to his political commissar with a dilemma. Two fellow workers, one with dirty hands and the other with clean hands, asked him for water. There was only enough water for one to wash his hands.

"Which one do you think deserves the water?" asked the commissar.

"The one with dirty hands," said the worker, "because he has the greater need."

"Wrong," said the commissar. "The one with clean hands should be rewarded for his habits of cleanliness."

Several days later the worker and the commissar met again. The worker said the problem had come up again, and proudly announced that he had given the water to the worker with clean hands.

"Wrong," said the commissar. "You should have given it to the worker with dirty hands; he had the greater need."

When the worker complained about inconsistency, the commissar said, "You're now beginning to understand dialectical materialism."[40]

Perseverance, guile, and opportunism are keys to conduct in the Bolshevik Code. "The Party leadership," according to Leites, "need not be concerned with consistency in its public statements. Again, only effectiveness is important."[41] Under the Soviet system, when the communist leadership declared a new reality, all the forces of the government, police, military, and propaganda coordinated their efforts to create a new political line. In fact, the falsification of reality has a tradition extending before the Soviets. Margaret Mead observed in her 1951 study of Soviet character:

> In Tsarist Russia there were attempts to give an appearance of reality and solidity to matters of dubious truth, as in the great insistence on written confessions as early as the seventeenth century or in the Potemkin villages. . . . In Bolshevik doctrine, what the leadership decides shall be done is what history has already ordained is going to happen (although it is also what needs the utmost effort to make it happen). . . . Nevertheless a great variety of falsifications and theatrical enactments of the ardently desired or deeply feared do occur.[42]

Even when the new reality failed to exist, government officials had to believe in and promote the general line handed down by the Politburo. If any intellectual leader dared to protest, his or her acts became a violation of the law or proof of mental illness requiring institutionalization.

In 1968 the Soviet press portrayed the Soviet invasion of Czechoslo-vakia as an attempt to suppress "counterrevolution" and "German revan-chism," a code phrase for the revival of German influence. Actually, the liberal government of Alexander Dubcek advocated "socialism with a human face," an attempt to reconcile communism and modernization. Coincidentally, I arrived in Moscow on August 28, 1968, the day after the invasion. There was a news blackout from Prague; there were no pictures or stories of Czech opposition. A wave of propaganda in the government-controlled press and television railed against the failure of the Czech government to prevent a return of counterrevolutionary elements that would have led to Western domination and German con-trol if Soviet troops had not arrived in time. When I went to a restaurant to sample opinions, a young worker and his wife quoted a *Pravda* story warning of "a revival of German revanchism"; my Russian-language tutor shook her head in wonder at the irony of a Czech rebellion when "you think of what we sacrificed to help them recover from the German occupation."

The readiness to falsify reality to justify repressive action is by no means a thing of the past. Witness Yeltsin's public insistence in Decem-ber 1994 that the bombing of the Chechen capital of Grozny had stopped, even though the world was watching television pictures of Soviet aircraft firing rockets at civilian targets.

The increased uncertainty in the post-Soviet era has intensified a willingness to deceive—a tendency that is not so different from twenty years ago, when a young Soviet consultant on foreign policy told jour-nalist Hedrick Smith, "Deceit is a compensation for weakness, for a feeling of inferiority before foreigners. As a nation, we cannot deal with others equally. Either we are more powerful or they are. And if they are, and we feel it, we compensate by deceiving them. It is a very important feature of our national character."[43] A more complex form of deception has taken hold during the post-Soviet period. It is shown in such episodes as the disappearance of $6 billion from the Vnesh-torg Bank (the central foreign trade bank) in 1991 and the sales of state corporations to selected private banks at prices far below their market value. This high-level corruption, occurring at the same time as Russia is asking for foreign aid, demonstrates the extent of the Rus-sian malaise.

Soviet cynicism in matters of truth went hand in hand with disdain for "bourgeois" values. Leites maintained that if the Soviets allowed conceptions of honor to enter into their political calculations, they had in essence surrendered to their enemy's control, because "a code of honor requires specific reactions to certain acts of others, and thereby allows an enemy to predetermine one's behavior." Therefore, Leites stated, "real Bolsheviks never permit themselves to put political questions on a sentimental basis."[44]

Instead, when it comes to negotiating style, the Soviets "strive to push to the limits of their strength, using verbal assaults as one of their means and trying hard and long for all their objectives, whether big or small. They fiercely resist anything which seems to be a concession unless a condition of duress requires them to retreat—then, perhaps, quite substantially."[45]

Soviet attitudes toward concession tallied closely with the traditional Russian view of compromise, which is culturally conditioned and has a different context and meaning than in the West. Lenin's definition of compromise is that it can be exploited as part of a tactical moment to achieve a goal.[46] In his 1989 work on Soviet negotiating behavior, Raymond Smith explained that "compromise, in Russian eyes, opens the gateway to domination. The word in Russian, *kompromis,* is not a native Russian word and, in the Russian mind, tends to have more the flavor of what a Westerner would understand as 'to be compromised' than to make reciprocal concessions to arrive at a mutually agreeable or beneficial agreement. A Soviet negotiator will, therefore, tend to disguise his side's compromises behind verbiage or bluster, or to decline to admit that his side's position has changed. Alternatively, he will trumpet a compromise as an enormous concession and go on the offensive, demanding an equal or greater compromise from the other side in return."[47]

In an early study of Russian negotiating behavior in 1951, Philip Mosley, adviser to several U.S. delegations and a specialist on Russia, likewise pointed out that the word "compromise is not of native Russian origin and carries a negative connotation." Giving up on a demand makes a Soviet negotiator feel "he is losing control of his will and becoming subject to an alien will. Therefore, any point which has finally to be abandoned must be given up only after a most terrific struggle.

The Soviet negotiator must first prove to himself and to his superiors that he is up against an immovable force. Only then is he justified in abandoning a point."[48]

In the view of human rights activist Vladimir Bukovsky, "Compromise is a bad word in the Soviet Union. In this, ideology reinforced cultural traditions. The traditional view of how a person should be is principled, strong, honest. Ideology reinforces this with the notion of no compromise with the class enemy. To call something a principled, uncompromising position is a compliment. In the West, it would be called rigid. There is a belief in Russia that there is one Truth, and that you are supposed to try and achieve it, not compromise it. This is reinforced by Marxism/Leninism."[49]

"The Anglo-American idea of a political compromise," observed Margaret Mead, "is based on the expectation of there being at least two sides to a question, so that the workable compromise represents a position somewhere between or among a series of positions each of which is sincerely believed in and stoutly defended. But the Bolsheviks' idea of the Line is more accurately represented by the figure of a lens which is correctly focused; there is only one correct focus for any given situation, and this is not seen as arrived at by finding some mid-point between lens readings which are too open and those which are too closed; rather, all settings except the correct focus are seen as deviations from the single correct position."[50]

Americans see compromise as splitting the difference and seeking a means for concluding a deal; Russians view the proposal of compromise as a sign of weakness that encourages them to press harder.

The reflexive suspicion of compromise and the impulse to push as hard as possible for as much as possible can be seen as extensions or symptoms of the acute sense of insecurity felt by the Soviet leadership. That insecurity also fueled the continual drive for recognition and acceptance from the West. "It is not so much understanding of, it is recognition by, the West the Russians crave," contended Ronald Hingley.[51] Hingley quoted Tibor Szamuely in *The Russian Tradition* (1974): "What really interests them is to know whether we admire them enough. What they are afraid of is that we should be ill-informed as to their merits. What they want from us is not information but praise."[52]

Soviet "congenital insecurity," even in official political dealings with the United States, is well illustrated in a story recounted by Henry Kissinger of his efforts to fathom the riddle of Soviet behavior: "A week later [in January 1970], [Soviet ambassador] Dobrynin came in with an extraordinary complaint that again demonstrated the congenital Soviet insecurity and at the same time put us on the defensive. He pointed out that in the recently published Presidential Foreign Policy Report, an epic of 40,000 words, the only foreign leaders mentioned by name were Presidents Thieu and Ceausescu. His leaders were likely to conclude that we were not taking them seriously. I turned this amazing point aside politely, somewhat disingenuously telling him that the report was written primarily for an American audience."[53]

Although Soviet negotiators insisted that their country be regarded as the equal of the United States in terms of international standing, they considered the Soviet Union superior to the United States in terms of moral legitimacy. The Soviets derided the profit motive as exploitation of the working class and attempted to place communism in a morally superior position. The impulse against profit had existed in Russia before the revolution of 1917, and only in recent years, as new fortunes have been amassed, have attitudes begun to change. The older generation of Russians still believes that communism was a morally superior system because it provided a level of security for the working masses.

For the younger generation the 1917 revolution, the "Great Patriotic War," and Stalin belong to the pages of history textbooks. The lure of Western-style consumerism eventually overtook exhortations to fulfill the millennial dream of workers of the world uniting under the red banner of proletarian internationalism. No matter how pronounced the Soviet sense of moral superiority, the fact of Western material superiority was inescapable. Awareness of the West's material success made the Soviets hypersensitive, defensive, and envious. The generation that grew up under Brezhnev was already yearning for blue jeans and the Beatles. An often quoted but unnamed Kremlinologist remarked, "The fall of the Soviet Empire began with the importation of the first pair of Gucci loafers." The contradictory impulses for a viable social safety net that retains the vestiges of the socialist dream and the ability to live a new, "normal life" with Western freedoms and financial structures underlie the negotiating process.

THE GORBACHEV INTERLUDE

The reign of Mikhail Gorbachev appeared to mark the beginning of the end for the Bolshevik Code. Gorbachev stood as a transitional figure between the tired, ideologically hidebound despotism of the Soviets and the chaotic and pragmatic pluralism of the Russian Federation. With some degree of hindsight, in fact, the years between 1985 and 1991 proved to be only a temporary aberration from Soviet norms. When Gorbachev and the Soviet Union fell in 1991, many Soviet-style characteristics reasserted themselves. Furthermore, while one should not underestimate the changes Gorbachev and his close associates wrought, neither should one exaggerate the degree of discontinuity with the past: Gorbachev sought not to destroy the Soviet Union but to reform it. His manner often exemplified typical Bolshevik traits, especially in bullying and beating down his opposition. His Bolshevik training was also expressed in his negotiating behavior. Secretary of State James Baker described Gorbachev's negotiating offer on Central America, at their first meeting in the Kremlin in May 1989, as "a double dose of trying to get something for nothing."[54]

In the end Mikhail Gorbachev rejected the use of Soviet repression that sustained Bolshevik power at home and in Eastern Europe. The "new thinking" in Soviet behavior under Gorbachev and his foreign minister Eduard Shevardnadze deviated from the Bolshevik Code in four major areas: the role of conflict in history; the nature of the capitalist world; the roles and tasks of the Soviet Union as the leader of world revolution; and the Soviet Union as the builder of a socialist world order. Gorbachev and his team gradually backed away from the orthodox Marxist-Leninist view of world conflict and unrelenting class struggle in favor of a more pragmatic approach to conflict resolution.

In the November 1986 issue of *Kommunist,* the journal of the Central Committee of the Communist Party, Gorbachev for the first time formally abandoned the inevitability of class struggle and conflict in Soviet ideology. Gorbachev quoted Lenin who, Gorbachev said, had expressed a "thought of colossal profundity—about the priority of the interests of social development and common human values over the interest of this or that class. Today, in the nuclear-missile era, the significance of this thought is sensed with special sharpness." In the

Aesopian language of Marxism-Leninism, Gorbachev was acknowledging that the Soviet Union's support of "class conflict" and the working class should be moderated for the sake of more important human values, namely, survival of the human race in the face of the danger of nuclear war.

Gorbachev developed this theme in a major speech in 1987, saying that "security . . . can only be mutual, and, if we take international relations as a whole, it can only be universal. The highest wisdom is not to be concerned exclusively for oneself, especially when this is to the detriment of the other side. It is necessary that everyone feel equally secure." In the same speech Gorbachev proclaimed that global problems "that affect all mankind" cannot be solved "through the efforts of a single state or group of states. What is needed here is cooperation on a worldwide scale." Commenting on the speech, Holsti noted, "These are not the vocabularies and concepts of Marxism-Leninism. Security and problem solving through world cooperation have little to do with traditional Soviet visions of world historical processes."[55]

Gorbachev abandoned not only Marxist dialectical materialism but also the Bolshevik doctrine of the implacable hostility of the capitalist world to the Soviet Union. Moving toward acceptance of the idea that the Soviet Union could cooperate with the West to create a more stable international order, Gorbachev's attitudes and policies implied that imperialism "may indeed have changed its fundamental characteristic, and not just because of Soviet policies."[56]

The Basic Principles of U.S.-Soviet Relations, signed by Brezhnev and Nixon at their 1972 summit, set forth a code of behavior between the United States and the Soviet Union that called for measures to reduce not only the risk of nuclear war but also tensions and conflicts, especially the kind that could involve major powers in their relations with other areas of the world.[57] But the agreement was practiced more in the breach than in the observance. Despite its signed approval of the Basic Principles, the Soviet Union failed to renounce its commitments to the world revolutionary process in Ethiopia, Angola, and Yemen. The "internationalist duty" of the Soviet Union was another ideological obligation stemming from Leninist doctrine and it became the rationale for the Soviet invasion of Afghanistan. By 1986, when the 1978 invasion of Afghanistan had turned into a debacle, Gorbachev

redefined the Soviet Union's concept of international duty and removed Soviet troops; Shevardnadze turned to the United Nations to
request that it play a mediating role in the Soviet withdrawal in 1988.

The year before, in September 1987, in his address to the UN General Assembly, Shevardnadze had stated that the Soviet Union would
like to see a world in which peace is secured by the United Nations. That
same month Gorbachev had urged the International Court of Justice
to expand its jurisdiction—an idea, noted Holsti, "that would have
appeared preposterous to any of his predecessors."[58]

Although able to effect a marked shift in Soviet relations with the
outside world, replacing ideology and confrontation with pragmatism
and cooperation, Gorbachev could not achieve a similar change in attitudes within the aging senior leadership at home. Glasnost and perestroika opened a crack in the closed door of Soviet policymaking, but
that crack was not wide enough to allow the forces of economic and
political reform to enter. It was wide enough, however, to allow domestic and foreign audiences to perceive more clearly the failings of the
Soviet system.

Internally, the biggest loss of credibility to the Communist Party
came on April 26, 1986, when an explosion occurred in the fourth
nuclear reactor at the Chernobyl nuclear power station in Ukraine. It
took two days before a public announcement of the accident was
issued and until mid-May before Gorbachev appeared on television to
discuss the disaster and express his sympathy.[59]

In his memoirs Shevardnadze writes in deep sorrow of "Chernobyl
Day," when the Politburo insisted on doing business as usual "by
the worn-out scripts of the past despite our proclamations of honest
openness":

> Chernobyl Day tore the blindfold from our eyes and persuaded us that
> politics and morals could not diverge. We had to gauge our politics con-
> stantly by moral criteria. Lest I be thought too sanctimonious, I shall say
> that moral politics is the credo of the pragmatist, a person whom life
> has taught that immoral politics goes nowhere. . . . Chernobyl was the
> first test of glasnost, and it failed. Now it's all up ahead, I told myself,
> we're just starting, but ahead lay the tragedies in Alma-Ata, Sumgait,
> Sepanakert, Baku, Tbilisi, Vilnius, and Riga, and the old mechanisms
> kicked in, simplifying, distorting or just eliminating the truth about
> events.[60]

When East Germans began fleeing to Hungary in 1988 and the Berlin Wall came down in 1989, the Soviet Union no longer was prepared to define and fulfill its international duty with force. The old bitter joke, "How do the Russians visit their friends?" "In tanks," no longer applied.

For his role in releasing the Soviet grip on Eastern Europe in the vain hope of saving the Soviet Union, Shevardnadze was forced from office by hard-line communists in January 1991.[61] Seven months later, the traditionalists in the Kremlin responded to Gorbachev's fundamental change in Soviet attitudes toward world order with the abortive coup of August 1991. By the close of the year the Soviet Union no longer existed.

The Communist Party and its controlling institutions, including the decisive Central Committee, were replaced by the Office of the President, led by Boris Yeltsin. The West expected that as Yeltsin rose, Russia would move away from its Soviet past and closer to Western ways of thinking and behaving. On the contrary, Yeltsin's ascent has meant a return to Soviet practices and outlooks that predated Gorbachev. This can be explained partly in terms of specific personalities, partly in terms of Russian culture. In Yeltsin's administration, party discipline has been replaced by the dictates of the President's Office. His inner team, most of them Communist Party officials who served under him in Sverdlovsk, moved to Moscow with him in 1985, when he became Moscow city party secretary, and remained loyal when Gorbachev forced him to resign in 1987. Many of these old Bolsheviks were Yeltsin's inner-Kremlin managers. They all followed the Bolshevik Code.

Westernizers such as Foreign Minister Andrei Kozyrev were ousted. First Deputy Prime Minister Anatoli Chubais, who carried out the privatization of state property, continued to fight an uphill battle for reform. Chubais was named Yeltsin's chief of staff after the 1996 election, recognition and reward for his role in the campaign and a move to please supporters of market reforms. Yeltsin, like his predecessors, played one faction against another, the Bolsheviks versus the reformers, to divide and rule until his declining health intervened.

President Yeltsin's initial appointment of General Aleksandr Lebed as the head of the Security Council was a skillful move to reach for nationalist support. Lebed immediately flew to Chechnya and ended the war there by recognizing the reality of the Russian defeat. He saw the devastated condition of Russian troops, who were paid in kind with cabbages or were forced to beg for food. Lebed's success in Chechnya aroused his appetite for power, and he was forced from the cabinet by Yeltsin and Chernomyrdin, his chief rival. Lebed, who won 15 percent of the vote in the first round of the presidential balloting in 1996, stands in the wings consolidating his political base for another run at the presidency.

After the election President Yeltsin's health became an overriding concern for the rest of 1996. Yeltsin underwent quintuple heart bypass surgery and later contracted pneumonia, forcing him to stop work an extended period of recuperation. During the eight months that Yeltsin was almost continuously ill, the government was run by Prime Minister Viktor Chernomyrdin; Chubais controlled the President's Office. Lebed repeatedly urged Yeltsin to resign.

On March 6, 1997, Yeltsin formally returned to office vowing to "restore order," end economic chaos, and root out political corruption. It was a different Yeltsin from the incoming president who had celebrated "Russia's evolution into a pluralistic democracy."[62] In an effort to start anew, Yeltsin fired most of his cabinet, representatives of the old Soviet *nomenklatura* and the so-called Sverdlovsk *mafiya*,[63] and named Chubais first deputy prime minister.

Chubais was empowered by Yeltsin to lead the battle against economic corruption, money-laundering abroad, and the refusal by major corporations to pay taxes. Yeltsin added Boris Nemtsov, the successful market economy reform governor from Nizhny Novgorod, to his Kremlin team to restart the economy and establish a viable tax collection system. New reform cycles appear from time to time, but the underlying continuity of past behavior patterns and the persistence of the Soviet legacy remain a drag against change.

■ 2 ■

The Durability of the Inheritance

Continuity versus Change

On all fronts, the Russian Federation has struggled to adjust to the chaotic aftermath of the collapse of the Soviet Union. The transition to a market economy has been uneven, unproductive, piecemeal, and painful. Abandonment of the socialist safety net has created deep fissures in the Russian body politic. Despite the reelection of President Boris Yeltsin in July 1996 by a fairly comfortable majority (he won 54 percent of the vote), there remains deep underlying sentiment for centralized leadership exercised by a strong figure who will retain the subsistence economics of Bolshevik socialism. The attitude embodied in the aphorism "They pretend they are paying us and we pretend we are working" lingers in the mills, mines, and defense industries that are months behind in paying wages supplied by the central government in Moscow. The industries that the Soviet government directed and supported have still to be absorbed and integrated into a market economy.

The exercise of governance has been greatly impeded by the breakdown of the Communist Party and Soviet institutional structure. On the international stage, Russia has found itself relegated from protagonist to supporting player, a demotion that the former superpower has yet to accept. The Russian Federation must decide what it wants to retain or re-create from its Soviet—and pre-Soviet—past and what it wants to disown.

The impact of this struggle on Russian diplomacy has been to raise doubt about its ability to deliver on its commitments. In this chapter we briefly examine the ways in which the demise of the Soviet Union has affected the institutional and political context within which Russian negotiators operate. We look first at the institutional chaos created by the sudden disappearance of the Soviet system; we then examine nationalism among the new or rejuvenated political forces that now influence the making and the execution of foreign policy. Although much has changed from the Soviet era, much remains the same, especially the style and the psychology that animate Russian negotiating behavior. We take note of the degree to which contemporary Russian officials have inherited traditional Russian attitudes and Soviet-style approaches.

COLLAPSE FROM WITHIN: THE LOSS OF INSTITUTIONAL COHERENCE

In the Soviet system, control of foreign political and economic policy was centered in the Politburo of the Communist Party of the Soviet Union and administered through the International Department of its Central Committee. The powerful Central Committee apparatus consisted of some forty thousand officials organized in secretariats to coordinate and expedite approval of decisions. Major decisions had to go to the Politburo for approval. Minor decisions were made within the Central Committee apparatus by the Central Committee secretaries.

When Mikhail Gorbachev came to power he began to modify the ideologically driven and confrontational foreign policy of his Soviet predecessors. He began to conduct diplomacy outside the elaborate and highly regimented Soviet system. The results, according to former Soviet ambassador to Washington Anatoli Dobrynin, were calamitous:

> In exchange for the generous Soviet concessions Gorbachev and his devoted lieutenant Shevardnadze offered the West, they could and should have obtained a more important role for the Soviet Union in European security and a stronger Soviet voice in European affairs. But they did not. Able but inexperienced, impatient to reach agreement, but excessively self-assured and flattered by the Western media, Gorbachev and Shevardnadze were often outwitted and outplayed by their Western partners. On occasion they went further than necessary in concessions in agreements on arms control, Eastern Europe, German unification, and on the Persian Gulf crisis, and they continued doing so right up to the breakup of the Soviet Union. Gorbachev in addition distorted the mechanisms of Soviet diplomacy by running a kind of personal back channel with high American officials to avoid criticism by his colleagues

in the Politburo and our corps of professional diplomats. They were increasingly kept in the dark. (The confidential channel I ran and all the deals struck on behalf of Moscow with Washington, had to pass through the entire Politburo for approval.) From 1989 on, Soviet diplomacy became progressively less effective because of the urgent pressure of Gorbachev's domestic political agenda and his efforts to sustain his weakening reputation at home by what appeared to be successes abroad. The result was a dramatic reduction in our capacity to adapt to the fast-changing international environment, provoked in no small degree by Gorbachev himself.[1]

Dobrynin is speaking for the Bolshevik Code, under which he was raised, and the order which it produced. Gorbachev's "new thinking" and its accompanying freewheeling style were heresy and anathema to the elder party faithful who relied on the Soviet state for their privileged existence. In Eastern Europe the promise of freedom raised expectations and released long-suppressed economic and political drives. In the Soviet Union the fear of change without strict direction from the top down created turmoil and disorder, the most dreaded enemy of the Soviet state. Gorbachev could not bring the hard-line conservatives in the Politburo along with him and in the end they destroyed him, which made Yeltsin's rise to power possible.

The diplomatic mechanisms "distorted" by Gorbachev remained more or less intact and provided a reasonably efficient framework within which to pursue Soviet foreign policy. However, when the Soviet Union expired in December 1991, and the Communist Party disintegrated, the Central Committee apparatus was entirely eliminated.

No new institutions were created to replace the Communist Party and the Central Committee system. President Yeltsin's Security Council and his foreign policy advisers have not been able to replicate the International Department of the Central Committee of the Communist Party either in organizational skill or bureaucratic authority. The lack of decision-making institutions, a feeble judicial system, and the absence of a coherent procedure to resolve policy differences have resulted in debilitating contradictions in Russia's conduct of international negotiations.

The gridlock in Russian-U.S. negotiations is broken on occasion by summit meetings between Presidents Yeltsin and Clinton or in high-level consultations between Prime Minister Viktor Chernomyrdin and

Vice President Al Gore. The Gore-Chernomyrdin Commission meets at least twice a year and prepares issues for top-level decisions in areas of trade, finance, and capital investment. A good working relationship between the vice president and the prime minister and heavy staff work have facilitated discussion of a number of high-profile issues. Gore and Chernomyrdin reached an agreement to let the Export-Import Bank finance the manufacture of new Russian passenger jetliner bodies with American engines in exchange for opening the Russian market to the sale of American-made jet aircraft.

However, the Gore-Chernomyrdin channel has failed to accelerate resolution of lower-profile issues, which fall victim to an unreliable, nonexistent, or corrupt banking and taxation system. Corruption at all levels of the Russian government has an unspoken but ever-present influence on economic negotiations. Corruption cannot be disregarded in any diplomatic negotiation where the expenditure of funds is involved.

On the level below Gore-Chernomyrdin, the U.S. Department of Commerce is part of a U.S. interagency group that is trying to develop intergovernmental cooperation and consultation in Russia. Ombudsmen from Commerce and the Ministry of Foreign Economic Relations investigate complaints and assist in achieving fair settlements. U.S. Commerce Department counselor Jan Kalicki's counterparts are Deputy Minister of Foreign Economic Relations Nikolai U. Drozdov and Deputy Minister of Fuel and Energy Anatoli Shatalov. The main objective is to cut red tape and move applicable legislation through the Duma (the parliament). The U.S. Department of Energy, the Treasury Department, and the Department of Agriculture maintain officers in the embassy in Moscow to coordinate the interagency process and work directly with Russian counterparts.

A senior American official involved in the effort explained, "A line of approach has been established—now the problem is how to accomplish the objectives. No single ministry can deliver the government. You have to check with a lot of people. There is no routine interagency process. Confidence building is necessary and the process is frustrating. Each item must be cleared in an ad hoc way. Yet if you look at how far they have come, and the fundamental forward steps they have taken from 1980 on, it is amazing how far they have gone. But the jury is still out on the final result."[2]

Compounding the difficulties are Russian sensitivity and ambivalence to the American role in building new institutions in Russia. Negotiators must deal with the countless decisions that are needed to implement actions when there is no institutional infrastructure to communicate and enforce decisions. "Life does not consist of major decisions; the vast majority are those decisions in which Gore-Chernomyrdin are not interested," said former Foreign Ministry negotiator Victor Israelyan, who in his career relied on the old Central Committee structure of the Communist Party. "Now that [structure] is gone. The challenge is how to solve problems without a centralized bureaucracy."[3]

A senior American diplomat involved in high-level negotiations with the Russians summed up the problem: "They don't have the Central Committee [CC] machinery anymore. The CC foreign policy section is not there in any coherent way. Communist Party discipline on the whole system is not there anymore. A bunch of institutions are in charge of running the country that were never meant to run the country. Institutionally there is no agreement on the decisions that are made. That is not real policy. The ultimate appeal mechanism is to refer the problem to the top. Politics of interest are being developed through the Duma, the regions, and the ministries. The decision-making process for a negotiation is far from transparent. There is no organized system. All kinds of decrees are issued, but nobody respects them. You have to build a consensus or go forward to the highest level to get a decision backed up."[4]

In this new era, confusion and uncertainty prevail. Where once the International Department of the Central Committee of the Communist Party mandated political authority and imposed bureaucratic discipline, coordinating the work of the ministries to achieve a single political or economic policy position, today it is every ministry for itself. After a draft is initialed by the Ministry of Foreign Affairs, American negotiators have to make their own deals with the other ministries involved. "Slavic complexity is never a straight line. In the West we had the two Richards, Burt and Perle, but still the system proceeded symmetrically. Now each time we negotiate in Russia it is a different way, with new rules established by them," explained former ambassador John Maresca.[5]

The degree of autonomy individual ministries enjoy today and their ability to conduct autonomous foreign economic policy is well illustrated by the case of the Ministry of Atomic Energy. Its head, Viktor N. Mikhailov, controls a one million–person industrial complex that is a major component of the Russian economy. Mikhailov has the ability to provide electric power and generate hard currency through the sale of nuclear reactors; with that power he has established a self-sustaining feudal barony.

In 1995 Mikhailov generated a crisis in U.S.-Russian relations when he signed an agreement with Iran to provide it with up to four light-water reactors. The Clinton administration strongly opposed the sales because it believed the reactors and accompanying equipment would give Iran the potential to develop nuclear weapons. The United States asked Russia to forgo the construction of even one reactor; the first was planned to begin in the autumn of 1995. Moscow was unresponsive to the administration's admonition that supplying reactors to Iran and training Iranian workers to operate them would accelerate Iran's efforts to develop nuclear weapons. Instead, Russian Ministry of Atomic Energy officials argued that U.S. complaints were aimed at undermining Russian reactor sales in a highly competitive market.

Although Russia was pledged to support a policy of nuclear non-proliferation, the ministry's primary concern was, and remains, competing internationally for the sale of reactors. The lack of a Russian interagency process and a confused and ineffectual chain of decision making created a power vacuum that enabled Mikhailov to move ahead to consummate the sale of the reactors. He acted in the face of continued American warnings of the proliferation dangers and Iran's inability to pay for the sale.

In September 1995 the Russian government reiterated its determination to proceed with the sale to Iran of four reactors, despite what a State Department spokesman said would be "a very serious issue in the U.S.-Russian relationship." Congress threatened to block economic aid to Russia if the reactor deal went through. The $250 million in aid involved was intended to help restructure the Russian economy, including the privatization of land and businesses, the reform of capital markets, the development of new businesses, and the creation of viable legal and regulatory institutions.[6]

The U.S. negotiators failed to convince President Yeltsin and his top aides that Russia's own national security and international concerns about Iran as a nuclear power were at stake over the sales. The Russian Atomic Energy Ministry presented the reactor sales in purely economic terms, and President Yeltsin, facing the presidential election, was unwilling to act against Minister Mikhailov's initiative after the lucrative contract was announced.

The Russian government, balancing the $1 billion in sales of reactors against the $250 million in U.S. aid, gave no indication of backing down. At one point in the debate, when the Russian sale of two reactors, valued at $500 million, was being discussed in Washington, Ambassador Yuli Vorontsov was heard to tell an American diplomat, "If you find the $500 million for the reactors we'll forget we ever heard of Iran." In the end the United States did not raise the aid package over $250 million, and the Russians rated the profit motive higher than the principle of nuclear nonproliferation. The ominous contract remains in force, but senior American officials question Iran's ability to pay for the reactors and insist that the case is not closed. They continue to protest the sale and raise it at Gore-Chernomyrdin meetings. They warn that Iran, as a nuclear power, will also be a threat to Russia.

A NEW STRUCTURE: "PRACTICAL INTEREST" AND RISING NATIONALISM

All negotiators seek to preserve and promote their country's self-interest. In postcommunist Russia, national interest is being redefined. Russia's interests are no longer equated with the furtherance of Marxist-Leninist ideology, nor—as Israelyan has observed—with realizing the short-lived dream of "partnership." Instead, negotiations are fueled chiefly by two forces: one is "practical interest"; the other, equally potent, is Russian nationalism.

For many long-serving Russian officials, the end of the Soviet system has generated confusion, disillusionment, and ambivalence. The plight of those who would have reformed the communist system was instanced at a meeting between the novelist John Le Carré and former KGB chairman Vadim Bakatin, appointed briefly in 1991 by Mikhail Gorbachev. A respected communist before he took over as KGB chairman,

Bakatin had become, said Le Carré, "a decent man deprived of his convictions. 'Where is the world going?' he wants to know. 'Where is Russia going?' 'Where is the middle way, the humanitarian one, between capitalist and socialist excess?' Bakatin described himself as a socialist. He grew up a socialist. 'Okay, things went wrong, power got into the wrong hands, the party took some wrong turnings, but I still believed that we were the moral force for good in the world. What are we now? Where is the moral force?' asked Bakatin.

"With Estée Lauder and Galeries Lafayette, I think of answering; with the gray queues of Moscow citizens waiting to spend a week's pay on a McDonald's burger," wrote Le Carré.[7] Consumerism and materialism have become significant social forces in today's Russia, filling the hole in the social fabric left by Russia's abrupt renunciation of Marxism-Leninism.

This change has made itself felt in high-level circles as well as among the public at large. Although some, like Bakatin, bemoan the loss of moral purpose, other officials (especially among the younger generation) are less perturbed and much readier to respond to material incentives. With the disappearance of ideology, money and what a senior American diplomat calls "practical interest" have emerged as driving forces in negotiations on a government-to-government level. "Showing you have achieved a practical or tangible plus is a very important thing for Russia. It could be money, employment, or benefit to a region. You have to show that you have not been taken advantage of and that you have received something specific," the senior diplomat said. Atomic Energy Minister Mikhailov's pursuit of a billion dollars from Iran illustrates "practical" if shortsighted interest.

Reflecting on the evolution of Russian diplomacy since 1991, Victor Israelyan noted that "after the fall of the Soviet Union in the first years of Russian diplomacy there was a new ideology of a rosy world in which we and the Americans were partners. It was an exaggeration trying to create a picture of a nonexistent world, a dream. It was . . . an ideal world, one that does not exist. Now negotiations are becoming based more on reality and national interest."[8]

Russian nationalism, reflected in the internal struggle for domestic political power, is now a primary operational element of foreign policy decision making. This is Russian nationalism stripped of its Marxist-

Leninist rationales. Internationalist rhetoric has been abandoned in favor of Russian rights and ambitions—chief among which is a return of the Russian Empire. President Yeltsin and, following his lead, Foreign Ministers Andrei Kozyrev and Evgeni Primakov have conjured up a Great Russia, reuniting the Soviet Union and championing the Slavs. Their vision of Russia harks back to a prerevolutionary imperialism that included the unity of the Slavic peoples of Russia who would dominate lesser Central Asian powers on its borders.

"What we are seeing now are the consequences of the breakup of a colonial empire. After the colonies obtain independence, the enduring animosities left over rise to the surface," argued John Maresca. He cited rearguard actions against ethnic nationalists in conquered territories trying to break away from Russian dominance.[9] In the Transcaucasus region, Lieutenant General Aleksandr Lebed was in charge of Moldova, where his Fourteenth Army protected Russians and prevented the region from breaking away. Lebed's actions in Moldova and his nationalist rhetoric have proved very popular with a significant sector of the Russian people, whose strong support for Lebed in the first round of the 1996 presidential elections prompted Yeltsin to name him the general head of the National Security Council. Thus empowered, Lebed ended the war in Chechnya, but his lust for power led to Yeltsin firing him, thus forcing Lebed to prepare his own campaign for the presidency.

Russian troops are in Tajikistan ostensibly to fulfill a peacekeeping role, but in reality their heavy presence indicates the reemergence of Russian control, a lesson to other newly independent Central Asian countries. Treaties with Armenia and Georgia have established Russian bases with Russian troops in both countries. Azerbaijan is under continual pressure as Russia seeks to gain a share of the rich Caspian Sea oil reserves and control Azerbaijan's oil exports through Russian pipelines.

For the former republics of the Soviet Union, dealing with Moscow has become more difficult because of internal disorder in Russia and strained relationships between Yeltsin and the Duma. In August 1993, Eduard Shevardnadze, president of the former Soviet republic of Georgia, asked the UN Security Council to send a peacekeeping mission to help resolve the conflict with the secessionist region of Abkhazia. This would give a clear signal to the world that the United Nations was supporting a Russian-led peacekeeping force. However, the Security

Council, fearing that Russia might use its peacekeeping force as a means to reimpose Russian control of Georgia, delayed nearly a year, until July 1994, and then sent only 136 military observers.

When the Security Council quickly agreed to U.S. proposals in November 1994 to send five thousand peacekeeping troops to Haiti to replace U.S. forces, Russian officials cried "foul" and "double standard." "We saw a different expeditiousness. Georgia was extremely slow, and Haiti was faster than we would like," said Sergei Lavrov, Russian ambassador to the United Nations. During the discussions on Georgia, the United States presented eleven questions for Russia to answer before Washington would vote for the resolution. The questions included such issues as how refugees would be resettled and whether the press would have free access. When then U.S. ambassador Madeleine K. Albright proposed a resolution to begin building up the UN force in Haiti, Lavrov presented the same eleven questions and demanded answers from the United States.[10]

The Russians have not yet publicly accepted the new asymmetry in the power balance between the United States and Russia. The United Nations was slow to back a Russian-led peacekeeping force in Abkhazia, watchful that it was not a ruse to reimpose Russian hegemony. Close coordination by the United States with the United Nations and direct UN participation preempted the fear that the United States would tip the geopolitical scales by simply imposing a peacekeeping force in Haiti.

Lavrov insisted in 1994 that Russia does not intend to dismantle its positive post–Cold War relationship with the United States. However, basic substantive differences remain between the United States and Russia over dealing with Iraq and Bosnia. The Russian position on Bosnia followed a shifting pattern from hesitant approval of Western proposals to open opposition, based on the ebb and flow of nationalist passions in Russian internal politics and the perennial Slavophile appeal that Russia is the guardian of the fate of the Slavic people, who have a sacred mission.

The Russian attitude toward NATO expansion has followed a similar shifting pattern, determined by the waxing and waning of nationalist sentiment and Russian assertiveness. Yeltsin has adhered to the Soviet style of continually shifting position: promising, withdrawing, threatening, backing down. Faced with parliamentary elections at the end of

1995 and a presidential election in the spring of 1996, Yeltsin and Kozyrev were immobilized on the NATO issue. They stalled for time; the closer Russia drew to elections, the more nationalistic President Yeltsin became and the stronger his opposition to NATO grew. On September 8, 1995, Yeltsin warned that expansion of NATO to Russia's western frontier "will mean a conflagration throughout all Europe."[11]

The behavior of Foreign Minister Andrei Kozyrev was likewise shaped by the pressure of nationalism. From 1994 to his dismissal in 1995, Kozyrev tacked to and fro, placating nationalist ambitions while striving to emerge as a serious partner in Western alliance policymaking.

Kozyrev accommodated a new political situation with "shock diplomacy" at the December 1992 meeting of the Conference on Security and Cooperation in Europe (CSCE). With no advance warning, Kozyrev rose to "announce some changes in concept of the Russian foreign policy, some of which particularly concern the CSCE." These changes were a complete reversal of Russian policy, which threw the conference into disarray. Kozyrev's comments reveal critical issues that remain unresolved and are part of the underlying structure of any negotiation with Russia:

> Firstly. Preserving on the whole the policy towards integration with Europe, we realize that our traditions come mostly, if not altogether, from Asia, which establishes certain limits on the rapprochement with Western Europe. Despite some evolution, we see the unchangeable principles of NATO and Western European Union which continue developing plans for their military presence in the Baltic and other regions of the former Soviet Union, as well as interference in Bosnia and the internal affairs of Yugoslavia.
>
> Sanctions against the Federal Republic of Yugoslavia were obviously dictated by this policy. We demand that they be lifted. If this does not happen, we will reserve the right to take all necessary unilateral measures to protect our interests, especially so because they are inflicting economic damage upon us. In its struggle, the present Serbian government can count on the support of Great Russia.
>
> Secondly. The territory of the former Soviet Union cannot be regarded as a zone of full application of CSCE norms. In fact, this is postimperial territory where Russia will have to defend its interests by using all available means, including military and economic ones. We will firmly insist that former Soviet republics immediately join a new federation or confederation. This will be a tough discussion.

Thirdly. All those who believe that they can ignore these peculiarities and interests, that Russia will repeat the fate of the Soviet Union, should remember that a state is a state that can stand up for itself and its friends. We are also ready to take a constructive part in the CSCE work, but we will be very cautious with ideas leading to interference in internal affairs.

Kozyrev then ceded the floor while reserving the right to express his opinion again. An hour later, with the conference deeply shaken by his remarks, Kozyrev returned:

I would like to assure you and all others present that neither President Yeltsin, who remains the head and guarantor of the Russian domestic and foreign policy, nor I, as minister of foreign affairs, will ever agree to what I read in my previous statement. I would like to thank you and all those present for the possibility of using such a rhetorical technique, but I did it out of the most serious considerations so that everyone realizes the real threats on our path towards a postcommunist Europe. The text I read out is a rather precise compilation of demands by the opposition, and not by far the most extreme opposition in Russia. . . . This is just a technique aimed to show the threat of a turn of events.

Kozyrev's arguing both sides of an issue and changing his role like a chameleon was the first display of a style he was soon to repeat: accepting, then denying, then threatening, then compromising, in an effort to balance his international position against the demands of Russian domestic political pressures. The general line from the Central Committee of the Communist Party has been replaced by the fluctuating influence of parliament and extremist nationalist threats. The result is inconsistent, erratic, and unpredictable behavior in negotiations, with the pattern being set from the top leadership on down.

In his approach to NATO expansion, Kozyrev initially followed President Yeltsin's lead; he was warm to the Partnership for Peace (PFP), which offers the countries of the former Soviet bloc many of the benefits of full NATO membership—short of formal security guarantees. Secretary of State Warren Christopher called it "a vision of an undivided and integrated Europe."[12] In May 1994, Russian defense minister Pavel Grachev told the NATO allies that Russia was prepared to join the PFP without any conditions, but added that Russia wanted a parallel "full-blooded strategic relationship" with the alliance, one that took into account Russia's status as Europe's largest country and premier nuclear power.[13]

At a NATO foreign ministers' meeting in Ankara on June 10, 1994, Kozyrev said he hoped to visit NATO headquarters in Brussels "soon" to sign the agreement, which the press said would dispel "months of doubt about his country's intentions." However, he did not specify a date. Kozyrev stated Russia had reached an understanding with the sixteen Western allies that Moscow's role in the PFP would be "a substantive program that would involve no mutual vetoes, reservations, or surprises."

Thus, Kozyrev revealed a time-honored Russian negotiating strategy, which was to agree in principle to a general statement but back away when it comes to actually working out specific details. Despite the appearance of sweeping and rapid improvement in its relations with the West, Russia insisted on a firm set of demands as its terms for military cooperation with the PFP. The dialogue on nuclear issues outside PFP, Russia demanded, should be settled in principle before Russia signed the agreement. The West, fearing Russian foot-dragging and delay, wanted signatures first and refinement of the relationship later.

Kozyrev also made it clear that Russia did not want Poland, Hungary, and the Czech Republic to enjoy full NATO membership so long as Moscow was excluded. In Moscow, Yeltsin said he saw no reason why Russia should not become a full member of the European Union in due course.

On June 22 Kozyrev traveled to Brussels and signed up Russia as a member of the PFP. Kozyrev told NATO members that large sections of the Russian public needed convincing that NATO was not intent on a "triumphant march eastward." Kozyrev said a "major psychological adjustment" would be necessary before Russians could accept the idea of former Warsaw Pact members joining NATO. However, he stepped back from previous demands that NATO be subsumed by the Organization for Security and Cooperation in Europe. When Yeltsin came to Washington in September 1994, President Clinton made the case to him for NATO expansion, promising that the process would be open and transparent and that there would be no surprises. He also held out the prospect of Russia's being admitted to NATO eventually.

In an October 1994 speech in London, Kozyrev reinforced his argument that Russia wanted, and felt it deserved, Western moral support and financial assistance to help shoulder the burden of peacekeeping in the Eurasian land mass and especially along the ethnic and religious fault lines of the Transcaucasian and Central Asian regions. "No substitute for our efforts here is in sight," said Kozyrev. "Russia's withdrawal from its peacekeeping role would threaten the former Soviet Union with a Yugoslav scenario." His speech drew sympathy from the *Financial Times*, which observed that "in some West European chancelleries support is growing for carefully monitored case-by-case Western backing for CIS [Commonwealth of Independent States] peacekeeping activities, together with the dispatch of small teams of Western observers to monitor the modalities."[14]

On the second anniversary of his use, and then denial, of "shock diplomacy," Kozyrev struck again. On December 1, 1994, at the NATO ministers' meeting in Brussels, Kozyrev disrupted the close of the meeting by objecting to plans for NATO expansion. He specifically objected to enlargement that would include former members of the Warsaw Pact: "Very frankly I must tell you that there are certain issues that must be clarified. If the strategy of NATO is to enlarge, that requires consultation." Russia did not sign the agreement on steps toward NATO expansion; the NATO ministers stopped short of guaranteeing NATO membership to various former Warsaw Pact members until certain conditions were fulfilled, thus effectively delaying for at least a year the controversial decision on who would be admitted and when.

Then, in January 1995, at an international conference in Budapest, Yeltsin frontally attacked the idea of NATO expansion, warning that it risked transforming the Cold War into a "cold peace."[15] This became the new Russian general line. In his speech at the United Nations in New York City in September 1995, Kozyrev warned of the "danger of a second cold war" and attacked "countries which rely on multinational military alliances rather than the UN to solve international disputes."

Kozyrev's political adviser, Galina Sidorova, complained about the Western tendency of simultaneously accelerating and putting the brakes on its partnership with Russia, remarks echoed by other Russian intellectuals. She said the West's reservations are based on a generally unspoken sense of Russia's "peculiarity" as a nation with "an allegedly eternal incompatibility with the surrounding world." Sidorova said this "duality plays into the hands of forces on both sides for whom continued enmity is useful. . . . If [the West] bases its strategy on a presumption of Russia's guilt—in her size, potential, geographic location and future sins—then our fragile partnership risks remaining in an embryonic state."[16]

The Russians were yet again seeking sympathy for their vulnerability. They were threatening to stem the tide of new political combinations in Europe, which they see as a classic example of "encirclement" and blatant notification of their reduced power. Under pressure because of his debacle in Chechnya and his impotence in Bosnia, Yeltsin appeared to be supporting the Russian military in its demands to back away from the 1992 Conventional Forces in Europe (CFE) Treaty. The treaty, signed by thirty nations, took effect November 17, 1995, and called for the destruction of thousands of heavy weapons. It permitted intrusive on-site inspections and limited troop and weapons deployment. The Russians found the commitment to reduce forces on their northern and southern flanks too restrictive. They wanted to deploy tanks and artillery for three additional divisions in the flank zones.

The first demands to revise the CFE treaty were voiced publicly by Colonel General Vladimir Zhurbenko, first deputy head of the general staff, at a news conference on December 5, 1994. Zhurbenko complained that the conventional forces treaty was "discriminatory as far as Russia is concerned. All other countries may deploy their weaponry as they see fit." Russian violation of the treaty, urged by Defense Minister Grachev, forced President Yeltsin's hand and raised basic questions about Yeltsin's and Russia's reliability as a partner.

In September 1995 Grachev called for a combined NATO and Russian command over a new international peacekeeping force to be sent to Bosnia. NATO and American officials rejected Grachev's proposal, saying Russian troops would be welcome in the Bosnia force, but only if they agreed to serve under NATO command. After two days of negotiations in the United States between Defense Secretary Perry and Grachev, the Russians agreed to assign a unit to serve in Bosnia under U.S.—not NATO—command.

President Yeltsin retreated further into his nationalist shell and behaved in an erratic manner, positioning himself for the parliamentary elections at the end of 1995 and the presidential election in June 1996. At a press conference before his departure to meet with President Chirac in Paris, at the fiftieth anniversary of the United Nations in New York, and later at a summit with President Clinton, Yeltsin threatened to fire Foreign Minister Kozyrev. In an unprecedented public rebuff of his foreign minister, Yeltsin said he planned to replace Kozyrev when he could find a suitable replacement: "My dissatisfaction remains. I see no improvement in his work. For now, since he is trying, let's not squash him; let him work. But my decision remains." Ironically, Yeltsin criticized Kozyrev for his failure to coordinate with and get along with other ministers. Kozyrev did not respond or resign, but dutifully showed up at the airport for the trip to the West. Yeltsin pointed to his silent, forlorn-looking foreign minister and said, "He is asking me if he should come. And I am saying, yes, yes, you should— for now."[17]

While the 1996 presidential election loomed, Yeltsin publicly humiliated Kozyrev and offered him as a scapegoat to the president's critics. Kozyrev had been the lightning rod for nationalist attacks on Yeltsin. In a face-saving move, Kozyrev ran for a safe seat in the 1995 year-end parliamentary elections. Russian law prohibits a member of the Duma from being foreign minister. Having served as foreign minister of the Russian Federation from October 1990, Kozyrev was finally fired in December 1995 and replaced by Evgeni Primakov, director of Russia's overseas intelligence agency.

Primakov began his career as a journalist with strong intelligence connections. He served as head of the Institute of World Economics and International Relations (IMEMO) before being named by Gorbachev to head the Foreign Intelligence Service, one of the KGB successor agencies devoted to foreign intelligence. A shrewd bureaucratic infighter with a broad base of support, Primakov has solid nationalist credentials and a strong anti-American record, though he has been careful not to openly offend the United States since becoming foreign minister. He is an experienced professional with expertise and contacts in the Middle East. He has heightened Russian activity in the "Near Abroad"—the states that, with Russia, constituted the Soviet Union—and worked for closer ties with former Eastern European satellites, especially Bulgaria and Poland.

Primakov's negotiating style on NATO expansion, which has been called "the root canal strategy" by Western diplomats, consists of making the talks as excruciatingly long and painful as possible. "The Russians . . . seem to think that dragging the talks out may produce more Western concessions and that if it gets too painful the alliance will never try expansion again," said a senior Western official.[18]

The Russians have accepted the inevitability of NATO expansion and the alliance's admission of the Czech Republic, Hungary, and Poland by mid-1999. NATO's formal decision to admit these nations was made at the Madrid meeting in July 1997; there was no formal prior approval by Moscow of who the new members would be. In the detailed negotiations conducted by Primakov with the United States and NATO in the spring of 1997, Primakov communicated a series of "red lines" that the Russians insist must not be crossed in further NATO expansion. Primakov demanded that there be a ten-year moratorium on consideration of any other Central European country for alliance membership; that no former republic of the Soviet Union—including Ukraine and the Baltic states—ever be considered for NATO membership; that no nuclear weapons be allowed, and no foreign forces be permanently stationed, on the soil of the new NATO member states; and that NATO not upgrade Polish airfields to handle nuclear-armed aircraft.[19]

The Russian aim is to derail the process of NATO expansion or to set such restrictive limits that it cannot proceed beyond the initial phase. Henry Kissinger has charged that the NATO-Russia Founding Act, signed in Paris on May 28, 1997, "seeks to reconcile Russia by diluting the Atlantic Alliance into a U.N. style system of collective security." The Founding Act, according to Kissinger, will give Russia not just a voice in NATO but a veto. Kissinger argues that under the Founding Act, "Article 27 provides that 'any action undertaken by the Russian Federation or NATO, together or separately, must be consistent with the U.N. Charter and the Organization for Security and Cooperation in Europe's (OSCE) governing principles.' If this becomes the operating principle, Russia can always insist that all NATO actions, even in the traditional NATO theater of operations, will have to be reviewed by institutions in which Russia has a seat."[20]

This is a wrong interpretation, insist Clinton administration officials, who argue that Russian consultations with NATO give Russia a voice, but not a veto. U.S. ambassador to NATO Robert E. Hunter noted that "NATO would in no way be bound by anything raised by the Russians unless all its members—without exception—agreed. NATO and the United States give up nothing, but gain a chance to engage the country whose future may be most consequential for European security." Hunter summed up the Clinton administration's negotiating dilemma: "At heart, the United States and its allies have faced a set of choices: whether to reach out to Russia or to isolate it; whether to provide a valid place for Russia in European security or to pursue a new containment; whether to encourage Russians who want to work with the West or to cut them off in advance. NATO has made its choices, while 'keeping its powder dry.' It will, at the same time, both enlarge its membership and engage with Russia—not as compensation for enlargement but because building a strategic partnership with Russia makes sense for the long haul."[21]

The debate over NATO enlargement created powerful pressures on the Clinton administration from foreign policy intellectuals such as George Kennan who opposed NATO expansion on the grounds that it would weaken the democratic forces in Russia and strengthen extreme nationalists. Russian efforts to split the NATO allies resulted in the compromise solution of the NATO-Russia Permanent Joint Council, which provides Russia with a voice but no rights to restrict independent decision making and action. For President Clinton, who forged the compromise with President Yeltsin, the Permanent Joint Council with Russian participation and an enlarged NATO add up to a new definition of the balance of power. In a meeting with journalists on May 30, 1997, celebrating the fiftieth anniversary of the Marshall Plan, Clinton reviewed his own foreign policy goals and his efforts to get Russia and Germany to participate in the economic and political evolution of Europe. "What we have done is to construct a balance of power that both restrains and empowers all the people who come within the framework of the agreement." For Clinton, the goal is a wider European security network that takes into account post–Cold War economic priorities, an openness to new political partnerships, and a new security agenda. "We will all, in a more open society, face common threats from terrorism and organized crime and weapons proliferators and drug traffickers," said Clinton. "That means that we have to define our balance of power in terms of our capacity to resist those [threats] and maintain the conditions for progress and prosperity and decency within our own countries, and that we need people who are neighbors to help us more than we need to try to be dominating them in an old-fashioned way."[22] The evolution of Europe is in play, and the outcome remains uncertain.

THE KING IS DEAD, LONG LIVE THE KING!

Yeltsin's public humiliation of Kozyrev was reminiscent of Khrushchev's humiliation of Gromyko, when the Soviet leader bragged publicly, "If I tell Gromyko to sit on a block of ice he will sit there until it melts."[23] Indeed, in many respects Yeltsin's behavior calls to mind the style and practices of his Soviet and pre-Soviet forebears. This should not come as a surprise. Although Yeltsin has espoused democracy and is seen in the West as a potential democrat, his own self-image is closer to the traditional Russian concept of the ultimate, all-controlling leader, the *vozhd*, a latter-day tsar. His training as a Communist Party boss in the heavy industrial center of Sverdlovsk has taught him to divide and rule. Like the tsars and Stalin, Yeltsin excels at playing off one faction against another to preserve his own political power.[24] He is a longtime student and practitioner of the Bolshevik Code.

Yeltsin's adherence to long-standing Russian and Soviet values is evident in his response to the Chechen drive for independence. Chechnya declared its independence from Russia in 1991 by refusing to sign the new Russian Federation treaty. Yeltsin, preoccupied with consolidating his own rule and moving toward a market economy, neglected the festering Chechen boil. By 1994, with renegade arms sales of Russian weapons from Chechnya mounting and the flow of oil through the Grozny pipeline threatened by rising unrest, Yeltsin was forced to deal with the problem. Yeltsin was determined to put down the secession movement, fearing it would spread to other autonomous regions of the former Soviet Union and destabilize the Caucasus region.

Nathan Leites wrote that "the typical Soviet solution . . . has been to project guilt onto others defined as enemies of the Party, and to convert one's own latent fears of being overwhelmed by destructive forces into a systematic, ever more ruthless and violent eradication of opposition—real or imagined."[25]

Yeltsin's military advisers told him it would be easy to subdue the Chechens with an overpowering application of force. Yeltsin abandoned his avowed democratic leadership values, such as obtaining legislative and popular support and informing the public. Instead he relied on the secrecy of the military, the Interior Ministry, and an inner team of Communist Party–trained officials to execute the war. When an undercover attempt to overthrow the Chechen leader Dudayev failed, Defense Minister Pavel Grachev told Yeltsin that the army could solve the problem in three days. Yeltsin ordered Grachev to mobilize the Russian armed forces against Dudayev, and a massive military assault on Grozny, with hundreds of tanks and air support, began in December 1994.

Only when Russian forces finally managed to kill Dudayev in early 1996 and when opinion polls suggested that the continuance of the Chechen war would cost Yeltsin his presidential office, did Yeltsin begin negotiations with the rebels and promise to end the war. He traveled briefly to Chechnya for six hours during the campaign, but never set foot in the capital, Grozny. As soon as the election results were announced in July, the fighting resumed. Aleksei Arbatov, deputy chairman of the parliament's defense committee, said that Yeltsin's statements about seeking peace in Chechnya "look like an election farce. I understand that the president does not issue commands to bomb and shell Chechen villages, but he is doing nothing to stop those that do."[26] Such traditional blustering, blatant duplicity, and the refashioning of reality to maintain control were straight out of the Bolshevik Code. Yeltsin's efforts failed because the media, both domestic and foreign, reported the realities of Chechnya to the world in near real time.

The psychological and behavioral legacy of seventy-five years of Soviet rule and of centuries of arbitrary despotism have not, of course, been inherited by Yeltsin alone. Members of the older generation remain deeply imbued with a longing for authority and security. They are ready to accept cynical means to justify the end of restoring the country's societal discipline and international status.

The influence of Soviet thinking is evident among the younger generation, too. Handsome, smooth Vice Foreign Minister Vitali Churkin initially appeared generous and friendly, "pretending to be a good guy. It was all an act to get us to give our position first so they could find a weakness to manipulate. They don't hesitate to lie and if they can't use the lie they back off arguing, 'I didn't say it that way,'" explained an Eastern European diplomat who still negotiates with the Russians.[27]

It would be wrong to suggest that the legacy of the past has been inherited lock, stock, and barrel. The Russian Federation is engaged in a process of redefining its relationship to its Soviet and pre-Soviet past and adjusting to its changing political and economic circumstances. Yeltsin might see himself as a *vozhd*, but the new reality is that he is an elected leader and must court public opinion if he is to remain in power. In the summer of 1994, just before he departed for a boat trip along the Volga to build popular support, Yeltsin met with a group of officials from the Baltic states and told them proudly, "No tsar has ever taken this trip." Here was Yeltsin, in many respects a latter-day tsar, trying also to behave like an American presidential candidate, aiming to retain his rule by working the crowds and selling himself and his programs. During the 1996 election campaign Yeltsin traveled the length and breadth of Russia dispensing money for churches, civic projects, and back wages.[28]

Russian nationalism, too, has changed from the self-assured days of the Soviet Union. The expression of nationalism is now less constrained than before. The trappings of communist ideology have been removed, allowing nationalist rhetoric to blossom in full, garish display. Ultranationalists like Zhirinovsky indulge in the most intemperate and demagogic appeals to national and racial pride, and politicians of all stripes have courted the same sentiments. However, the pursuit of nationalist goals is more difficult than before. The breakup of the Soviet Union has meant loss of control over territories acquired by Moscow over the course of several centuries. Russia is working hard to regain this power, and there are now Russian troops and bases in all the former republics except the Baltic states, Ukraine, and Azerbaijan.

Dissolution has meant loss of the status and influence of a superpower. Russia has yet to publicly accept its reduced role in regional and global affairs, but the sense of wounded pride is patently obvious. The hurt is all the greater because Russia is heavily dependent on support from the West. The net effect of these changes has been to accentuate traditional Russian traits: fear of dependence on external forces; desire for recognition from the West as an equal partner; and perception of the outside world as dangerous and threatening. Seen in this light, Russian protests against its "encirclement" by an eastward-expanding NATO, Russian attempts to frustrate U.S.-led peacekeeping initiatives at the United Nations, and Russian actions to reassert control over the Near Abroad can be understood both psychologically and strategically.

The context within which Russian negotiators operate is thus a mix of the new and the old; it is an environment in which the advent of institutional chaos, "practical interest," and unfettered nationalism have occasioned a redefinition of Russian identity. The redefinition has been partial rather than comprehensive. When we turn to examine the actual process of negotiation, we find a similar picture: despite recent changes, contemporary Russian negotiating behavior remains recognizably a product of the past. The style and traits, the strategies and tactics, of Soviet (and even pre-Soviet) negotiators have been inherited largely intact. In many respects, new circumstances have only accentuated pre-existing fears, instincts, and patterns of thought and behavior.

■ 3 ■

The Negotiating Process

From the torturous opening moves to the furious pace of the pressured closings, negotiations with the Russians follow a predictable pattern. The essential elements remain consistent in a multilateral or a bilateral government-to-government encounter, a person-to-person or a team negotiation. The style is similar whether the discussions are about the control of nuclear weapons, real estate deals, shipments of goods, or consular rights.

Observing and analyzing negotiations by representatives of the Soviet Union, and now the Russian Federation, we can discern a behavioral map with clear indications of goals, timing, speed, detours, and tactical moves. In overview, the negotiating pattern might be characterized as demonstrating strategic continuity with new tactical emphases. The core negotiating style—formal, often stiff, unpredictably hostile, aggressive, or unresponsive—remains essentially unchanged. The biggest change is that ideology has been replaced by "practical interest," national prestige, international status, and money. The role of money to build institutions and resolve economic problems is a new and powerful negotiating tool, but it must be used with skill and wisdom. Money alone does not crack the Bolshevik Code.

As the preceding chapters have shown, the pattern of behavioral norms that dominates Russian negotiating style reflects the enduring influence of Russian culture and the Soviet mind-set. Under the top-down command system of Communist Party control, orders were given and obeyed without dissent. High levels of the Soviet bureaucracy processed information, then fed it down to the negotiators. Soviet diplomats needed skill, agility, and intellectual power to build and sustain a successful career with the highly disciplined, secretive, and mistrustful authoritarian system. Personal contacts, family relationships, long-standing Communist Party connections, and occasional good luck were the ingredients for individual advancement. The most important goal of the negotiator was to please the boss in Moscow. The negotiator's survival depended on not irritating or embarrassing the foreign minister or the Politburo. Soviet negotiators operated on a tight leash, fearful of retribution from the top should they suggest unauthorized initiatives. James Goodby, a former delegate to the Strategic Arms Reduction Talks (START) and head of the U.S. delegation to the Conference on Disarmament in Europe, has observed that despite the dissolution of the Soviet Union, Russian negotiators still have very little substantive flexibility.[1]

Soviet negotiators saw a world shaped by the dynamics of an omnipresent class struggle; in this Marxist-Leninist worldview, the West was cast as the perpetual enemy. In their intellectual frame of reference, means justified ends; the logic of dialectical materialism, not the rule of law, dictated negotiating strategy and behavior.[2] Soviet negotiators had a tendency to make sudden reversals of policy, which did nothing to encourage cooperation with the West but did a great deal to engender frustration among Western diplomats. Negotiating with the Soviets, a British diplomat said, felt "like putting coins into a broken vending machine. You could kick it and shake it, but you could not get it to cough up anything. You could not even get your coin back."[3]

The demise of the Soviet institutional mechanism for policymaking has not improved things; in some instances it has made the situation worse. Except in those cases where top-level officials of the Russian Federation are directly involved, negotiations often lead only to gridlock. Russian negotiators are now limited to dealing with specific issues such as the allocation of contracts or the disposition of nuclear weapons to be destroyed or moved. Politically well-connected ministers and economically profitable ministries have begun to make their own foreign policy, forcing Western negotiators to deal directly and separately with each ministry involved in a negotiation—not only the Foreign Ministry, as was customary in the past.[4]

Since the fall of the Soviet Union, Marxism-Leninism has been replaced by nationalism, and to a lesser degree by "practical interest," as the motive force driving Russian foreign policy. A variety of new variables can now influence the negotiating process. Demands by the opposition in the Duma must be taken into account on such issues as approving strategic arms control agreements and permitting foreign investment in oil and gas. The negotiators' essential style, however, has not changed. The Russians still enter negotiations distrustful of their counterparts, defensive because of their self-perceived weakness relative to the West. They are disdainful of compromise and insistent on securing their maximum demands. They persist in conducting long, arduous sessions in which agreement is usually achieved only in the concluding moments under the pressure of time. On some issues they may conclude that it is not in their interest to proceed; they deny they ever agreed or simply back away from a prior agreement and go their own way.

It is instructive to refer to Henry Kissinger's comparison of Chinese and Soviet styles of diplomacy:

> The Soviets tend to be blunt, the Chinese insinuating. The Soviets insist on their prerogatives as a great power. The Chinese establish a claim on the basis of universal principles and a demonstration of self-confidence that attempts to make the issue of power seem irrelevant. The Soviets offer their goodwill as a prize for success in negotiations. The Chinese use friendship as a halter in advance of negotiation; by admitting the interlocutor to at least the appearance of personal intimacy, a subtle restraint is placed on the claims he can put forward. The Soviets, inhabiting a country frequently invaded and more recently expanding its influence largely by force of arms, are too unsure of their moral claims to admit the possibility of error. They move from infallible dogma to unchangeable positions (however often they may modify them). . . . The Soviets, with all their stormy and duplicitous behavior, leave an impression of extraordinary psychological insecurity.[5]

Every negotiation has its own rhythm and time frame. Summits at the highest level have a preset agenda and time limit. Long-running negotiations on arms control, environmental issues, civil aviation, or economic issues are subject to shifting political winds, domestic political pressures, and the course of world events. The different phases of negotiation vary in character and length according to how pressure tactics are applied and when a decision is made to move to a midgame fallback position. Domestic political considerations, elections, economic crises, or opposition challenges can expedite or draw out the timetable.

However, the approach and the style employed by the Russians are predictable. No matter the negotiating forum, the subject under discussion, or the personalities of the negotiators, the same tactics are called into play and the same psychological and behavioral traits are evident while the negotiation advances from prepositioning, through opening moves and midgame, to endgame and implementation.

PREPOSITIONING

Before the negotiators formally assemble around the long, green baize conference table set stiffly with mineral water, chocolates, and hard cookies, the process of prepositioning begins, which sets the tone for the subsequent negotiations. The late foreign minister Andrei Gromyko's advice to a young negotiator, recounted by a senior Soviet diplomat, typifies the Russian approach: "Ask for something that does not belong to you, ask for more than they will want to give. Then if you have to retreat you will still have gained something that did not belong to you. The principle is 'What's mine is mine and what's yours is negotiable.'"[6]

The same way the Soviets did, Russians size up their counterparts in an effort to assess strength of character, ideological commitment, intellectual breadth, and who has most influence with top-level decision makers. General John R. Deane's memoir of his service in Moscow during World War II offers a classic insight into prepositioning and testing by his Soviet counterpart. His first call to the Soviet chief of staff General Antonov was particularly striking:

> I have never had a reception of more studied coldness [Deane wrote]. There was not the slightest spark of cordiality as he shook hands and asked me to be seated. [Antonov then went on to berate Deane about U.S. efforts in Italy.] . . . By this time I had become thoroughly chilled except under the collar and recited a few plain truths. I pointed out that we had liquidated Rommel's forces in Africa, forced Italy out of the war, taken on a second front in the Pacific without the help of our great Red Ally, and, at the same time, run the gauntlet of the German submarine menace to deliver supplies to Russia. With that he asked me if I had any further business, indicating that our conference was concluded. This time when we shook hands there were two pairs of eyes which belied any cordiality in the process. My subsequent meetings with General Antonov were extremely pleasant, and I attained the utmost admiration for his intelligence and ability.[7]

R. F. Smith argues that Deane took the right approach in responding to Antonov's testing. "If he had not stood up for himself and his country, if he had bent over backward to be 'reasonable,' his subsequent meetings with Antonov would not have been 'extremely pleasant.'"[8]

During prepositioning the Russians are careful to cultivate personal relations for later exploitation. Their sociability is an attempt to discover personal or bureaucratic cracks in the team's discipline. Since the administration of President Franklin Roosevelt, the American propensity has been to think that a good personal relationship can overcome all negotiating obstacles, especially when dealing with the supreme leader, the *vozhd.*

Russians draw on intelligence gathered about the opposite negotiating team, probing and testing to see where they can capitalize on tensions within the U.S. delegation. They quickly back away when faced with U.S. solidarity. The probes include efforts to establish dominance by insisting on the rightness and strength of the Russian position or eliciting sympathy for Russia's economic or political woes. At the same time, they demand recognition of their country as a superpower and an equal of the United States.

Intelligence Gathering

The Russians, like their Soviet predecessors, rely heavily on intelligence to position themselves for a negotiation. The Soviet Union placed a high premium on espionage to provide insights into American intentions and plans. This mission, once conducted by the KGB, has been inherited and underscored by the KGB's successors, the Foreign Intelligence Service (SVR) and the Federal Security Service (FVS).

As in the days of the KGB, so today the local head of the Foreign Intelligence Service, the *rezident,* operates under diplomatic cover and reports directly to headquarters (The Center) in Moscow through his own coded communications channel. Military intelligence, the GRU, has been reinforced since the fall of the Soviet Union and its clandestine role has been enhanced, according to American intelligence officials.[9]

Included in the formal instructions to negotiators are briefs of issues and personality profiles of members of the U.S. delegation. Since the Yalta Conference in 1945, the Russian intelligence agencies have studied U.S. negotiators and tried to foreshadow issues, attitudes, and the behavioral style that Soviet leaders would have to face.[10] The Americans' positions in their own power structure, an assessment of their relationship to the president, their susceptibility to flattery, and their sympathy for Russia are elements of the profile.

Soviet delegations placed great emphasis on the use of informal contacts and casual conversations, and spent a great deal of time on lengthy probing of their Western counterparts. Their objective was to find out what was on the top of and what was new to the U.S. agenda. They reported this intelligence to senior Soviet negotiators for evaluation and action.[11] The Soviets were extremely cautious and examined Western positions carefully before entering into negotiations. If, during an information-gathering sweep, a lack of resolve was found at some level of the Western negotiating pyramid, "the Soviets would conclude that the position of the Western representative was negotiable."[12] American negotiators report that this practice is still pursued but is not as rigorously executed as in the days of Communist Party discipline.

Cultivating and Signaling Counterparts

Another high-priority prepositioning tactic that remains very much in use is the attempt to "cultivate" an American negotiator and establish a "special" personal relationship. Henry Kissinger described how, after being named national security adviser to President Nixon after the 1968 election, he was invited to a reception at the Soviet embassy. Ambassador Anatoli Dobrynin, recovering from the flu in his second-floor apartment, invited Kissinger up for a chat. Dobrynin began by suggesting they call each other by their first names, since they would work closely. Dobrynin remarked that he had just returned from the Soviet Union after a medical checkup in the same sanitarium frequented by Politburo members Brezhnev, Kosygin, and Podgorny. He said he had an oral message from his leaders that he wanted to deliver to the new president.

Dobrynin then explained to Kissinger that he had been in Washington since 1962 and had experienced many crises. "Throughout," recorded Kissinger, "he had maintained a relationship of personal confidence with the senior officials; he hoped to do the same with the new administration, whatever the fluctuations of official relations." Then, after his effort to impress Kissinger with his close ties to the Soviet leadership, Dobrynin tested Kissinger by musing that "great opportunities had been lost between 1959 and 1963." Dobrynin, who had been head of the American division of the Soviet Foreign Ministry during that period, said he knew that Khrushchev had wanted an accommodation with the United States. "The chance had been lost then; we must not lose the opportunities at hand today," said Dobrynin.

Kissinger, aware that he was being probed and assessed, told Dobrynin that the United States was prepared to relax tensions on the basis of reciprocity and that "we did not believe that these tensions were due to misunderstandings. They arose from real causes which had to be dealt with if real progress were to be made." Kissinger recalled the two Berlin ultimatums, Khrushchev's "brutal behavior toward Kennedy in Vienna," the Cuban missile crisis, and the Soviet Union's unilateral breach of the moratorium on nuclear testing. "If the Soviet leaders sought an accommodation with the new Administration by these methods, crises would be unavoidable; more 'opportunities' would be lost. Dobrynin smiled and conceded that not all the mistakes had been on the American side. I promised to arrange an early meeting with Nixon."[13]

Throughout the Cold War, American presidents attempted to cultivate friendship with their Soviet counterparts on a man-to-man basis: Eisenhower and Kennedy with Khrushchev; Nixon, Ford, and Carter with Brezhnev. Gromyko, however, was foreign minister for all the Soviet leaders who followed Stalin, and he retained the style and content of the Bolshevik Code. The thaw in superpower hostility increased drastically under Gorbachev, who decreed that the Soviet Union would deem "human values" more important than ideological considerations.[14] U.S. officials were encouraged to make their own attempts to cultivate key Soviet figures. Secretaries of State George Shultz and James Baker both made efforts to establish strong personal relations with their counterpart Eduard Shevardnadze, who replaced Gromyko in July 1985, and both were successful.

Under President Clinton, personal diplomacy between the heads of state has reached a new level of cooperation. Clinton backed Yeltsin's efforts to win reelection in June 1996 and urged the International Monetary Fund to support Yeltsin's economic program.[15] Although Yeltsin can be stiff and aloof, both he and Clinton have worked hard to establish a personal relationship in which they call each other by their first names, speak on the telephone, and exchange letters. Clinton considers Yeltsin "a true democrat . . . also an old-fashioned Russian patriot."[16] The positive side of such a relationship is that Clinton can appeal directly to Yeltsin on issues of personal or political concern, as he did successfully in regard to the withdrawal of Russian troops from the Baltic states. When lower-level negotiators have reached an impasse, the Bill-and-Boris connection has sometimes broken the deadlock.

The political downside is that President Clinton has been attacked for not taking a stronger public stand against the war in Chechnya and for being used by Yeltsin for his own political agenda. Such critics of Clinton foreign policy as Henry Kissinger have noted that, despite the close relationship between Clinton and Yeltsin, Russian sells nuclear power plants and submarines and other arms to Iran, in opposition to American policy. Russia also lifted the embargo on Iraq and has so far refused to delineate its borders with Ukraine and Estonia.[17]

Face-to-face contacts—Clinton and Yeltsin met no fewer than seven times between 1993 and 1996—and personal letters and telephone calls to produce rapid negotiating results have added a new intensity to U.S.-Russian negotiations. Considering the strength of the Yeltsin-Clinton link and the importance to Russia of the American connection, such high-profile personal diplomacy at the presidential level is likely to continue. It is useful to both sides. However, effectiveness depends on the individuals involved, and of course, the personal dimension ends with their terms in office.

OPENING MOVES

Russian negotiators never open discussions with a position close to the final position. Russians rarely make an attempt to establish a mutual framework of agreement; rather, they first wait for the other side to reveal its position and then, relying on carefully prepared instructions, open with a maximal demand. They make a concerted effort to intimidate their negotiating partner and establish a position of dominance and superiority. Despite their country's current position of weakness, the Russians bluster and threaten that the world will be worse unless they get their way.

Waiting for the Other Side to Reveal Its Position

Henry Kissinger often joked with Brezhnev that the Russians would never go first whether they were hosts or guests. He was remarking on the Russians' preference to wait until the other side has outlined and explained its position before exposing their own.

From 1973 to 1975, at the Conference on Security and Cooperation in Europe, U.S. negotiator Ambassador John J. Maresca found the Soviet negotiators to be organized, disciplined, and patient.[18] Only after the Western position was clearly understood would the Soviets introduce their counterposition. After the opening statements, Maresca noted, "the Soviets invariably insisted upon dealing with their own points first. Usually their point was that unless their problems were resolved, negotiations could not proceed. The Soviets often publicly ridiculed the Western proposal, then privately asked delegates what they really wanted to achieve with their proposal. The Soviets asked many delegates the same question, added up the answers, and acted accordingly. They thought they were determining just what could be dropped from the Western proposal."

Through this process they tried to find areas where the West would give up or modify its position. If they received a multiplicity of answers, they further ridiculed the West by publicly stating that "the West cannot even agree upon what it wants."[19] The Soviets became adept at identifying Western delegates most willing to compromise on a given subject. They tried to strike private deals, or at a minimum tried to sow dissension among the Western negotiating teams.

The style and practice continues. In the 1996 Conventional Forces in Europe negotiations, the Russians waited for the West to present its position before offering their ideas on how to reposition Russian forces.

Adopting an Aggressive Stance

After they have heard their counterparts' position, the Russians present their own opening position, one that is used as a battering ram to break down the negotiating partner's defenses. Many reports chronicle the Russian tradition of opening negotiations with aggressive and abusive remarks directed at the American position and American intentions. Examples include wartime meetings between Stalin and Ambassador Averell Harriman, and Khrushchev's treatment first of President

Eisenhower during the U-2 incident and then of President Kennedy at their first meeting at Vienna.[20] The tactic, with variations, remains an arrow in the quiver of negotiating weapons. At an arms negotiation meeting outside Washington in 1995, the Russian lead negotiator opened by saying that his counterpart's reference to their friendship was inaccurate, and proceeded to describe an adversarial relationship between Russia and the United States. He was trying to test his counterpart while carefully following instructions; he put forth a position that would protect him from criticism in the nationalist press and in the Duma in Moscow.

Curiously, when this aggressive behavior pattern was described to Viktor Sukhodrev, a skilled Russian diplomat and interpreter who was present at many summit opening sessions, he objected strongly to the view that opening remarks were intended to set a hard line. In no way, said Sukhodrev, was the Russian's behavior intended to be harsh or nasty; it was simply intended to take the measure of the other side. The opening position was a demarcation line that could always be referred to as an ideological defense wall, proof that instructions had been followed. He insisted these opening thrusts were meant to establish a serious tone that would not put the Russians at a disadvantage by making them vulnerable to personal appeals or arguments for compromise from the other side. This technique was applied to U.S. presidents as well as to heads of delegations. A tough opening, he explained, established blame and eradicated any idea that the Russian leader or delegation could be manipulated by appealing to the bonds of friendship. As such, the tactic adhered to the Bolshevik Code, which stressed that personal sentiment must never color the expression, or obstruct the promotion, of the party line. It protected the delegation from charges back home of weakness or deviation from the party line or official policy, a not-to-be-neglected consideration.

Such aggressive assertions of strength can also be seen as symptoms of a deep-seated insecurity. They are attempts to build a rhetorical wall of such height and strength that it will be able to withstand all the arguments that the other side may throw at it. The process of constantly testing the strength of the wall and the other side's ability to breach it is a defining element of Russian opening moves.

Making Maximum Demands

Russian opening statements are aggressive not only in tone but also in content. In the Soviet era, after listening to and assessing the American position, the leader of the Soviet delegation would present unrealistic demands in an ideologically approved, extreme statement of the Soviet viewpoint. By replacing communist ideology with the dictates of Russian nationalism, negotiators from the Russian Federation have found their own justification for excessive and uncompromising statements of their initial position.

Brent Scowcroft, national security adviser to Presidents Ford and Bush, cautioned that in a negotiation with the Russians it is advisable "to start not too far away from your bottom line. If not, you will never finish a negotiation because you will always be looking for the bottom line."[21]

Former SALT negotiator General Edward Rowny analyzed why the Russians enter with maximum demands, and why they believe their American counterparts do the same. "The Soviets always opened negotiations with extreme positions, while we traditionally opened with proposals closer to the final outcome we sought. I once tried to explain to General Trusov how Americans developed their opening positions. We would appoint two teams, I said, one representing U.S. interests and the other advocating what we thought would be the Soviet point of view. After debating the matter, the U.S. team would leave some negotiating room, but would come to the table with a position close to our desired outcome. We wanted to appear reasonable and fair. 'Let us assume that the best outcome for both of us lies in the middle of this room,' I explained. 'While we enter with a position a meter from the middle, you Soviets come in with a position over at that wall.'

"'Don't do us any favors,' Trusov said. 'If you feel we begin with a position over at that wall, then you should come in at the opposite wall. After all,' he said, 'we can't go back to Moscow admitting that we gave up more than you did.'

"It was of no use trying to explain to Trusov that Americans were simply unable, psychologically, to enter a negotiation with an extreme position. It was a good example of the cultural gap that divided us."[22]

Relying on Prepared Instructions

Moscow restricts the parameters permitted to Russian negotiators before negotiations begin. Russian diplomats are expected to follow carefully prepared, if not always detailed, instructions, without deviation. The extent to which Moscow decides to limit the scope of the negotiating position plays a critical role in determining the outcome of the subsequent negotiations. Although the head of the Russian delegation usually drafts the negotiating instructions, they are sent to the foreign minister and the President's Office for approval.

In arms control negotiations beginning with SALT I in 1969 a Politburo commission was established to supervise the process. The commission was made up of representatives from the Central Committee of the Communist Party, the Ministry of Foreign Affairs, the Ministry of Defense, the KGB, and the Military Industrial Commission of the Council of Ministers (the VPK). The group became known as the Big Five, and its meetings were usually attended by the heads of the agencies or their deputies. Formal reports to the Politburo were always signed by the principals themselves. The Big Five resolved practical issues related to preparation of the Soviet negotiating position and provided guidance for Soviet negotiators. The Big Five reported to the Defense Council, headed by General Secretary Leonid Brezhnev, on high-level strategic and more general problems. When the negotiations reached an impasse on strategic issues, negotiators referred back to the Big Five, who then asked the Defense Council to resolve the stalemate with new instructions.[23]

Victor Israelyan, a career diplomat who headed the bureau of international organizations within the Soviet Foreign Ministry, described the process of preparing instructions during the Soviet period: "The draft is the first step; then, of course, the Ministry of Defense, the KGB, and other interested ministries have to approve. Next, the Politburo blessed it, and finally the formal instructions were issued. Our instructions were very general." "In this way we were very similar," said Israelyan, referring to the similar process of interagency clearance performed within both the U.S. and the Soviet governments. However, he often believed his American negotiating partners "were more equipped with factual material than we were."

The instructions were the bible, to be followed without breaking new ground, said Israelyan. "When negotiations began on the reduction of armed forces, reduction of weapons, or prohibition of weapons I would have some two pages of instructions. One page and a half was blah blah blah, you have to be guided by the speeches of the general secretary of the Communist Party of the Soviet Union, Comrade Leonid Ilyich Brezhnev or Comrade M. S. Gorbachev, and the decisions of the plenum or the Party Congress. Then half a page would be more or less on the specific problem of the negotiation. If it was verification, the instructions would say you can agree with occasional on-site inspections. Sometimes my American partners liked the statement I made, but when they studied it they understood that all my illustrations and comments were based on published statements. There was nothing new in them."[24]

For American delegates, the opening sessions were instructive because they provided the framework for assessing maximum Soviet demands. The opening statements provided an opportunity to mine for nuances that might indicate opportunities for new formulations or flexibility. American delegates listened carefully, hoping to find within the standard ideological rhetoric and the boilerplate the keys to Soviet demands and the possible areas for compromise. The early meetings indicated who was in charge of the Soviet team and how strong his influence was, whether he was bringing new ideas or digging in his heels.

Listening carefully and analyzing Soviet documents was part of a Cold War science of textual analysis known as Kremlinology.[25] Often new ideas would be included in the text of documents or floated in officially sanctioned interviews in the Soviet press. In the post-Soviet period the new ideas are still offered through official statements or interviews, but Kremlinology has faded along with the power of the Central Committee, which devised and disseminated the Communist Party's general line.

Ambassador Max Kampelman recalled that during the strategic arms negotiations in Geneva in 1985 he "learned or confirmed several items of importance during the first round of our meetings. Although the plenary sessions were formal and repetitive, they served a useful purpose. They probably did not persuade either side to change its views, but I was speaking to Moscow with these formal statements as much as to the negotiator in my presence. Everything written would be sent to Moscow precisely as delivered. The plenaries permit you to make a case and lay out a position; in something as complex as nuclear arms and disarmament, that takes time."[26]

At the CSCE negotiations in Madrid in 1983, the U.S. position had been worked out in advance with the NATO allies. Thus the Western position had little flexibility and was close to a final position. In its initial position, the Soviet Union put forth a series of extreme demands that were not based on a unified position with the Eastern Europeans. They did not need one; Soviet diplomats simply dictated the position, based on Moscow's instructions. In that sense the Soviets had more flexibility than the West, but their proposal was unrealistic; it was based on testing Western resolve and trying to extract concessions from the West.

Attempting to Hide or Set the Agenda

Russian delegations often arrive at negotiations ready to negotiate on the basis of a concealed agenda, one that is responsive not to the issue on the table but to other, more pressing policy concerns in Moscow or to internal political pressures in Russia. At the CSCE meetings in Madrid from 1980 to 1983, Soviet Ambassador Dubinin was tasked with creating a disarmament conference that would blunt the U.S. effort to place intermediate-range missiles in Europe. "What was unsaid publicly about Madrid and never written up," explained Ambassador Kampelman, was Dubinin's specific assignment: to get a disarmament meeting going as part of CSCE. "They were still trying to fight the basing of Pershing and Cruise missiles in Europe. They would go to the Europeans and say, 'Why do you need Cruise missiles if we are having a disarmament conference?' The French proposed a meeting for confidence-building measures. I said it was not in our interest to have a short meeting," said Kampelman. What was to have been a three-month meeting in Madrid was extended by the United States to three years to avoid what the Soviets had proposed, the convening of an all-European CSCE disarmament conference before deployment of Pershing medium-range missiles could be accomplished.

Even when Russian delegations do come to the table prepared to tackle the ostensible subject of the negotiations, they typically try to control or reset the agenda by shifting the emphasis from specific goals to generalized statements of principle. For the Soviets, the goal in a negotiation often was a generalized position that both sides could agree upon. They wanted a vague, unspecific agreement in principle that would serve to undercut Western demands for specifics and provide material for propaganda in the communist and third worlds. The Soviet delegation would then interpret the general goal as its own and claim that the West had agreed to the Soviet position. "The Soviets," Kissinger noted, "are much addicted to declarations of principles. Probably they see them as an acknowledgement of equality and a device to create the impression that major progress is taking place in bilateral relations. Perhaps there is something in Russian history that leads them to value ritual, solemn declarations, and visible symbols."[27]

During a secret trip to Moscow in April 1972 to arrange a summit that was held later that spring, Kissinger met with Brezhnev, who proposed a step of "immense significance," namely, the idea of a Soviet-U.S. understanding not to use nuclear weapons against each other. Nixon also wanted an agreement to limit nuclear weapons, but not before he obtained Soviet cooperation in ending the Vietnam War. Brezhnev's priority was to press for a Brezhnev-Nixon Declaration of Basic Principles, an idea first proposed in 1971 but not adopted until Brezhnev's visit to the United States in 1973. The declaration of principles emphasized broad goals such as mutual restraint and noninterference in the affairs of other states.

In contrast, Kissinger's agenda, as ordered by Nixon, was to obtain Soviet pressure on North Vietnam to end the war. Kissinger and Gromyko had agreed on a statement making public Kissinger's visit, the text of which spoke of "important international problems as well as bilateral matters" to be dealt with preparatory to the summit meeting in May. "Important international problems" was an obvious reference to Vietnam, for Hanoi had launched a major offensive only three weeks earlier. Before he departed for a Politburo meeting Brezhnev dropped the announcement on the table and said it was acceptable except for "some minor alterations." What Brezhnev had done was to return to the original Soviet version, leaving out mention of Vietnam and nuclear disarmament, and thus creating the impression that the United States had asked for the meeting and that the talks were solely about summit preparations.

Kissinger was furious and "exploded." Gromyko said the choice was between Brezhnev's draft or none. Kissinger and Gromyko jousted until Gromyko agreed to go to Brezhnev in the Politburo meeting and see if the wording could be modified. He returned with agreement to use the phrase "important international problems" but to drop a phrase describing the talks as "frank and useful." Gromyko agreed that Kissinger could use this phrase in briefings and that the Soviets would confirm it. "In other words there would be a version for America and another for Hanoi. The episode is significant precisely because it was so petty. Anything that could conceivably be gained by such a crude maneuver must surely be outweighed by its powerful reminder that in dealing with Soviet leaders one must be constantly on one's guard. It is illustrative of the Soviet tendency to squander goodwill for marginal gains and of a nearly compulsive tendency to score points meaningful only, if at all, in terms of the Politburo's internal rivalries. After that stormy session, all was again serene and jovial, in the way of Soviet negotiators when they have at last discovered what the negotiating limits are," wrote Kissinger.[28]

Was the episode really so "petty"? In the rarefied atmosphere of the communist world, Gromyko was thinking of how the statement would be read in Beijing and Hanoi. The Chinese would attack the Soviet Union for colluding with the Americans; Kissinger's proposed statement would erode Hanoi's trust in Moscow. The negotiator must take into consideration the various audiences who will read or overinterpret intentions through apparently minor word changes. Holding firm to one's position and being constantly on guard for political recriminations or backlash are essential to a skilled negotiator.

The Soviet negotiators pursued general agreements in principle because they were useful for their political and propaganda impact. Israelyan recalled, "We would prefer an agreement in general terms and say, let's reduce arms by 15 or 20 percent, while our American and European partners would stress the details of practical implementation. Our mentality is to agree that we will have dinner. Okay? You will say, I have some problem with my stomach; if I go to the dinner I won't eat. I say, let's agree to go to the dinner and then we will negotiate the details later. This is a mental mind-set and a defining characteristic."[29]

At the conclusion of the CSCE conference in 1975, Ambassador John Maresca noted this pattern of behavior in action. "The Soviets wanted the Conference to produce a very brief final document, consisting almost solely of a list of principles guiding relations among states, with a central place to be given to the all-important idea of inviolability of frontiers. They also hoped to squeeze out any undesirable proposals under the other subject headings of the agenda."[30]

The U.S. government, wrote Raymond F. Smith, "prefers to negotiate an agreement that spells out obligations in detail and, in the implementation phase, assuming the good faith of both parties, to lay stress on the spirit of the agreements. The Soviets prefer more broadly worded agreements but expect in implementation to be required to do no more than what is precisely laid out in the written documents."[31] Americans have learned not to expect "goodwill" in going further than the minimum in fulfilling written obligations—which reinforces the U.S. interest in specifying agreements in as much detail as possible.

MIDGAME

Russian negotiators listen to and assess the other side's opening position and deliver an aggressive statement of Russian demands. Their next task is to probe again for weaknesses in the Western position and divisions among the Western team. The Russian tendency is to test the locus of strength and authority, then attempt to overthrow it if the negotiator hesitates or indicates lack of resolution. In pursuit of this goal, a wide variety of tactics is employed, some abusive (verbal battering and threats), some exasperating (stalling and repetition), some ingratiating (emphasizing "special" relationships). The Russian team also makes an effort outside the formal negotiating arena, notably through the use of the media, to influence the course of a negotiation. Soviet negotiators made high-level efforts to bypass the normal diplomatic channels and conduct negotiations through back channels, such as journalists and business executives with high-level access.

At the same time that they seek to extract the maximum concessions from their negotiating partners, Russian diplomats must also keep a watchful eye on Moscow so as to discern shifts in the political tides at home and avoid provoking the anger of their bureaucratic superiors.

The Heavy Hand of Moscow

Russian negotiators are kept on a tighter rein by their political masters than are diplomats of most Western countries. As a consequence, Russian negotiators are typically slow to respond to new initiatives and severely limited in the options they themselves can propose. The process of securing interagency consensus preceding an international negotiation is often extremely trying for Russian negotiators. Even more difficult is the process of securing a change in instructions once negotiations are under way. With the institutional chaos left by the demise of the Soviet system and the Communist Party, the problems of establishing bureaucratic and political consensus have been exacerbated. There is no formal coordinating mechanism, and Russian negotiators "are nostalgic about the old interagency coordination method chaired by the Central Committee," explained Igor Khripunov, a former Soviet strategic arms negotiator.[32]

Even before the Soviet Union disappeared, Russian negotiators faced severe constraints. If the Americans came up with a new proposal, recalled Soviet negotiator Victor Israelyan, the Russian delegation head was unable to reply without referring to Moscow for new instructions. This prospect was painful. "Moscow hated questions. This was the worst thing."

Israelyan and other Soviet heads of delegations disliked going back to Moscow for new instructions because it meant they could no longer work with the basic guidelines that had been arduously cleared through the system up to the Politburo for final approval.

"When I would ask for new instructions you can imagine the anger of the minister, the fury. 'You fool, you yourself have prepared the instructions, now you are asking what to do because the Americans came with some new suggestion.' I didn't like new American proposals because I would have to ask for instructions and that would mean that I had prepared myself poorly. It was the worst thing to inform Moscow of a new American proposal without giving your comment on how to deal with it. You had to know whether or not it would be liked in Moscow. When you were in Moscow it was more or less easy; I had colleagues on my level I could ask. Sitting in Geneva or somewhere else and asking for new instructions and to suggest how to respond was very difficult," remembered Israelyan.

The result was that negotiations were stalled until the Soviet delegation returned to Moscow for a New Year or summer vacation break. Freewheeling or "creative" American negotiators may not have understood their counterparts' problems in obtaining new instructions, but they knew they would have to await the return of the delegation from Moscow for any new momentum in their talks.

Soviet delegation leaders often made suggestions in the name of their American counterpart so as not to lose face in Moscow if the initiative was rejected. During the SALT negotiations, in order to avoid committing themselves to a position while raising a possible point of compromise, Soviet delegates presented the Americans with a nonattributable document. General Rowny received the document from his Soviet counterpart when they were leaving a meeting; the Soviet negotiator told him, "Here's a non-paper, you can read it if you wish. But if you attribute it to me, I'll deny it." The Soviets expected the Americans to consider the idea set forth in the paper. If it was appealing, Rowny could present it at the next meeting as his own. According to this scheme, Rowny explained, "the Soviets would then send the 'American proposal' to Moscow for analysis. If Moscow approved, 'our proposal' would be adopted. If Moscow did not agree, the Soviet negotiators could not be accused of having suggested it."

If the American delegates thought the Soviet idea needed refinement, they could send a written reply, but they had to designate it a "non-paper reply" to the Soviet delegation's "non-paper." This was for the Soviet delegation's use only, and not to be relayed to Moscow. "If we heard nothing back from them, it was a signal that they did not like our changes. But at times, they would reply to our 'non-paper' with another 'non-paper.' It was by such unconventional and often silly games that the negotiations moved forward," explained Rowny.[33]

Although delegation heads were given little room for maneuver by Moscow, their instructions did include a fallback position. This practice has been inherited from the Soviet Union and continues. Israelyan noted, "You never come out with your last or final position, that is clear. You start with a first position and then you have a '*zapasnaya* position,' a fallback position, a second position. I always had a fallback position in my instructions."

The Soviets always carefully calculated the midgame; the timing of when to place a new position on the table was critical, explained Israelyan:

> Some Soviet negotiators would stick to the first position and be happy to report back to Moscow that they had stated our position several times and rebuffed the Americans. Others, whom I considered more practical and professional, would not waste too much time before going to the second position. But if you go to the fallback too soon you don't have anything more in your pocket. If you make your second position known the second day, then you don't have anything left and you will be forced to ask for new instructions. The minister will then ask, what did you rush for? Why didn't you try to convince the Americans? Here, much depended on the character and the experience of the negotiator to find the right time to make the concession or introduce a new proposal.
>
> I was part of a negotiation on the withdrawal of Soviet troops from Afghanistan, and our position was that it was up to us alone and we were not going to negotiate, so we just shut up. I understood this was a waste of time. If there is a negotiation, you agree to negotiate a second or third position. Usually there is only a second position, and it depends on the art of the negotiator.
>
> I had in the delegation a representative of the KGB and the Ministry of Defense and, in the chemical weapons negotiations, a representative of the Ministry of Chemistry. First, I had to get their support because they had the right to report to their bosses. After I obtained a consensus I sent cables to Moscow.
>
> What would be convincing for Moscow? First of all I had to inform them that the experts agree with the opinion I express. Then I had to reflect the position of our allies. Sometimes the Poles, the [East] Germans, or the Hungarians would express something on their own. Their arguments in support of my position would say something I could not say. I used them to make a point. My colleagues would feel my attitude, and in expressing their views they would give me an additional argument.
>
> Very important of course is the position of the nonallies—India played an important role, so did Yugoslavia, Egypt, the Arabs. If they said that they would welcome such a development, I would report it.
>
> Then I would come with my second position or recommend accepting the American position. This is the art of the negotiator, you have to know what the reader of the cable wants, what he is interested in, what kind of result he wants.

Israelyan's retrospective description of the process explains why most American negotiators found that informal sessions were immensely important in finding new directions for the negotiations. Soviet KGB and military people felt freer to speak informally and more informatively than members of the Soviet foreign service.

In the postcommunist period American negotiators find that the Russians "still stick to set speeches in formal settings," but are inclined to discuss broader issues in informal settings. In this context, pending issues come into the open and can be resolved. During these informal sessions American diplomats work hard to acknowledge Russian equality as a superpower. Later, at the bargaining table this assurance is essential in evoking Russian responses.[34]

Just as Russian diplomats must remain keenly attuned to the wishes of their superiors in Moscow, so Moscow itself must now adapt its foreign policies to suit political pressures inside Russia. Shifts in the Russian Federation position on NATO expansion have clearly reflected the rise of Russian nationalism. Accused by nationalist and communist politicians of sacrificing Russian national interests by working too closely with the United States, President Yeltsin and his foreign ministers opposed NATO's move to include former Soviet bloc states such as Poland, Hungary, and the Czech Republic. Yeltsin flouted the restrictions placed on Russia for the IMF loan of $10 billion during the 1996 election campaign; he illegally used $1 billion to pay back wages and fulfill campaign promises, but he returned close to compliance by tightening the government budget once he was reelected. The promise of great power acceptance of Russia in the Group of Seven (the G-7; now the G-8) and continued IMF support of the Russian government were strong incentives for Yeltsin to reach a compromise on NATO expansion. Feeding Yeltsin's own political popularity and raising the money to sustain it were important negotiating weapons skillfully wielded by American negotiators.

Secrecy

The Soviet Union kept its negotiators not only on a tight rein but often in the dark. The Soviets jealously guarded access to details on weapons capabilities and numbers even from those charged with representing Soviet interests in negotiations. Victor Israelyan has said that he and other Soviet arms negotiators were not kept abreast of the latest developments in weaponry, and often learned the extent of Soviet weapons stockpiles only when Western delegates revealed the secret information during negotiations. Only by revealing the information could the West establish a basis for arms reductions. In many ways, the arms control negotiations served as a seminar to teach Soviet diplomats the technical intricacies of arms control and the details of their own country's capabilities and deployments.[35]

During the chemical warfare negotiations that took place during the Geneva Conference on Disarmament from 1979 to 1987, Israelyan, who headed the Soviet delegation, could not, under instructions from Gromyko, admit that the Soviet Union possessed chemical weapons. In his memoirs, the former Soviet ambassador to Washington Anatoli Dobrynin declared, "The shroud of secrecy caused bitter suspicion abroad. Except for Gromyko himself, even the very top Soviet diplomats including myself were completely ignorant of the Soviet military's expansion programs and discussed such matters with their foreign counterparts on the basis of figures that were out of date. On some occasions we actually did not tell the truth on Moscow's instructions without knowing it, as in the case of the Krasnoyarsk surveillance radar designed for tracking space missions."[36]

Speaking in 1996, an American negotiator with more than twenty years' negotiating experience observed that "the Russian attitude to secrecy has changed some, but not that much. In discussing military numbers and technical details there is still a basic feeling that these are sensitive subjects that shouldn't be divulged. There are all sorts of agreements at the summits to exchange information, but that has not happened and is hard to implement. They are a little more open within the government than in the past. However, the long tradition of secrecy is still there hiding weakness and there is a lot of weakness to hide."[37]

Stalling and Repetition

Stalling was a standard maneuver for Soviet delegations. This annoying practice was perfected by Foreign Minister Vyacheslav Molotov, who, as William Taubman has written, "resorted to three tactics: he tried arguing, then bargaining, and when all else failed, he stalled."[38] Molotov's legacy is still a standard Russian practice. Frequently, Russians refuse to answer letters or telephone calls, announce that they are not available, and insist on postponing or changing dates. Accompanied by bad manners and rudeness, stalling is a deliberate effort to wear down an opponent and force concessions, especially from a goal-oriented opponent, as the Russians conceive the Americans to be. In post-Soviet times, stalling is also an indication of the chaos and disorganization of the Russian government.

In his memoirs Henry Kissinger pointed out how the Soviets used their traditional "stalling tactics" to further their goals with the United States. After one month of high-level discussions and requests on behalf of Nixon to schedule a summit with the Soviets to focus on a "new stage of U.S.-Soviet relations," Dobrynin responded in a perplexed and slightly dense fashion that he was unclear what message he should be taking back to Moscow—could it be that the United States wanted a summit to discuss a new stage in U.S.-Soviet relations?[39]

These stalling tactics were employed in order to keep raising the potential stakes in the negotiations. The Soviets kept increasing their demands and expanding their wish lists. Just how much would such a summit cost the United States? The more desirous of the summit the United States seemed to be, the more the Soviet demands grew. President Nixon hoped for a U.S.-Soviet summit in the summer of 1970. The Soviets, through Dobrynin, stalled for more than a year. In this case, however, the Soviet delaying tactic backfired: Kissinger's secret trip to Beijing in July 1971, and the prospect of a U.S.-Chinese summit between President Nixon and Chairman Mao, shocked the Soviets and prompted Moscow in September 1971 to agree to a summit. The United States, though, now chose to delay, and put the Soviets off until after Nixon's trip to China in February 1972.

Soviet stalling tactics are legendary. General Rowny recalled how Soviet delegates kept reiterating their opening positions rather than engage in discussion:

> During the SALT II negotiations in 1974, I became exasperated with the stalling tactics of one of my Soviet military counterparts, Col. Gen. Ivan Beletsky. He kept repeating the same statements and would not enter into a serious discussion of the merits of our respective positions. I told Beletsky that I was elaborating on the rationale for our position and that he should do the same with respect to theirs. "It takes two to tango," I said.

"No," retorted Beletsky, "it takes one to tango." He then told me about the way young men met young women in his hometown: "In my day, we went to Saturday night dances looking for a date. All the young women seated themselves along the walls of the dance hall. Rather than ask one of them to dance, a young man would pick up a chair and dance with it.

"As I danced the tango, I kept looking at the expressions on the young women's faces. When one smiled and nodded approvingly, I knew I had gained her favor. I then asked her to dance, and we became friends.

"It's the same in our dealings with you," he continued. "We simply keep repeating our positions, expecting that one of you will smile or nod approvingly.

"So you see," he concluded, "it takes one to tango."[40]

This stalling technique can be seen as reflecting a deep-seated sense of insecurity on both a personal and a political level. At the personal level, it is safer to tango alone and wait for a signal from the other side than to take the chance of appearing weak in the eyes not only of one's negotiating partners but also of one's superiors in Moscow. For Russian negotiators, no results are often a victory, especially when internal policy considerations are taken into account. Russian stalling on the NATO Partnership for Peace is a case in point: an ambiguous, hedged policy on acceptance of NATO expansion has served President Yeltsin's political agenda in his battle with nationalist elements. At the political level, the long history of invasions of Russia has bred a fear and suspicion of the outside world, sentiments that were exacerbated by the Soviet view of the West as an implacable foe in the unremitting struggle between capitalism and communism. The painfully acute sense of diminished status on the international stage that pervades the Russian Federation has further accentuated Russian insecurity.

Pressure Tactics

Stalling, repeating positions, not returning phone calls, postponing meetings, and generally making it appear that progress is impossible are part of the arsenal of pressure tactics long employed by Russian negotiators. Such tactics can be as unsubtle but nonetheless effective as calling meetings at odd hours in the expectation that Russian negotiators will outlast their counterparts physically.[41] It is a large and varied arsenal on which negotiators draw in the attempt to extract maximum concessions from the other side while yielding little or nothing on the Russian side.

In the Yeltsin years the disorganized bureaucracy and the lack of a centralized decision-making mechanism have led to poor, often appalling Russian failure or inability to respond. Russians are notoriously negligent about meeting deadlines for written replies or proposals. What may seem like a subtle form of pressure is actually an inability to act, and American negotiators must often take the initiative to move negotiations forward, remaining cautious not to make concessions in their efforts to keep talks on track.

Abuse, Intimidation, and Ridicule

Foreign Minister Gromyko's long-winded repetitions of Soviet demands and abusive verbal battering of his adversary led to his reputation as a worthy successor to Molotov, whose nickname was Mr. Iron Bottom. Sitting out an American opponent was a standard Soviet tactic, especially when dealing with American negotiators whose time frame for a specific negotiation was linked to a presidential election or presidential appointment and whose culture values efficiency and expeditious problem solving.

The Soviets were quick to try to take advantage of a nonprofessional negotiator appointed by the president. The classic example was Stalin negotiating with Averell Harriman and Lord Beaverbrook for Lend Lease assistance in 1941 before the United States entered the war. At their first meeting Stalin described the Soviets' most urgent combat needs, with tanks leading the list, followed by antitank and antiaircraft guns. Harriman left the meeting "flush with satisfaction. He had prepared himself well and it had gone perfectly. One more meeting and an aid package could be tied up for Roosevelt and Churchill. But when he and Beaverbrook returned on the following evening, they encountered an altogether different reception. Stalin was restless, boorish, and spiteful, angrily puffing on his pipe, pacing the floor, interrupting them to make telephone calls, and accusing them of being niggardly in their offers."[42] By the end of the session nothing had been accomplished but an agreement to meet a third time. At a third meeting Stalin listened "patiently, nodding his approval over and over as Harriman ticked through the revised lists developed by working groups." Stalin interrupted Harriman and Beaverbrook only to ask for more scout cars and trucks. The first wartime agreements with the Soviet Union valued at $1 billion were concluded in deceptive harmony.[43]

In his comprehensive study of Soviet diplomacy and negotiating behavior, Joseph Whelan noted, "Though the Soviet Union was then facing its greatest peril as the German armies were approaching within 30 miles of Moscow, and though its needs for Allied assistance in great quantities were immediate and most acute, still Stalin was the tough-minded negotiator who could and did, by employing the tactic of abuse, throw off balance his negotiating counterparts. By placing them on the defensive, he reversed the role of petitioner and donor, thus creating a psychological mood and relationship that could give greater assurance that his needs would be met. Perhaps on no other occasion was Stalin able to demonstrate more dramatically this historic Russian negotiating position of strength out of one of weakness."[44]

At the CSCE meetings from 1973 to 1975, recalled John Maresca, intimidation of Western delegates "was carried out through public ridicule, heaping abuse on a delegate or his position in an open meeting, or usually in more private circumstances, by a sometimes unnerving display of anger, complete with threats to a delegate's career." The Soviets embarrassed Western delegates by criticizing their positions to their superiors (especially if the delegates seemed to contradict positions expressed by Western leaders) before the delegates had a chance to fully explain the situation to their superiors. The Soviets would also reiterate, albeit in a dozen different ways, the same question—"What do you really want?"—seeking both to ridicule a Western proposal and to isolate its essential points. Then the Soviets concluded that the Western delegates would be willing to drop all the other points that were not defined as essential.

Public ridicule was part of what Maresca termed "the steamroller," which also involved exploiting procedural rules, manipulating friendly Western delegations, and using maximum pressure to force through a measure. Western delegations at the CSCE hesitated to fight back unless the issues were clear and easily defensible because they and their political leaders did not want to appear to be obstructing détente.[45]

Persistence, Silence, and Intransigence

The Russians never take no for an answer, explained Maresca. "A 'no' is never accepted by Russians as an initial response. Believing that every response can be manipulated and changed, they will repeat their requests over and over again, adding a new twist every time."[46]

While they persist in interrogating their negotiating partners, Russian negotiators can themselves be decidedly unforthcoming. They will simply refuse to reply to a proposal they do not like or are not ready to deal with. By refusing to communicate or ignoring the point of their counterparts' remarks, the Russians hope to create the impression of being an aloof and remote negotiating partner, one that their opponents will finally seek to placate by making concessions.

Ambassador U. Alexis Johnson, frustrated by a lack of give-and-take during SALT negotiations, resorted to asking direct questions. His counterpart, Minister Vladimir Semenov, reacted by searching through a stack of index cards he kept at hand to see if he could answer Johnson's questions. When he found a card that answered a question Moscow had anticipated, he read it. More often, however, he simply read the answer to a question for which he had an answer, even though it had no relevance to the question asked. When Johnson complained that Semenov was not answering his question, Semenov, with a straight face, told Johnson he was not asking the right questions. Johnson at one point decided not to let it pass. "I insist," he said, "that I asked the right question."

"Well," said Semenov, "I gave the right answer, but you didn't listen between the lines."[47]

Timing of Concessions

During the first three years of the CSCE meetings from 1973 to 1975, the Soviet delegation used Western governments or trusted sources in the media to release one or two concessions immediately prior to high-level East-West visits or Western meetings. This technique ensured that whenever the senior political levels of Western governments focused on the CSCE, which they did only rarely, the latest reports would be of Soviet concessions and progress.[48]

During the SALT II negotiations, pressures on both President Gerald Ford and Leonid Brezhnev prevented convening a summit to conclude the treaty. In October 1976, according to Ambassador Anatoli

Dobrynin, President Ford took him aside after a White House meeting and explained that before the coming American presidential elections, Soviet-American relations were heading for a "time of troubles." Dobrynin quoted Ford as saying: "Let Brezhnev give me anything, at least something of a positive nature, to be able to continue the dialogue on a constructive, not totally pessimistic note."

In his memoirs Dobrynin reported that Moscow was in no mood to oblige because of strong pressure from the Soviet military, which demanded restrictions on U.S. cruise missiles. At the same time, the Soviet leadership underestimated the importance of domestic constraints on American presidents. "Moscow believed that all requests of this kind from Washington had only one objective—to wring some further concession from the Soviet side," wrote Dobrynin.

Nor did the leadership pay any attention to Dobrynin's reports about the serious differences of opinion among factions within the American cabinet that Ford could not disregard. "The Kremlin was convinced that a president was the boss and had the power to decide unilaterally, especially given his desire and need to reach an agreement. So, instead of attempting some goodwill gesture toward the president, we fell into our habit of prolonging the argument. Usually we would make some concession at the end, but often only at the time when the moment for doing so had passed, and the only thing we would get in exchange was the enmity that arose from a deepening of the rift between the leaders of our countries. The history of Soviet diplomacy was marked by such wasted opportunities."[49]

Concessions and Compromise

Russian negotiators ratchet up the pressure on their counterparts to make concessions, but fiercely resist offering their own compromise solutions unless forced to do so. At the CSCE meetings, recalled Maresca, despite the order of presentation of proposals, the Soviets invariably insisted on dealing with their own points first. "They took the position that unless their problem points were resolved, negotiations could not proceed. The Russians hinted at flexibility if their demands were met, but in the situations where the Western side also wished to settle a dispute quickly and acceded to Soviet wishes the Western side was invariably disappointed afterwards."

American negotiator Raymond F. Smith cautioned, "Never grant a tangible immediate benefit in return for a promised future one. You will wind up negotiating again for the promised Soviet action and will more likely have to give up something else to get it. You may even find that your magnanimous gesture, intended to create a better atmosphere, may indeed have contributed to a worse one." Smith also warned, "If you give your Soviet counterpart a bird in the hand, you are going to wind up beating the bush for a long time."[50]

Soviet negotiators and most present-day Russian diplomats were trained to follow Lenin's adage: "If you strike steel, pull back; if you strike mush, push forward."[51] American negotiators "should expect the Soviets to go on the offensive when the United States makes concessions and should have their counter-strategy prepared. The Soviets expect that we will go on the offensive after we have made a concession," explained Smith. "Although the Soviets are ready to move quickly away from unreasonable demands if they meet a firm rejection, they will dig their heels in and insist upon some accommodation to their request if the initial reply is vacillating."[52]

Ambassador Warren Zimmermann described a favorite Soviet tactic of making concessions and then retracting them while the talks were moving ahead at top speed. The Soviets calculated that the Americans were so engaged in negotiations that they could not withdraw and would tolerate the Soviet act of bad faith. The Soviets used this tactic in an effort to restrict access by dissidents and human rights activists to the Human Rights Conference scheduled to be held in Moscow in 1991. The Soviet Union wanted the access question agreed upon in 1989 so that the human rights issue could be preempted and disposed of. While pushing for agreement that Moscow would be the site of the conference, the Soviet delegation agreed to full access; however, as soon as it was agreed to stage the meeting in Moscow, the Soviets pressured the smaller nations they could use as intermediaries to push for changes in the language regarding access, making the relevant wording less specific and thus allowing the Soviet government to limit access of dissidents to the conference. Zimmermann was called and asked if he would accept the change. "Knowing that would be a deal breaker I immediately said no and the Russians backed down," Zimmermann recounted.[53]

The Russian equivalent to compromise is bartering or trading off issues, especially when quantitative values are involved. "Any concession has to be on a quid pro quo basis," explained Bryant Wedge and Cyril Muromcew in their analysis of Soviet negotiating behavior in the SALT negotiations.[54] The quid-pro-quo mentality is evident also when Russian negotiators are faced with unacceptable proposals from their Western counterparts. In order to negate, or at least seriously weaken, such proposals, the Russians respond with what Maresca has termed "the equally disagreeable counterproposal," which is designed to be no less disquieting and uncomfortable for the West than the Western proposal was for the Russians.[55]

For Russians, compromise is replaced by a counting mentality, one-for-one trading. Anthropologist Geoffrey Gorer noted: "In negotiations with Russians, a successful outcome is most likely if negotiations are phrased in terms of the most concrete and symmetrical equality: man for man, ton for ton, acre for acre, town for town, and so on. In the view of the Russians, the only alternative to the utmost rigorous equality is for one of the parties to be completely subordinate; and they always have the fear that they may be forced into the position of absolute weakness."[56]

A British Foreign Office paper, "Negotiating with the Russians," advised that Soviet negotiators "tend to see negotiations as a form of horse-trading or a series of unrelated individual bargains. Soviet counter concessions must therefore be obtained on the spot, not with delay, as a condition of concessions, otherwise they will probably not be obtained at all."[57]

In negotiations for Mutually Balanced Force Reductions (MBFR), American diplomat Jonathan Dean found similar behavior. "Soviet negotiators are decidedly close-fisted with their negotiating assets. They carefully husband negotiating resources, demanding a formal quid pro quo for every move and refuse to go further until NATO participants respond with a move of their own. Even a small Western move may suffice to fulfill the requirements of this mechanistic reciprocity, which does not seek to weigh the relative importance of moves made by either side."[58]

Developing and Maintaining Special Relationships

Russian tactics run the gamut from abuse and rejection to conviviality and embrace. After months of maintaining a cool, formal distance from their American counterparts at the CSCE, Russian delegates turned to the Americans and spoke about "We Great Powers," stressing the importance of Soviet-American cooperation. The Russians then tried to be chummy with the United States, claiming that the "petty details" presented by European allies were disrupting the vital agendas of the United States and the Soviet Union. The points at issue, Maresca noted, were not at all minor and "despite their apparently lofty attitude, [the Soviets] themselves were almost never willing to yield on 'minor details.'"[59]

After friendly high-level visits and successful summits, the Soviets approached specific Western delegates and tried to develop private relationships in the glow of the new harmonious atmosphere. For bait they offered to make a (minor) concession if a favorable solution to the issues at hand could be found. The Soviets stressed the need for secrecy in this new atmosphere. Usually meeting in private, the Soviets offered little of significance but "pursued this technique effectively on several occasions, sometimes using to their advantage the fact that Western delegates were not always privy to what had taken place between their own political leaders and the Soviets."[60]

Friendly overtures from Russian diplomats are not always, or at least not entirely, motivated by cynicism. Russians are susceptible to what former negotiator Yale Richmond called "the big and beautiful syndrome." Russians see themselves and Americans as citizens of two superpowers destined to play leading roles on the world stage: "Joint endeavors between Russians and Americans are therefore seen as natural. Indeed, Russians get a psychological lift from working with Americans, regarding such cooperation as recognition of their coequal status. But they also expect Americans to accept them as equals, to return their admiration, and they are disappointed and puzzled when they do not," wrote Richmond.[61]

Despite the breakup of the Soviet Union the Russians still claim equality and superpower status. Their political and economic difficulties have made the Russians acutely conscious of their reduced importance materially, but have heightened their Slavic sensitivity and sense of mission. The Russian need for recognition and approval from the West has been intensified at the highest levels, with a warming of relationships between Gorbachev and Bush, Yeltsin and Bush, and Yeltsin and Clinton.

The rules for friendship and cooperation are not readily or easily apparent, however. Ambassador Rowny recalled inviting the Russian delegation to take an excursion boat on Lake Geneva. Small talk was not working so Rowny took out his harmonica and played popular Russian tunes, including "Mi Communisti" (We Are the Communists). On hearing it, the members of the delegation formed a conga line and stomped around the boat. At the end of the song Minister Vladimir Semenov took up a collection of dollars, rubles, and Swiss and French francs from the astonished onlookers. "We'll divide 50:50," Semenov said. But when Rowny stretched out his hand, Semenov put all the money in his pocket. "You had 100 percent of the pleasure playing. I'll have 100 percent of the pleasure of spending the money," he said, "50:50." "This was their idea of fairness," noted Rowny, with no suggestion that Semenov was pulling his leg.[62]

Maintaining "special relationships" is a high priority for Russian negotiators. The personal relationships cultivated during the prepositioning phase, whether between top-ranking officials or lower-level diplomats, are carefully tended throughout the negotiating process by means of lunches or dinners and social outings for recreation. The famous walks in the woods between negotiators Paul Nitze and Yuli Kvitsinsky in July 1982 in Geneva led to resolving the impasse on limiting intermediate-range nuclear forces (INF).[63]

The Russian penchant for personal ties and approval from their American counterparts is an important ingredient in the negotiating mix. In the final days of the Soviet Union both Gorbachev and Yeltsin sought the approval of President Bush, whom they held in high esteem. Both of them, noted Anatoli Dobrynin, "called Bush as if he were a supreme judge—to give him their own versions of the fateful events."[64]

Russians seek the approval of their Western opposite numbers, but they will not do so at the expense of Russian national pride. Aware of their country's inferiority to the West in economic development, Russians nonetheless are proud of their country's history and assert their moral superiority. For the Soviets, the struggle by the "working masses" against the forces of "reactionary imperialism" implicitly conferred moral superiority on the Soviet leadership. Today, nationalists proclaim the unique role and achievements of Russia. A recurring theme has been, and remains, the sacrifices made by the Russian people: Russian negotiators refer to the heavy losses incurred in the war to defeat Napoleon and the twenty million Russian lives lost in the "Great Patriotic War" against Nazi Germany. Paul Nitze learned how sensitive Russians are to their patriotic values and love of the motherland during the INF talks. In *Deadly Gambits*, Strobe Talbott describes a meeting between Nitze and Soviet negotiator Yuli Kvitsinsky in which Nitze pointed out "unmanned cruise missiles 'can sustain much higher rates of attrition than piloted aircraft.' In that sense, he added wryly, the drones are 'infinitely courageous.' The Soviets bridled at even this touch of humor. They thought it contained an aspersion on the bravery of Soviet pilots or on the willingness of Mother Russia to sacrifice as many of her sons as necessary to defend herself. 'We don't care about attrition,' replied a military officer on the delegation, A. I. Ivlev. 'That is not a factor for us.'"[65]

Exploiting Entertainment

Entertaining has played an important role in Soviet negotiating behavior and continues to be an integral part of doing business with the Russians. Typically, a breakthrough in negotiations will be announced not at a formal negotiating session but at an informal occasion. Russians use informal meetings as an intelligence-gathering arena and, with drink, hope to throw their opponents off guard to obtain insights into their characters or personal weaknesses. A drinking bout provides an opportunity to demonstrate the Russians' ability to consume alcohol in prodigious quantities. Drinking is also the excuse for being maudlin and expressing sentiments a Russian man might be ashamed to reveal when sober. This is a chance to show one's spiritual side, including generosity toward one's counterpart and love of mankind. Such expansiveness usually ends with professions of peace and friendship and the promise of personal loyalty and trust.

Russians like to quote the old proverb "More people are drowned in a glass than in the ocean." This is a rueful commentary on the extent of alcoholism among Russians and a veiled warning against the dangers of revealing secrets when inebriated. Even a morning meeting is likely to include a glass of cognac accompanying tea or coffee. Contemporary diplomatic style continues to borrow from the French manners of the imperial court of St. Petersburg, with an ever-present bottle of brandy, scotch, or wine to establish an atmosphere of good fellowship on first meeting. Drinks also offer the opportunity for toasts, which for Russians are an intricate part of diplomatic positioning used to transmit hints, allusions, and veiled, coded messages regarding the potential for new openings or a change in position.

The renowned French observer of Russian behavior, the Marquis de Custine, wrote in 1839 of Russian fondness for drink, and his insights are still relevant: "The greatest pleasure of these people is drunkenness; in other words, forgetfulness. Unfortunate beings! they must dream if they would be happy. As proof of the good temper of the Russians, when the muzhiks get tipsy, these men, brutalized as they are, become softened, instead of infuriated. Unlike the drunkards of our country, who quarrel and fight, they weep and embrace each other."[66]

For Russians, drink is liberating and inspiring, an escape from the meanness of life or the tensions and fury of politics. For Russian negotiators, well-lubricated lunches, cocktail hours, and dinners provide an opportunity for personality assessment, position probing, and the resolution of deadlocks. Ambassador Rowny noted, "During SALT I, alcohol had been served during the informal meetings; the Soviets were as fond of our bourbon and scotch as we were of their vodka. Not surprisingly, some of these sessions had reportedly become quite boisterous and incoherent. This practice was carried over into SALT II, but when Ambassador Johnson, who appreciated good scotch as much as anyone, realized after the first several sessions that the Soviets could hold their liquor and their tongues better than we could, he decided not to serve alcohol."[67]

Soviet negotiators consistently tried to seek advantage, even in a relaxed social setting, and to play up Russian superiority and culture. Ambassador Kampelman cited an encounter at dinner in Madrid with the Soviet head of the CSCE delegation, Yuri Dubinin: "Dubinin—a cultivated man who spoke good Spanish and later learned English when he became ambassador to Washington—was often unable to resist the temptation to take advantage. That evening, after caviar and a beautifully boiled fish with a delicate white sauce, he offered me a chocolate from a red box with a large picture of the Soviet Olympic mascot, Misha the bear. The United States had just boycotted the Moscow Olympics, but he unnecessarily explained to me just who Misha was. Not wanting to offend, but compelled to make a point, I reminded him (in some detail) of the reason that my country had not taken part in the Olympics, after which I felt free to take a chocolate, and did so."[68]

Russian president Yeltsin, while jockeying for power with Soviet president Mikhail Gorbachev, tried to take advantage of President Bush during a summit in July 1991. At Gorbachev's official dinner for President and Mrs. Bush in Saint Vladimir's Hall in the Great Kremlin Palace, Yeltsin waited until the last minute to make his grand entrance. Then he tried to escort Barbara Bush into the dinner, making it appear to the press that he was the host. At the end of the evening, Bush "grumbled to his aides that Yeltsin had been a 'real pain,' exploiting him in order to upstage Gorbachev. Scowcroft said, 'That guy's got to be told we're not going to let him use us in his petty games!'"

The next day National Security Council aide Ed Hewett took Ambassador Jack Matlock aside and asked him to complain to Foreign Minister Andrei Kozyrev: "Tell him that there are certain agreed upon norms of gentlemanly behavior. Let's not get into the habit of surprising each other."[69]

Using the Media

The Soviet Union treated the press and other media as an appendage of the state and government, and at weekly meetings the Central Committee's Department of Ideology would lay down the general line the Soviet press was to follow. Since the fall of the Soviet Union, the Russian press has grown much bolder, often voicing outspoken criticisms of Yeltsin and his government. Nonetheless, most Russians still view the press as the servant of political power—and the media's distinctly partisan support of Yeltsin during the 1996 presidential elections (fueled by fear of a communist victory) suggests that journalists have yet to adopt the political independence cherished in the United States.

Foreign media have likewise been assumed to lack real independence. "The Soviets," observed Max Kampelman, "did not know how to read events in a democratic context. For all their sophistication, they were victims of a Pravda complex, believing that if something important appeared in the paper, someone in power had approved its appearance."[70] Russian officials still believe that the U.S. press is controlled by Washington.

Despite this misapprehension, the Soviets have demonstrated skills in manipulating the U.S. media. Perceptions of initiative and advantage play an important role in negotiations, and the Soviets employed their own "spin doctors" to influence media interpretations of events in a light favorable to the Soviet Union at summits. Georgi Arbatov, head of the U.S.A. and Canada Institute and a Central Committee member, was the best-known Soviet propagandist. Arbatov, Henry Kissinger noted, "was especially subtle in playing to the inexhaustible masochism of American intellectuals who took it as an article of faith that every difficulty in U.S.-Soviet relations had to be caused by American stupidity or intransigence." Arbatov, Kissinger added, "was endlessly ingenious in demonstrating how American rebuffs were frustrating the peaceful, sensitive leaders in the Kremlin, who were being driven reluctantly by our inflexibility into conflicts that offended their inherently gentle natures."[71] By developing a public personality in the West, Arbatov emerged as an English-speaking spokesman for the Soviet position. His U.S.A. and Canada Institute was the choke point that assessed and passed on invitations to U.S. senators, congressmen, journalists, and academics, all of whom were carefully screened and reported on by KGB officers working under cover at the institute.

The Soviets were sensitive to every nuance of positioning themselves favorably in the public media. Anatoli Dobrynin recalled how Mikhail Gorbachev learned quickly from President Reagan's "singular knack for publicity through the use of the symbols of protocol." At their first meeting in Geneva on a cold November day, Reagan was the official host at Fleur d'Eau, a nineteenth-century lakeside chateau where Reagan was staying. Gorbachev wore an overcoat and a winter hat, bundled up against the cold. When he arrived, Reagan came out to greet him in a suit without a topcoat or hat. The photographs and television coverage of the arrival, transmitted around the world, showed Reagan looking youthful, energetic, and physically strong compared with Gorbachev. "They both looked the same age," wrote Dobrynin. "We learned later from Reagan's aides that the president had been waiting for Gorbachev in the hall, also dressed in an overcoat. But as soon as he saw Gorbachev through the window, he pulled off his coat and walked outside to meet the Soviet leader. Reagan's instinct worked, and Gorbachev quickly made a mental note of it. When it was our turn and Reagan came to our residence, Gorbachev also came out coatless to meet him."[72]

Both sides in a negotiation believe that once a position has been revealed in press reports, negotiating leverage has been lost. At the Reykjavík summit in October 1986, the Russians positioned themselves in advance to place the United States on the defensive. Before the meeting, Ambassador Dobrynin in Washington bragged that Gorbachev would present surprise proposals that would trap the United States and make it appear unresponsive.[73] Initially, the American press interpreted the results as a failure, but in fact the discussions between Presidents Reagan and Gorbachev led to the START Agreement to reduce nuclear weapons that was signed by Presidents Bush and Gorbachev in July 1991.[74]

Posturing in favor of peace and arms reductions at summits and leaking proposals to gain approval for new initiatives are standard practices for delegates of all countries. However, at lengthy bilateral or multilateral negotiations, press leaks can disrupt negotiating progress. At the CSCE meetings the Soviets protested when Ambassador Kampelman briefed the Western press. "The Russians complained that I was violating the rule of confidentiality of our meetings by meeting with the press. I told them that in my meetings with the press I never discussed what any of the other delegations said. I said the people of my country have a great voice in the decisions of my country and I have an obligation to inform the American people of what our delegation is doing and I advised him to do the same with his press. The arms negotiations were too sensitive and we did not want to distort the process by appealing to the press but we held a press conference at the end of each round."[75]

In joint press conferences at all summit meetings of Soviets and Americans, the two sides agreed to observe strict protocol and establish advance agreement on who would speak and what issues would be covered. This agreement did not hold, however, in July 1991 at the Bush-Gorbachev summit in Moscow. The United States became the victim of internal jockeying for power among the Russians. Russian president

Boris Yeltsin used every occasion to embarrass Soviet president Mikhail Gorbachev and underscore Gorbachev's continuing loss of power. Yeltsin refused to attend a small private Kremlin luncheon with Bush, saying he would not be part of a "faceless mass audience." After the luncheon Bush agreed to meet Yeltsin in his new office in the Supreme Soviet building on the Kremlin grounds. Yeltsin kept Bush waiting for seven minutes, then stretched the scheduled fifteen-minute meeting to forty minutes. Although the two sides had agreed in advance that there would be no press conference afterward, when Yeltsin and Bush emerged from the room, a beaming Yeltsin told a group of waiting reporters and camera crews that he had high hopes for "normalizing" American-Russian ties. He added that Bush had "agreed" with him on economic cooperation, the code word for the United States increasing direct economic assistance to Russia.

Michael R. Beschloss and Strobe Talbott recounted, "Bush felt sandbagged. He did not wish to confirm the impression that behind Gorbachev's back, he and Yeltsin had opened a new era in direct U.S.-Russian relations, but neither did he wish to contradict him. Thus he ignored Yeltsin's comments about the future and said instead that the Russian president had made 'a big hit' during his trip to Washington the month before. . . . As he climbed into his limousine, Bush complained to [National Security Adviser] Brent Scowcroft that he had been 'ambushed' by the Russian leader: 'Yeltsin's really grandstanding, isn't he?'"[76]

Negotiators often use their contacts in the media to plant stories that reflect their point of view, hoping to influence the course and outcome of the negotiations. News stories can influence public opinion, float new positions, or threaten dire consequences to the position of an adversary. During negotiations to resolve the Cuban missile crisis, a willing journalist acted as an intermediary to float new ideas or carry conditions outside the formal negotiating arena.[77] If these proposals had been rejected, both sides could have pretended they had never been offered because the intermediary was an unofficial voice.

The Rise and Demise of Back-Channel Diplomacy

During the Cold War both the Soviets and the Americans tried to conduct negotiations independent of formal diplomatic channels through secret "back channels." The Soviet intelligence organizations—the KGB and the GRU—operated clandestine structures parallel to the open, governmental diplomatic chain of command. Bureaucratic rivalry within the Soviet system led to the KGB and the GRU competing to develop their own direct lines of contact to the White House, which became known to Americans as "the back channel" and to Russians as "the confidential channel." Former secretary of state Henry Kissinger sometimes called it the "Presidential channel."

The back channel contributed to a crisis in the 1960s when Nikita Khrushchev used it in an attempt to deliberately deceive President Kennedy. He used GRU Colonel Georgi Bolshakov, who was operating under cover as the chief of the Washington bureau of the Tass news agency. Bolshakov, who reported directly to Moscow through the Soviet military attaché, established a confidential relationship with Attorney General Robert Kennedy and Presidential Press Secretary Pierre Salinger. After returning from a meeting in Russia with Khrushchev in August 1960, Bolshakov, on instructions, assured Robert Kennedy in September that there were no Soviet missiles in Cuba. On October 6, Bolshakov, continuing the deception, called on Robert Kennedy with another message from Khrushchev. The atmosphere of their meetings, usually informal, had changed to formality. Bolshakov told Kennedy, "Premier Khrushchev is concerned about the situation being built up by the United States around Cuba, and we repeat that the Soviet Union is supplying to Cuba exclusively defensive weapons intended for protecting the interests of the Cuban revolution."[78]

Nine days later President Kennedy was shown the U-2 photographs of the Soviet missile sites under construction in Cuba. Presidential adviser Theodore Sorensen summed it up: "President Kennedy had come to rely on the Bolshakov channel for direct private information from Khrushchev, and he felt personally deceived. He was personally deceived."[79] The Bolshakov channel was exposed in an article by journalist Charles Bartlett, who had close contact with the Kennedys. The Bolshakov channel was redirected to Ambassador Anatoli Dobrynin, who reported to Foreign Minister Gromyko. Gromyko "of course disliked the very existence of a special channel run by the Defense Ministry and not by him," explained Dobrynin.[80]

In his memoirs, Dobrynin discussed his own role in the confidential channel when it played its most active role in superpower diplomacy. "Richard Nixon used it to circumvent the diplomatic bureaucracy he so distrusted and even bypassed his Secretary of State, William Rogers. . . . This mode of communication existed for many years while I served as ambassador, continuing with varying intensity, although it was more restricted during the Reagan era when all contacts went through the Secretary of State. . . . It provided the freedom of personal chemistry which is an essential of diplomacy, and made it possible to explore uncharted diplomatic territory, which was often what was needed to break the stalemates that characterized the Cold War."[81]

Despite the continuity of duplicity demonstrated in the Bolshakov case, the Soviets regarded the back channel as fundamentally a demonstration of trust, a symbol of legitimacy and equality, and a means by which the Americans and Russians could resolve serious issues outside the spotlight of domestic and international criticism. The back channel provided an opportunity for calm decision making without public pressure in negotiations that could, if they failed, lead to military conflict. A successful example of quiet back-channel diplomacy replacing dramatic confrontation was the Soviet attempt to establish a naval base at Cienfuegos, Cuba, in 1970, which the United States was able to rebuff without obliging the Soviets to make a humiliating public withdrawal.[82]

In his memoir, *White House Years,* Kissinger portrays the Soviets as relying heavily upon private, back-channel conversations and exchanges of messages with the United States in order to advance their policy positions.[83] For Ambassador Dobrynin, though, the back channel was often difficult to manage because he found himself whipsawed between Secretary of State William Rogers and National Security Adviser Kissinger, who clearly had Nixon's support. In his memoirs, Dobrynin noted, "Moscow also preferred to use 'the Kissinger channel,' especially for confidential questions of great import, because the Kremlin knew from experience this channel was far more effective than the State Department."[84]

Inherent in back-channel communications is the peril of one level or group of diplomats being unaware of what another is doing. When Kissinger and Dobrynin negotiated through a secret back channel on SALT and the ABM (antiballistic missile) Treaty, the official U.S.

delegation under chief negotiator Gerard Smith was left completely in the dark. Acting either on his own initiative or at the behest of Foreign Minister Gromyko,[85] Vladimir Semenov, the Soviet SALT negotiator in Vienna, proposed to Smith a deal that, though it represented a bigger concession than the Soviets had previously conceded at Geneva, had already been rejected by Kissinger, who had negotiated a better deal with Dobrynin. When Kissinger heard of Semenov's proposal, he "vehemently accused the Soviet side of neglecting the confidential channel and ignoring the President's eagerness to keep in touch personally with the Soviet leadership," recalled Dobrynin. "The Soviet side, he said, preferred routine diplomatic channels, although it was perfectly aware it could spring leaks which could make things difficult for both Nixon and Kissinger himself. 'We can just stop using the channel,' he warned.

"I replied that it was up to either party whether to use the channel, but I was sure this incident was based on a kind of misunderstanding or misconduct that could never be excluded in the difficult conditions of two-tier talks. . . . In any case, the SALT negotiations continued, with Semenov still in charge of our delegation but without information on what was passing through the confidential channel."[86]

In another case of using the back channel in 1983, rivalry between the KGB and the Foreign Ministry prevented positive action. Ambassador Kampelman, who headed the American delegation to the CSCE in Madrid, wanted the Soviets to release the Pentecostalists taking refuge in the American embassy in Moscow and allow them to emigrate. Kampelman met privately in Madrid with Sergei Kondrashev, a KGB general who was deputy head of the Soviet delegation to the CSCE and with whom Kampelman had developed a personal rapport that enabled him to establish an effective back channel. Kondrashev had indicated that he had his own channel to Moscow. Kampelman told him that President Reagan wanted to see action on the release of the Pentecostalists. At first Kondrashev accused Kampelman of trying to blackmail him and said there would be no results; then he said it could be done.

"Only you and I, nobody else knows in Washington but the President and the Secretary of State," insisted Kondrashev.

"What about Gromyko?" Kampelman asked, to which Kondrashev replied no, indicating he was not to be included.

However, the ambassador to Washington, Yuri Dubinin, found out from a State Department aide who thought Dubinin was in the loop. Dubinin informed the Foreign Ministry, which sent a message to the head of the delegation, Kovalev, which was read to Kampelman. "In effect, the United States was being criticized for interfering in Soviet internal affairs; the Soviets would not change their policies or practices just to please us, or to end the CSCE meeting; we should disabuse ourselves of any illusions that the Soviets had promised or would promise us anything about their behavior; if, in pursuit of their national best interests, they do adopt a policy that pleases us, it is purely coincidental and nothing more," recalled Kampelman. He accepted the Soviet note and said he would study it.

The internal Soviet bureaucratic overtones of the incident became increasingly evident when Kampelman learned a few weeks later that Aleksandr Bessmertnykh, then one of Foreign Minister Gromyko's aides, had told an American embassy official in Moscow, "'Max talked to the wrong person,' implying that I should have dealt with the Foreign Minister rather than the KGB. I was certain that this was wrong. I had probed with Ilichev, Kovalev and Dubinin, all of whom had sternly rejected my overtures. Both Al Haig and George Shultz found Gromyko totally cold on human rights. Gromyko was far less flexible than Andropov, who had indeed permitted Kondrashev to deal with me and had, at least minimally, delivered."[87]

Since Kissinger left government, there has been a move away from back-channel negotiations that exclude normal interagency consultations, and toward direct, personal contacts. Both Kissinger's Republican successors, George Shultz and James Baker, eschewed secret back-channel diplomacy for direct contacts with Mikhail Gorbachev and his foreign minister, Eduard Shevardnadze. The fall of the Soviet Union at the end of 1991, and the accompanying end to the coordinating process overseen by the Communist Party Central Committee, has meant that it now falls to the president of the Russian Federation to make numerous final decisions on foreign policy matters. The precarious nature of the Russian political condition has accentuated this situation, with a greater number of issues getting bucked to the highest level for judgment than previously. The result has been the development of a direct personal relationship between Presidents Yeltsin and

Clinton. This Bill-and-Boris connection is maintained through telephone calls and periodic summits. The utility of high-level personal contacts has been underlined by the regular, twice-yearly meetings between U.S. vice president Al Gore and Russian prime minister Viktor Chernomyrdin.

Preparatory work for these high-level encounters at the level of the secretary of state and foreign minister and their deputies has increased the number of meetings of lower-level working groups. Informal working groups have addressed specific problems in negotiations on the removal of nuclear warheads and the destruction of missile silos. A nascent move away from secrecy to what has been labeled "SIT" (Safety, Irreversibility, and Transparency) now characterizes such negotiations.

The American strategy has been to engage all levels of the Russian bureaucracy and appeal to Russian self-interest and self-esteem in the interest of resolving issues of concern to both sides. (We will examine specific examples of this issue-oriented, problem-solving negotiating style in the next chapter.)

ENDGAME

Following Gromyko's dictum that "it is the last twenty minutes of a negotiation that counts," Soviet negotiating behavior relied heavily on the endgame. So too does the current Russian style, partly because of the inheritance of the Soviet attitude, and partly because thorny issues with domestic political liabilities are reserved for presidential decision. Once the final outcome of a major negotiation is in sight, it is easier to reciprocally resolve other, lesser issues. The Russians tend to wrap up smaller issues quickly at the very end if they have reached an internal leadership consensus. It is important to understand this Russian trait and exercise patience in the midgame phase of a negotiation.

The Russians are skillful at hiding their cards and playing their hand in a low-key manner unless they are under direct pressure from Moscow or forced by domestic political needs to conclude an agreement. At the CSCE follow-up meetings the Russians seemed to be more relaxed about the timetable than the U.S. side, and they tried to use this to their advantage. CSCE follow-up meetings that started in 1986 were scheduled to end in January 1989 at the end of the Reagan administration. The U.S. delegation's instructions were to end the conference before the president left office. For a time, the Russians thought the United States was tied to that deadline and thus could be forced to make concessions, but they found that in fact the United States was prepared to stick to its fundamental objectives and let the talks continue with a new administration.

At that point the Russians realized they should quickly settle. They were eager to gain acceptance for an international human rights conference to be held in Moscow, and to secure the continuation of the CSCE with arms control talks, thus bringing in all the CSCE states as a way to undercut NATO. The human rights conference finally took place in Moscow in the fall of 1991.

The rules for negotiating the endgame grow out of the issues at stake, the political atmosphere, and the personal chemistry between the principals. If the negotiators can convince their principals in Moscow and Washington that their instructions have been followed, or that variations on the instructions are fair to both sides, or that the other side has given up more, they are free to reach an agreement. The key is for the negotiator to be aware of his adversary's minimum needs and the political pressures he is facing.

Timing is important, especially if a minor negotiation can be fitted into the context of a major agreement. A prime example was a trade of spies for dissidents during the Carter administration. Two Soviet UN employees, Valdik Enger and Rudolf Chernayev, were arrested in May 1978, tried, convicted, and sentenced to fifty years in an American prison. After an interagency dispute over whether jailing the two Russians would lead to reprisals or worsened relations with the Soviet Union, President Carter, overruling State Department hesitations, decided there should be no exceptions to the law. When Enger's and Chernayev's convictions were imminent, National Security Adviser Zbigniew Brzezinski initiated conversations with Ambassador Dobrynin about the possibility of an exchange.

Dobrynin offered to free two hijackers convicted in the Soviet Union. Brzezinski said the offer was totally unacceptable and pressed for the release from prison of Anatoly Sharansky, the Jewish dissident, and Aleksandr Ginzburg, a well-known Russian dissident. The negotiations continued for several months, quibbling over numbers and people.

Finally, with agreement on SALT II near, at the end of April 1978, and a June summit in sight, the two sides struck a deal. The Soviets agreed to release five dissidents in return for their two intelligence officers; in a side agreement, a Soviet citizen sentenced to death for espionage on behalf of the United States was spared, but that was not part of the official public announcement.

"Because our side had stood firm, a favorable agreement was in fact negotiated, and the Soviets respected it scrupulously; more importantly, five genuinely heroic individuals and their families gained their freedom, and that injected into the often impersonal conduct of foreign affairs a deeply gratifying human dimension," wrote Brzezinski.[88]

The importance of political competition within the U.S. president's cabinet, within the Soviet Politburo, or within the Russian Federation leadership is not to be underestimated in forcing endgame resolution. Summits help build a Russian or American leader's image and popularity, and strengthen his power. The desire for a summit meeting and the need to keep political momentum rolling can be important stimuli for forcing resolution of difficult issues. The following account of the Daniloff episode in 1986 illustrates such a historical moment.

In late August 1986, a week after the FBI had arrested a Soviet intelligence officer, Gennadi F. Zakharov, in a sting operation, the Soviets seized Nicholas S. Daniloff, the Moscow correspondent for *U.S. News & World Report* magazine, on a trumped-up charge of spying. Clearly, the Soviets hoped to use Daniloff as a bargaining chip in a swap for Zakharov.

Secretary of State George Shultz, who was assured that Daniloff was not working for the CIA, spoke out strongly in a speech on September 5 against Soviet hostage-taking as an instrument of policy. Shultz insisted that the Reagan administration had ruled out a trade of Daniloff for Zakharov. Reciprocity in this case was unacceptable.

On September 8, in a back-channel effort, the KGB *rezident* in Washington contacted the Hearst Corporation's foreign editor, John Wallach, and proposed that both Daniloff and Zakharov be remanded to the custody of their respective ambassadors in Moscow and Washington. The Soviets approached Wallach to act as an unofficial intermediary because they wanted a positive signal from Shultz before officially making the proposal. If the United States refused and the approach became public, the Russians would be in a position to deny it had ever been made.

Shultz agreed, and on the evening of September 11 the Soviets said they were ready to proceed with the first step remanding Daniloff and Zakharov to their respective embassies. The final resolution awaited Soviet foreign minister Eduard Shevardnadze's arrival in America a week later for meetings scheduled earlier in the year. His first meeting was at the State Department, and Shultz, who "had long since learned in negotiations that personal confidence and a personal touch can be helpful," decided to break with precedent and go out of his office to meet Shevardnadze in the Treaty Room nearby. For two and a half hours they argued. Shultz proposed a three-step scenario: Daniloff is released; Zakharov, after trial, is released; Soviet refuseniks are released. Each of the three steps would stand alone, Shultz said. Shevardnadze listened and said the Soviets wanted an immediate trade of Daniloff for Zakharov and no trial for Zakharov. Shevardnadze said he had brought a letter for President Reagan from Gorbachev, which contained a proposal for a presummit meeting for two days in London or Reykjavík.

Shevardnadze was taken to see President Reagan in the White House, and they met for an hour. In his memoirs Shultz recalled that "the President did nothing to relieve the tension. He made it obvious to Shevardnadze that no progress could come in the U.S.-Soviet relationship without Daniloff's release. I knew Ronald Reagan was an accomplished actor, but this was no act."

When Shultz and Shevardnadze returned to the State Department they agreed on how to solve remaining problems at the CSCE conference, and Shultz gave Shevardnadze a list of Soviet dissidents and Soviet Jews who should be permitted to emigrate from the Soviet Union. Also at issue was the U.S. insistence that the Soviet mission to the United Nations be reduced to no more than 218 people, including 25 intelligence officers.

At the same time Shultz, a master negotiator, told Shevardnadze that Reagan had reacted favorably to Gorbachev's proposal for a presummit meeting, but could make no public response until the Daniloff problem was settled.

On September 23 Shultz and Shevardnadze met in New York for the opening of the UN General Assembly, but made no progress on the

Daniloff issue. After two more meetings that week there was still no progress, but Shevardnadze told Shultz that Gorbachev wanted to get the Daniloff case settled so he could meet Reagan in Reykjavík from October 10 to October 12.

Shultz returned to Washington to report to President Reagan and work out a compromise approved by the president. The proposal agreed upon was for the Soviets to permit Daniloff to leave the USSR. Then, twenty-four hours later, Zakharov pleads nolo contendere (no contest), a legal equivalent of guilty, and the United States expels him. As soon as Zakharov departs, the United States announces that human rights activist Yuri Orlov and his wife will be allowed to leave the Soviet Union. The Soviets acquiesce to the reduction of the number of personnel at the Soviet mission to the United Nations. Finally, on September 30, both sides announce that Reagan and Gorbachev will meet in Reykjavík from October 10 to 12, 1986. The agreement was sealed with a handshake and, with several near misses, carried out.[89]

The endgame was precarious and pressured on both sides, but the desire of Gorbachev to subordinate a tactical propaganda victory to a summit with Reagan clearly won the day. Both sides were forced to finesse the question of a trade, and did so because they had a larger purpose, a summit of historic significance.

At the Reykjavík summit in 1986 Gorbachev tried to turn what was billed as a meeting to prepare a summit into a full-fledged negotiation on strategic arms control. Reagan and Gorbachev agreed in principle to major reductions in strategic offensive forces, but Gorbachev's proposal to eliminate all nuclear weapons if the Americans would abandon the Strategic Defense Initiative (SDI) was not accepted by President Reagan. Gorbachev could not get Reagan to yield, and the meeting ended on a bitter note. However, the talks produced the basis for later progress. The decision of President Reagan not to be pressured, nor to extend the talks, prevented hasty action that would have been destabilizing to Western Europe and the NATO alliance. Gorbachev's behavior was typical of the Soviet penchant for wanting to press for a breakthrough and agreement, on the spot, during the endgame of a negotiation. Reykjavík was billed as a "meeting," not a summit, but Secretary of State George Shultz noted, "in the eyes of the world, Reykjavik would become the epitome of the very word 'summit.'"[90]

Gorbachev's behavior pattern echoed that of earlier Soviet leaders. Khrushchev and Brezhnev struck quickly, needing to retain Politburo support once approval had been given on a fast-moving endgame agreement. "One of Brezhnev's most striking characteristics," Kissinger has noted, "as of almost all Soviet negotiators, was his anxiety to get matters wrapped up once he had decided on a breakthrough. He could haggle and stall for months, even years. But once his own cumbersome machinery had disgorged a design, his domestic standing seemed to depend on his ability to get it implemented rapidly."[91]

Gorbachev carefully balanced his rising foreign standing against his falling domestic popularity and in the end gave way to the West on major negotiations in an effort, never realized, to obtain funds to sustain and rebuild the Soviet economy. Although he received less than 1 percent of the vote in the 1996 Russian presidential elections, Gorbachev's popularity remains high in Europe and the United States.

Domestic considerations play no less of a role today. Indeed, domestic Russian political pressures often demand and force a solution causing a foreign policy shift. In the face of the 1996 presidential election, adjustments to the Conventional Forces in Europe (CFE) Treaty signed in June 1996 by the Russians were expedited by the need for Yeltsin to show he was in charge. These changes showed Yeltsin could deal with the West on issues affecting Russian security and national pride. However, the nationalist opposition to NATO expansion caused Yeltsin to vacillate on Russian support for the Partnership for Peace and NATO enlargement.

IMPLEMENTATION

Russian negotiators, like their Soviet predecessors but unlike their American counterparts, view the signing of an agreement not as the end of a negotiation but as one stage in an extended process. Longtime arms control negotiator Jonathan Dean summed up the difference: "Americans tend to consider an agreement, once achieved, marks the end of the problem under discussion, and that the solution will administer itself. With a more accurate view of the ongoing character of East-West relations, the Soviets see the implementation of an agreement as a continuing negotiation."[92]

Negotiation does not end with the signing of an agreement. Coming to terms does not assure implementation of the agreed settlement, which must be constantly monitored. Instances of noncompliance must be protested and, if necessary, the terms of agreements must be renegotiated. With a characteristically Soviet disdain for the rule of law, Russians will renege on agreements should they decide that changes in political realities dictate a new approach. A British Foreign Office paper on negotiating with the Soviet Union warned:

> Soviet representatives are not persuaded by eloquence or reasoned arguments, but rely on a calculation of forces. They see any agreement as an arrangement codifying the momentary relationship of forces, a snap-shot of a power equation or of the relative positions of the parties at a particular moment. Since these relationships are not static but an ever changing reality, an agreement has no intrinsic moral binding force. The Soviets tend to respect its letter, as long as it is sufficiently detailed and precise. But when conditions change, they expect to be free to renegotiate, modify, ignore, abrogate or apply it selectively as the new circumstances dictate. There is for them no such thing as a permanent or absolute "settlement."[93]

The implementation process thus depends on verification and determined follow-through by Russia's negotiating partners. The SALT and ABM agreements produced quarrelsome violations, which the Joint Consultative Committee, established to reconcile disagreements, was unable to resolve. "Some violations were minor exploitations of ambiguous language; others were of potentially strategic significance," wrote George Shultz in his memoirs.

"The clearest and most important violation, in this case of the ABM treaty, was the Krasnoyarsk phased-array radar station, located deep inside the Soviet Union, where it could serve a 'battle management' function in a potential antiballistic missile system. The Joint Chiefs of Staff had told us that the fundamental balance of forces was not affected by these Soviet transgressions. In military terms that might be true, but the political consequences were vast."[94]

Shultz's approach to dealing with the problem offers a model for enforcing implementation. In 1983, arms control talks had been suspended by the Soviet Union following NATO deployment of intermediate-range nuclear missiles in Germany, Great Britain, and Italy to counter Soviet SS-20 missiles. The United States was equally dissatisfied with the Soviet Union for violations of the 1972 ABM Treaty.

The ABM Treaty prohibited construction of long-lead-time radars except on the periphery of the United States or the Soviet Union and oriented outward. The Krasnoyarsk phased-array radar provided full coverage, unlike traditional "dish" radars that rotate to view the horizon lighthouse-style. Its potential role in an antiballistic defense made the violation important.

In January 1984 Shultz met with President Reagan to plan a strategy that would rectify the Soviet violations of the ABM Treaty and institute a "realistic reengagement" of negotiations. For Shultz the question was "how high a decibel level to put on those violations at this stage of the game. My preferred course of action, I told the president, was to keep the public decibel level down but to tell the Soviets flatly that their violations of solemn agreements would have to be rectified before any new understandings could be reached."[95]

Over the next year the Soviets took no action. On February 1, 1985, the Reagan administration filed a report to Congress charging the Soviets with a clear violation of the 1972 ABM Treaty and a number of other violations.[96] The Soviets refused to engage, but privately Soviet foreign minister Aleksandr Bessmertnykh questioned Marshal Sergei Akhromeyev, chief of the General Staff and first deputy minister of defense, on why the military insisted on violating the treaty when they knew the Americans would discover the radar site and protest. "First let us build it, then we will discuss it," Akhromeyev told Bessmertnykh.[97] At the time the Soviet Union was bitterly protesting American research on SDI to develop a defense against nuclear missiles. The internal dynamics of Soviet strategic arms policy dictated the necessity for the violation, even on a conditional basis, explained Bessmertnykh, implying that the Soviet military was creating a bargaining chip to be traded for SDI. It was not until the farewell meeting of Presidents Reagan and Gorbachev after George Bush's election in November 1988 that Gorbachev agreed to dismantle the Krasnoyarsk radar, pointedly meaning Shultz when he said the action was "another victory for the secretary."

The CFE Treaty, signed in November 1990, is an example of how changing geopolitical realities have required alterations in an agreement. The treaty achieved significant cuts in Soviet and Warsaw Pact manpower, tanks, armored personnel carriers, and artillery. No sooner had the treaty been signed than there were disagreements that took until June 1991 to resolve.[98] The fall of the Soviet Union in December 1991 and the resulting realignment of the newly independent states again created differences over interpreting requirements of the treaty.

The Clinton administration again negotiated Russian adherence to the treaty. The agreement called for the Russians to be permitted to increase their forces on their northern and southern flanks but did not include the Russian city of Novorossiysk in the exemption. Agreement was also reached on ABM theater missile defense issues between Presidents Clinton and Yeltsin at their April 1996 meeting in Hyde Park, which set the stage for the final signing of the revised CFE Treaty in June. The mechanism for reaching agreement was detailed staff work undertaken on the level of deputy secretary of state and deputy foreign minister in preparation for the summit agreement, followed by final negotiations on the expert level.

A similar pattern of negotiating behavior took place before the Helsinki summit between Clinton and Yeltsin on March 21 and 22, 1997, their twelfth meeting. After blustering by Foreign Minister Primakov and by Yeltsin himself that NATO enlargement was a "serious mistake," the Russians backed off. Although they continued to disagree on NATO enlargement, a joint statement said that "in order to minimize the potential consequences of this disagreement, the two presidents agree that they should work both together and with others, on a document that will establish cooperation between NATO and Russia as an important element of a new comprehensive European system." Yeltsin would seek a political accommodation with the United States. In return for assurances that an expanded NATO posed no military threat to Russia, Yeltsin would sign a document agreeing to cooperate with the alliance.

The summit was loaded with a broad range of issues. The list included further progress to create transparency of strategic nuclear warhead inventories. Another issue was the destruction of strategic nuclear warheads and strategic arms reductions. This would set the stage for START III talks, as soon as START II was ratified. To sweeten the pot President Clinton committed the United States to a joint initiative to stimulate investment and growth in Russia. The United States agreed to support Russia's entry into the World Trade Organization in

1998 and support Russian participation in the major industrial nations' Group of Seven, thereafter to be called the Summit of the Eight. Yeltsin denied that he had traded off a NATO compromise and arms control agreements for American support on economic initiatives. "I categorically disagree with the formulation that . . . we sort of bartered here and, as a result of that we have come up with these ideas. . . . This was not a case where we used this as a poker chip."

President Clinton said he and Yeltsin had not come to Helsinki "expecting to change each other's mind about our disagreements. We did come here expecting to find a way of shifting the axis from our disagreements to the goals, the tasks, and the opportunities we share. And we have succeeded."[99]

The U.S. military had begun working on Primakov during his visit to Washington in mid-March 1997. They invited him to the war room in the Pentagon and gave him a two-hour briefing on NATO's military capabilities. The U.S. generals used slides and audiovisual aids to convince Primakov that NATO troop levels were sharply reduced from the levels of the Cold War. Primakov wanted concrete guarantees that there would be no eastward movement in NATO's military structure. He insisted that Washington agree to a "sufficiency" rule, setting a maximum limit on NATO holdings of certain specified military equipment. When Secretary of State Madeleine Albright went to Moscow at the beginning of May, there was still no agreement, and her first days of meetings produced no breakthrough. It was a classic endgame holdout by the Russians. Only when Albright was about to return to Washington empty-handed did Primakov offer a new Russian proposal dropping the "sufficiency" rule. In return Albright hinted that the alliance was ready to make a statement ruling out the use of old Warsaw Pact nuclear storage sites by NATO.[100] The results were the signing in Paris of the Founding Act between NATO and Russia, and Yeltsin joining the G-7 at its Denver meeting in June 1997 as the eighth member, making it the G-8. Symbolism is important in negotiations, and by playing to Russia's need to retain its great power status as a member of the G-8, Clinton won Russian cooperation on NATO. In the depths of the Cold War the Russians would have raised the Iron Curtain of ideology; in the 1990s money and international prestige are the new negotiating tender. Deputy Foreign Minister Georgi Mamedov summed up Russia's place at the G-8 when he said, "The fact that we are taking part in it is the best evidence of Russia's role as a great power. We are being approached—we are not regarded just as a country that has economic difficulties, that cannot make ends meet."[101]

Rapidly changing realities in Russia—notably, the end of the war in Chechnya and the deterioration of the Russian armed forces—continue to demand new strategic assessments of the balance of forces. To a greater extent than during the Soviet era, signing an agreement with the Russian Federation is only a step in the process of establishing working terms of reference. This places a still higher premium on assessment. Realistic and accurate intelligence must be the basis for treaty implementation. Clinton's engagement of Yeltsin has become a critical factor in U.S.-Russian negotiations. American officials say Yeltsin once told Clinton, "I know you trust me. But I know it's because you are afraid of what may come after me."[102] In the endgame it is the two presidents meeting each other's need for a mutually favorable or win-win outcome that has produced interim results. The willingness to continue negotiations with incremental progress, but without final resolution of the outstanding issues, remains the heart of the process in dealing with the Russians.

▪ 4 ▪

Counterstrategies and Countertactics

There are important differences that define Russian and American negotiating styles. Russians rely on a who-whom, winner-take-all mentality aimed at dominating or destroying their opponent. Americans are pragmatic and try to create a win-win solution in which both sides believe they have accomplished many if not all of their negotiating objectives. Under the Soviets, ideology created an adversarial negotiating atmosphere in which the substance of agreements was often less important than the appearance of who had come out on top.

Today, in the post-Soviet world, new problems confront negotiators. While the Russians still seek to emerge from a negotiation without political liabilities—and ideally with propaganda advantages—substance is now much more important than appearance. Moreover, the nature of that substance has changed. The Soviets sought concrete gains that would bolster their imperial position and advance their ideological interests. The Russians today seek two goals: to defend and assert their embattled national pride, and to secure money and material advantage. The most notable difference is that institutional disarray in the Russian policymaking arena makes it difficult for Western diplomats to know with whom they need to reach agreement and, after it is reached, whether the agreement will be implemented.

Negotiating with the Russians requires heightened insight into the Russian fear of foreign penetration, of the loss of internal unity, and of Russia being plundered of its natural resources by marauding capitalists with advanced technology and vast funding. To negotiate with such a proud but vulnerable rival requires firmness and new skills in balancing self-assurance with reassurance.

Throughout the process the Western negotiator must continually recognize how cultural differences and Russian sensitivities regarding national pride and self-esteem affect negotiating encounters, without falling prey to pleas for compassion and "understanding" of Russia's problems. The task for contemporary American negotiators is three-fold: to engage an effective institutional partner who can deliver on an agreement or contract; to ascertain what incentives will persuade the Russians to conclude a deal; and to assert U.S. resolve and avoid being manipulated into an unfavorable position by the Russian side.

PERCEPTIONS AND FALSIFICATIONS OF REALITY

For American negotiators, dealing with Russian counterparts requires an ability to stand firm and distinguish reality from fantasy. The Soviets attempted to establish their own versions of reality. In Hungary in 1956 they were "crushing counterrevolution"; in Czechoslovakia in 1968 the Red Army was beating back "German revanchism." This trait has not disappeared.

In the cases of Chechnya, NATO expansion, and Kozyrev's threats to the CSCE at Stockholm (see above, pages 49–50), Russian perceptions of reality were far-fetched or falsified. Although Foreign Minister Prima-kov warned of public concern over NATO expansion, public opinion polls contradicted him. They indicated that personal economic con-siderations, such as nonpayment of wages and pensions, and fear of crime were the primary issues affecting the Russian public. In dealing with Russian officials who attempt to advance the Russian position by altering or interpreting reality, American negotiators must understand the Russian tendency toward distortion based on the Bolshevik Code by which the means justify the end. Whether this becomes merely a short-term ploy or a sustained effort depends on many factors, not the least of which is the ability of the negotiator to engage with and estab-lish a shared standard of truth with his Russian counterpart.

ENGAGEMENT

In his study of Chinese political negotiating behavior, Richard Solomon noted: "The objective of a negotiating strategy must be not only to reach agreements consonant with American interests, but to gain control of the dynamics, the rhythm, and stratagems of the friendship game as they are expressed in the negotiating process."[1] The "friendship game" has been played with different techniques by the Russians, but the goal is the same. The Chinese use friendship to overcome a cultural gap and offer it as a prize. The Russians stress their cultural similarity to Americans and assure them that it will lead toward common goals. Solomon's analysis holds true for dealing with Russia in its emphasis on controlling the course of negotiations—or at least not losing the initiative and being subject to manipulation. The Soviet determination to eliminate sentiment from negotiations and conduct them instead on the basis of hard-nosed calculation of objective forces has softened slightly in recent years. The Russians play the "good cop" and "bad cop" routine by singling out a member of the American delegation and offering an inside track on why they are sticking to a tough position in an effort to win sympathy. Another member of the delegation will stress the downside to the Americans if they do not accede to the Russian demands.

Key to securing control is engagement of the Russian side. "Engagement" here means a range of moves designed to open and maintain communication with Russian officials, to create negotiating momentum by educating them in the advantages to be gained in achieving common goals, and to persuade the Russians that negotiations need not be a zero-sum game in which one side's gain is a loss for the other side, but can instead yield win-win outcomes in which both sides benefit.

Engaging the Bureaucracy

Even during Stalin's reign, U.S. diplomats recognized that control of the Soviet decision-making process did not reside with any one individual. George Kennan, who served as ambassador to Moscow from 1952 to 1953, remarked in his memoirs that "the top level is physically incapable of encompassing the whole range of our dealings with the Soviet government and of assuring collaboration which we are seeking. Agreements reached there can be—and frequently are—sabotaged successfully . . . on the lower levels. We must train the Russians to make their whole machine, not just Stalin, respond sensibly to our approaches."[2]

American government negotiators from the president on down are still engaged in conditioning the Russians to respond constructively to our approaches. Indeed, the current organizational chaos that exists within the Russian government has made this job all the more important. The problem for U.S. negotiators is to identify how and where decisions are taken within the Russian bureaucracy and to discover the means to facilitate that decision-making process.

When the Communist Party of the Soviet Union was abolished at the end of 1991, down with it came the International Department of the Central Committee, the closest Soviet equivalent to the U.S. president's National Security Council. Russia's foreign policy was left without a coordinating body. In an interview in June 1996, Deputy Secretary of State Strobe Talbott, who oversees negotiations with Russia, explained, "It was a party organ. When the Communist Party ceased to exist there was a vacuum that was never filled. We tried to help the Russians develop an interagency process because it is in our interest that they have one.

"We set up a Strategic Stability Dialogue, which meets on a regular basis and alternates between Moscow and Washington. They used the existence of a quite sophisticated interagency structure on our side to replicate one on theirs."[3]

The Strategic Stability Dialogue, which meets two or three times a year, is run by Talbott and his counterpart, Deputy Foreign Minister Georgi E. Mamedov. Those participating in the dialogue include senior officials on the deputy level from the Office of the Secretary of Defense, the Joint Chiefs of Staff, the National Security Council, the State Department, the Treasury Department, and the Central Intelligence Agency. While the Strategic Stability Dialogue has attracted little public attention, it has served as a major forum for communicating on what Talbott calls "over-the-horizon issues" such as regional peacekeeping, strategic defenses, NATO enlargement, and confidence-building measures.

These informal close encounters provide an opportunity for Americans to create an atmosphere of shared goals and convince the Russians that negotiations should produce a win-win result, not become a traditional *kto-kogo* (who-whom) relationship in which the aim is to destroy the opponent and pocket all the benefits. Such meetings provide an opportunity to do business "on the side" on arms control or summit issues. The Russians still tend to give set speeches to avoid coming to grips with issues. The American tactic is to attempt total immersion in an issue and then project benefits and liabilities. This approach has produced results in moving toward mutual problem solving.

Progress toward the same end can also be enhanced by such measures as the creation of a mutually shared database to establish a common frame of reference. Military secrecy and the lack of rudimentary computer networks and databases have put Russian negotiators at a disadvantage with their Western counterparts. By sharing data and placing Western knowledge of Russian military capabilities on the table, the move to "transparency," open knowledge of the balance of forces, has progressed rapidly and expedited negotiations. Russian negotiators are less disposed to openness than are their U.S. partners, owing partly to a lack of information and partly to what Victor Israelyan has called "the old legacy of negotiating with 'capitalists.' Assisting the Russian partner in obtaining necessary information will make negotiating more effective and less time consuming."[4]

Engaging the Leadership

The United States is most likely to achieve its desired aims in negotiating with the Russian Federation if U.S. officials can simultaneously engage the Russian bureaucracy and the Russian leadership. It holds true both for President Yeltsin and for his ministers. Such an approach helps avoid the all-too-common frustrations of securing an agreement in principle with one or another Russian ministry only then to see the agreement founder because of the lack of detailed follow-up or obstruction by another ministry. There is often a lack of consistency between the different levels of the same ministry, with American diplomats finding to their dismay that junior negotiators on the Russian side are on occasion openly at odds with their seniors.[5] Such actions, unthinkable in the Soviet past, are a sign of the growing political differences in Russian society. Dissenting diplomats can appeal to the communists and nationalist groups in the Duma. Although such developments may be seen as indicating some progress toward political democracy, pluralism and lack of discipline make the task of American negotiators more difficult.

Reflecting on the differences between the Soviet Union and the Russian Federation, Strobe Talbott noted the increased importance of securing close relationships with the top tier of the Russian leadership:

> During the Soviet period, the Soviet system, while not as monolithic as it seemed to us on the outside, was still very coherent from the top down. If a Soviet desk officer in Washington went over and talked with a second secretary at the Russian embassy on 16th Street he would get essentially the same pitch that President Ford or Carter or Reagan would get talking to whoever was the general secretary of the Communist Party at the time. Obviously there was still a lot of utility in having high-level negotiators negotiate, but you were negotiating with a unit that was the Soviet government. That is nowhere near true in the post-Soviet period; Russia is much more pluralistic than the Soviet Union was and the current Russian bureaucracy is less bureaucratic.
>
> There is good news and bad news in that. The bad news is that it's hard to deal with a government that is all over the lot. On the other hand it creates opportunities: if you have the right relationship between the guys at the very top we could get a logjam broken, we could get a breakthrough that we wanted on our terms.

Talbott cited the example of "the Missile Technology Control Regime in the first year of the administration. This was to persuade the Russians not to sell rocket engines to the Indians because we were convinced the Indians wanted the rockets to make ballistic missiles. It was an anti-ballistic missiles proliferation deal. We got the Russians to agree to cancel the sale of these rocket engines to India in exchange for access to commercial satellite launches. The mechanisms we used were the Boris-Bill presidential connection and the Gore-Chernomyrdin connection. We got the president and the prime minister of Russia to over-rule the bureaucracy."

President Clinton's first-name relationship with President Yeltsin has resulted in several other important accomplishments for the American-Russian negotiating agenda. Conscious of the value of the relationship, the U.S. administration has been careful not to endanger it by sharp criticism of the Russian leader. Although Clinton and his top foreign policy aides were privately critical of the war in Chechnya, the president soft-pedaled the issue by comparing the secession of Chechnya with the role of the South in the American Civil War.

Such analogies are hard to defend with historical facts, and there are risks in the president of the United States being so closely identified with a Russian leader, or indeed with any foreign leader. Personal friendship can keep up the momentum of high-level dialogue, but it cannot substitute for resolution of issues affecting national interest and security.

For the United States the primary negotiating goals are progress in Cooperative Threat Reduction (CTR), the destruction of nuclear weapons, and dismantling of nuclear warheads. Under legislation introduced by Senators Sam Nunn (D-Ga.) and Richard Lugar (R-Ind.) during the Bush administration, the United States has authorized expenditures of more than $1.6 billion in an unprecedented enterprise to dismantle nuclear weapons. The Bill-and-Boris relationship has provided the political momentum for the program and the presidents' direct intervention has been instrumental in breaking impasses at critical moments. The program calls for cooperation among the United States, Russia, and Ukraine, with U.S. funds being used to pay for plutonium waste that could otherwise be reprocessed into nuclear weapons.

"In early 1994 it was very nip and tuck on both sides with the Ukrainians and the Russians," explained Talbott. "It took President Clinton going straight to President Yeltsin to get the thing done. If Ukraine had decided to keep its nuclear weapons, we never would have gotten the kind of political agreements we got between Russia and Ukraine. Kazakhstan would not have given up its nukes and God knows what would have happened with Belarus. That was a huge deal. We devoted a lot of time to that in 1993. We worked a great deal at lower levels but on several occasions we needed to call Yeltsin to write [Ukrainian president Leonid] Kuchma and to call Kuchma."

Clinton accomplished the removal of Russian troops from the Baltic states in August 1995 because he chose his goal and pursued it directly with Yeltsin. Clinton promised American financial support for housing of Russian officers being repatriated from the Baltic states. The tactic was to take the issue out of normal negotiating channels and raise it to a personal summit level between the two presidents. "That was not a traditional arms control negotiation, that was a matter of political will. Once again that was President Clinton appealing to President Yeltsin, explaining why it was in Russia's interest," said Talbott.

The presidents deal primarily with national security issues. Vice President Al Gore, cabinet members, department secretaries, and their immediate subordinates have established consulting and decision-making relationships to address economic and financial policy issues. Since 1993, Gore and Russian prime minister Viktor Chernomyrdin have met at least twice a year; they are charged with breaking road-blocks to increased American investment in Russia, banking reforms, and the establishment of a securities market. The Gore-Chernomyrdin Commission's mandate is virtually unlimited, and it serves as a court of last resort on issues that cannot be resolved by the bureaucracies and their ministers. The commission has served as the intermediary for American businesspeople who cannot penetrate or deal with the Russian government structure; it has urged Russia to pass a production-sharing law that will allow foreign oil companies to invest in the country. Under the commission there are eight joint committees chaired by cabinet members from both sides that work on a broad range of issues including defense conversion, public health, space cooperation, science and technology, energy, agriculture, and commerce.

Even before the fall of the Soviet Union, American officials recognized the value of cultivating personal relationships with top-tier Russians. With the forced retirement of Andrei Gromyko and the appointment of Eduard Shevardnadze as foreign minister in 1985, a change began to take place in Soviet negotiating style. Americans were quick to note that the old-line Foreign Ministry professionals looked down their noses at Shevardnadze because of his background as a former KGB and Interior Ministry official in Georgia. His main qualification was that Gorbachev trusted him. Max Kampelman was "surprised at the patronizing attitude shown toward Shevardnadze by others in the delegation, particularly Dobrynin, who repeatedly interrupted Shevardnadze in a manner that some of us thought rude. The new foreign minister had risen to power too quickly for them, and the old hands seemed intent on making certain he made no errors and kept his inexperience hidden." At their first meeting in Helsinki in August 1985 Secretary of State George Shultz looked to a warmer relationship with Shevardnadze than had been possible with his predecessor, Gromyko. Shultz said directly that he and Shevardnadze had a special opportunity to accomplish great things.[6]

This was to be the first of many meetings in which the Shultz-Shevardnadze connection and then the Baker-Shevardnadze connection were to play a major role. American tactics of building trust by cultivating a personal relationship, first by Shultz hosting a private dinner for the Soviet foreign minister at Shultz's home in Washington, D.C., and later by Jim Baker entertaining Shevardnadze at a cookout at Baker's ranch in Jackson Hole, Wyoming, succeeded.[7] When the Soviet empire crumbled from within, personal relations between the U.S. secretaries of state and Shevardnadze stabilized the relationship.

Recognizing Russian Sensitivities

American diplomats have become increasingly sensitive to the ambivalence in Russian self-identity. Russian negotiators in the 1990s are more inclined than their predecessors to work through an issue rather than maintain a "principled" ideological stonewall. This does not, however, make them any less tenacious or skillful as negotiators. At the negotiating table there is an unresolved tension between a sulking sense of inferiority and a thrusting superpower assertiveness. This contradiction, intensified by the collapse of the Soviet empire, presents both pitfalls and opportunities. Post-Soviet Russians are no less defensive than their Soviet forebears, but they are less hobbled ideologically and are motivated by the prospect of producing real solutions to problems with the help of American and international funding.

U.S. defense secretary William Perry exploited the opportunity in this ambivalence when he reached out to persuade the Russians to participate in the Bosnian peacekeeping operation. The Russians refused to be under NATO control or to cooperate directly with their longtime adversary, NATO, which was in the process of enlarging but not including them. Perry approached the problem directly; he worked diligently and skillfully to convince Russian defense minister Pavel Grachev of America's respect and high regard for the Russian military. "Perry really converted Grachev and he did it through psychological means. He made Grachev feel like an important player. He brought him not only to Washington and gave him a twenty-one-gun salute and marched an honor guard past him, but he took him to NATO and had him treated like a big shot. He used all the trappings of the U.S. military and the alliance structure to overcome this inferiority complex that Russia has and the Russian military in particular has," explained a senior U.S. official involved in the negotiations.[8]

By the time that Presidents Yeltsin and Clinton achieved a positive framework for the deal at their summit in Hyde Park in April 1996, the hard work had already been done at the Grachev-Perry level. Through an exchange of visits, Perry and Grachev built a personal relationship. In the end, the Russians refused to serve in Bosnia under NATO command. However, they agreed to a formula, approved by Clinton and Yeltsin, that put Russian troops under American command, not technically under NATO. A senior American official noted, "That made all the difference to them and I think it tells you something about their attitude to the United States."

The Russian desire to be seen as an equal with the United States and the Russian belief that "the two of us together can settle things" are important ingredients in establishing a common frame of reference to foster mutual problem solving. Remarks by U.S. representatives on the shortcomings of Russian society smack to Russians of superpower chauvinism and play on the Russian inferiority complex. Former negotiator Victor Israelyan noted, "Unless it's imperative, touching upon multiethnic Russia's complex and controversial national problems will hardly facilitate negotiations."[9] In Soviet days, U.S. negotiators found it useful to play on Soviet weaknesses. In the postcommunist world the asymmetry between American and Russian power makes that technique obsolete. The problems have reached a new plane. U.S. negotiators are certainly aware of Russian weaknesses, but they must not appear to delight in reciting those deficiencies, and should instead emphasize their wish to help their Russian partners solve Russia's problems.

When the massive loss of life during the war in Chechnya threatened to destabilize Russian society, the U.S. government limited its criticism and practiced a policy of noninterference. America's official reticence to state its disapproval of Russian violence in Chechnya was symptomatic of the extreme change in the relationship between the United States and Russia. The Clinton administration believed that strong overt disapproval of Russian behavior would have weakened President Yeltsin and led to his downfall, negating the achievements of nuclear arms control in Russia and the former Soviet Union. The Clinton administration's negotiating style has focused on nurturing the relationship with Russia and building institutions rather than attacking or accentuating Russian weaknesses. The alternatives to Yeltsin—no government, a return to a communist government, or a military takeover—are sobering restraints on a policy of outspoken criticism of current Russian conduct.

ASSERTING U.S. RESOLVE

Engaging the Russians and respecting their sensitivities are important elements of an effective counterstrategy, but by themselves they are insufficient to yield success in negotiations. No less important are the assertion of U.S. resolve and the articulation of American democratic norms. Russian negotiators must be left in no doubt that although their American counterparts are willing to develop structures and relationships that will advance negotiations, the Americans are not prepared to sacrifice U.S. interests to achieve agreement. U.S. negotiators should, therefore, project consistency, determination, and strength. Israelyan advised: "Don't be intimidated. Don't be self-conscious or self-deprecating. Don't be put off by the Russians' put-down, negative approach to issues. Don't copy their negative style. Remember you have something they want."[10] A seasoned negotiator from the Office of the United States Trade Representative stressed the importance of "treating the other side respectfully. Do not condescend or lecture. Try to listen. Explain your point of view. Just keep explaining your point of view. Put the ball in their court and ask them how they are going to solve your problem. Tell them you can't work on solving their problem until they start working on your problem."[11]

When the Russians tried to stonewall a trade negotiation, the U.S. negotiator kept the talks going until midnight and did not call for breaks until the Russians asked for them. Being firm and direct can have an impact on Russian negotiators, but is best done in small groups or with the head of a delegation plus one other official. The rule to follow: If you show weakness you are in trouble. Be firm and strong.

Unlike the Russians, do not say an issue is nonnegotiable when there is room for discussion. A senior U.S. negotiator advised, "'This is very difficult or highly unlikely' still leaves room to talk, but if an issue is nonnegotiable say it is not on the table and maintain the position. Be clear about what is negotiable and what is not. The Russian style is to say an issue is not negotiable, but often it is and the way to find out is to listen carefully. The single most difficult thing is finding out what they really care about. You must probe and ask questions. The Russians are not like us. We are always spilling our guts and revealing information. Our society is based on transparency. Their society was based on secrecy, and transparency does not come naturally or easily to them."[12]

Recognizing the Limitations of Personal Relationships

Personal relationships can be useful tools for promoting give-and-take and pursuing win-win outcomes, but they can also be exploited by those intent on prevailing in what they see as an adversarial zero-sum encounter. U.S. negotiators should not attempt, in former ambassador Averell Harriman's term, "to bank goodwill" with the Russians. The concept is still alien to the Russian mind-set, and reference to it is taken as a sign of sentimentality and weakness.

Henry Kissinger recommended a "hard-headed" approach toward negotiating with the Soviets. "For while the men in the Kremlin do not mind playing on Western preconceptions that identify diplomacy with good personal relations, they really do not know how to deal with a sentimental foreign policy. . . . Soviet leaders have come up through a hard school," Kissinger explained. "They have prevailed in a system that ruthlessly weeds out the timid and the scrupulous. Only a great lust for power—or near fanatical ideological conviction—can have impelled them into careers in which there are few winners and disastrous penalties for losers. Personal goodwill, that mirage of western diplomacy, cannot move them. Their ideology stresses the overriding importance of material factors and the objective balance of forces."[13]

The Soviet readiness to dispense with personal goodwill when political considerations dictate a change of approach was illustrated at the Moscow summit of 1974. President Nixon, crippled by Watergate, tried to link the accomplishments of U.S.-Soviet relations to his friendship with Brezhnev. In a toast Nixon said the improvement in relations between the United States and the USSR had been made "possible because of a personal relationship that was established between the General Secretary and the President of the United States." The Soviets backed away from Nixon by dropping the word "personal" in the translations of the toast carried by TASS, the official Soviet news agency.

The Soviets also modified Nixon's toast by dropping his reference to Brezhnev's return visit "next year," refusing to commit to a target date. "No explanation was offered. None was necessary. The Soviets were cutting their losses," noted Kissinger.[14]

Despite the friendlier atmosphere that began to develop in relations with the West during Gorbachev's presidency and has since grown under Yeltsin, cordiality has by no means supplanted national interest and the instinct for political survival. The need for American and Russian leaders to carefully balance their personal relationships against their domestic political demands generates an ongoing tension in the relationship between Presidents Clinton and Yeltsin. Both sides put a good face on the relationship at their summit meetings, and Clinton openly but skillfully supported Yeltsin for reelection in 1996. Nevertheless, Russians are still ready to disregard established personal ties when political necessity demands. Yeltsin has chosen an openly nationalistic foreign minister, Evgeni Primakov, to maintain a profile that does not appear subservient to the West. Thus Yeltsin maintains both his friendship with the U.S. president and operating leverage with the Russian parliament and his domestic critics.

The risks of forging overly close ties with Russian counterparts are not limited to the possibility that those ties will be exploited or disregarded when deemed advantageous by the Russians. Unless U.S. diplomats maintain a professional distance, they may also embarrass and perplex their Russian colleagues.

Although his experience dealing with the Soviets was during the depths of the Cold War, George Kennan's cautionary remarks are no less applicable today:

A. *Don't act chummy with them.*
This only embarrasses them individually, and deepens their suspicions. Russian officials abhor the thought of appearing before their own people as one who has become buddies with a foreigner. This is not their idea of good relations.

B. *Don't assume a community of aims with them that does not really exist.* There is no use trying to swing Russians into line by referring to common purposes to which we may both have done lip service at one time or another, such as the strengthening of world peace, or democracy or what you will. They had their own purposes when they did lip service to these purposes. They think we had ours. For them it's all a game. And when we try and come at them with arguments on such common professions, they become doubly wary.

C. *Don't make fatuous gestures of good will.*

Few of us have any idea how much perplexity and suspicion has been caused in the Soviet mind by gestures and concessions granted by well-meaning Americans who sought to convince the Soviets of their friendship. Such gestures of good will upset all their calculations and throw them off balance. They immediately begin to expect that they have overestimated our strength, that they have been remiss in their obligations to the Soviet state, that they should have been demanding more from us all along. Frequently, this has exactly the opposite effect from that which we are seeking.[15]

Conveying Strength and Determination

Kennan also recognized the importance of projecting U.S. determination and strength. He advised:

Do not be afraid to use heavy weapons for what seem to us to be minor matters.

In general, it may be a bad practice to take a sledgehammer to swat a fly. With the Russians it is sometimes necessary. Russians will pursue a flexible policy of piecemeal presumption and encroachment of other people's interests, hoping that no single action will appear important enough to produce a strong reaction on the part of their opponents, and that in this way they may gradually bring about a major improvement in their position before the other fellow knows what's up. In this way they have a stubborn tendency to push every question right up to what they believe to be the breaking point of the patience of those with whom they deal. If they know that their opponent means business, that the line of his patience is firmly established and that he will not hesitate to take serious measures if this line is violated even in small ways and at isolated points, they will be careful and considerate. They do not like a showdown unless they have a great preponderance of strength. But they are quick to sense and take advantage of indecision or good-natured tolerance. Whoever deals with them must therefore be sure to maintain at all times an attitude of decisiveness and alertness in defense of his own interests.[16]

A Russian attempt to exhaust the patience of an adversary occurred in mid-May 1985, when Foreign Minister Gromyko met with Secretary of State Shultz in Vienna during celebrations of the thirtieth anniversary of the Austrian State Treaty. The Soviets made it clear to the State

Department in advance that they considered the meeting a preparation for the proposed summit between Presidents Reagan and Gorbachev. The meeting began at 2 P.M., and Gromyko, who was a proficient speaker of English, proceeded for more than two hours to discuss, in Russian, arms control issues, refusing to comment on Shultz's protest of the killing of a U.S. liaison officer in East Germany and never mentioning the Reagan-Gorbachev summit. Shultz, determined to show Gromyko he would not be intimidated by such behavior, proceeded to deliver rebuttals from position papers on the subjects Gromyko had mentioned.

At 6 P.M. Gromyko commenced a counterattack that lasted until 8:15 P.M., when Gromyko noted that they would be late for the gala reception being hosted by the Austrians to commemorate the State Treaty. When the two delegations gathered their papers and moved toward the door, Gromyko invited Shultz to a private conference in a corner of the room. "Do you have anything more you want to say to me?" the Soviet minister asked in English, without interpreters or aides present.

"No, we've covered everything," Shultz replied.

"What about the summit?" demanded Gromyko.

"What about it?" countered Shultz.

Gromyko crumbled and suggested they discuss the time and place for the summit, finally naming a date in late November. In his account of the meeting Don Oberdorfer notes that "Shultz ended the brief but intense conversation which lasted only two or three minutes in contrast to the six hours of roundabout talk preceding it, by saying he would take Gromyko's suggestions back to Reagan and be in touch."[17] By showing determination, skill, and physical endurance, Shultz convinced Gromyko he could not be intimidated, thus gaining the foreign minister's respect.

Demonstrating Consistency

Consistency is a key to successful negotiating strategy. Back channels, personal relationships, and private agendas appear to be shortcuts, but they can also open up opportunities for the Russians to play on real or apparent bureaucratic differences, thus disrupting policy coherence and creating confusion. Once the U.S. president sets a policy direction, his negotiators and associates must follow the line or risk setting up the potential for a foreign policy disaster.

In his memoirs Soviet ambassador Anatoli Dobrynin argued that on Soviet policy "Carter himself proved unable to give solid and consistent direction." Dobrynin asserted that President Carter, Secretary of State Cyrus Vance, and National Security Adviser Zbigniew Brzezinski were "reminiscent of the fable by the Russian poet Ivan Krylov about the incongruous team composed of a swan, a pike and a crayfish. . . . Hence the constant struggle of Carter's main advisors to gain the president's ear."[18] The Krylov fable mocks the inability of the three animals to perform the same task and is a cautionary tale against dividing responsibility when clarity of purpose and bureaucratic discipline are needed.

By the second year of the Carter administration the differences between Vance and Brzezinski on how to approach the Soviet Union were openly apparent; the team of Vance and his senior adviser on Soviet affairs, Marshall Shulman, vied with Brzezinski to win the president's confidence. In March 1978 President Carter delivered a speech at Wake Forest University in which he stressed U.S. determination to defend its national interests and preserve American values. Carter warned that "our strategic forces must be—and must be known to be—a match for the capabilities of the Soviets. They will never be able to use their nuclear forces to threaten, to coerce, or to blackmail our friends." Brzezinski, who had presented Carter with a draft of the speech, was pleased until he found out that Marshall Shulman had "reassured the Soviet Embassy—without the knowledge of the White House—that the president's speech should be viewed primarily as designed for domestic consumption and therefore should not be interpreted as indicating declined U.S. interest in SALT or accommodation."

Sending mixed signals to Moscow by first underreacting to the Soviet-backed deployment of Cuban troops in Ethiopia, and then overreacting to the announcement of a Soviet combat brigade in Cuba in the fall of 1979, was a serious mistake. Brzezinski argued that such swings in behavior, evidence of uncertainty or lack of clarity in long-range perspective, emboldened the Soviets—"and the final nail in the coffin was the Soviet invasion of Afghanistan."[19] Lack of discipline, resulting in inconsistency within the Carter administration, permitted the Soviet Union to go its own way without serious restraints or consideration for American concerns, a point underscored by Dobrynin in his memoirs.[20]

Demonstrating consistency is a complex equation, especially when the issues are divisive and a policy consensus is difficult to achieve. The Clinton administration's record of consistency is still being written on the issue of NATO enlargement. NATO enlargement cuts to the heart of Russia's self-image as a superpower. Critics argue that the Partnership for Peace, which prepares Eastern European nations for full membership in NATO, avoided the issue. It only aggravated the Russians and those nations that want to join NATO but must await an American decision on timing. The Clinton administration deferred resolving the question during the Russian election campaign in the spring of 1996 and the American presidential elections in the fall. The Clinton administration's hopes of building a consensus with the Russians and the East Europeans led to intense negotiations during 1997, billed as the decisive year to enlarge NATO.

REWARDS AND PENALTIES

Being firm and consistent in pursuit of an authorized negotiating objective is not always enough. A judiciously balanced combination of incentives and penalties is often the right formula for securing Russian agreement.

"Make no requests of the Russians," urged Kennan, "unless we are prepared to make them feel our displeasure in a practical way in case the request is not granted." Kennan warned against taking requests to a higher level because it only encourages the Russian bureaucracy to be uncooperative. Instead of this, Kennan urged, "we should take up matters on a normal level and insist that Russians take full responsibility for their actions on that level. We should take a retaliatory or corrective action promptly and unhesitatingly when we do not obtain satisfaction on the lower level. It is only in this way that we can teach the Russians to respect the whole range of our officials who must deal with them."[21]

When Kissinger tried to enlist Soviet pressure on North Vietnam to end the war, he found "the deepest reason for Soviet immobilism in 1969, however, was undoubtedly that conditions had not yet generated

incentives and penalties of sufficient magnitude to impel decision."
Kissinger found that the Soviets faced no penalties for evading American requests, and in hindsight he believes it was a mistake to heed
Soviet warnings against American escalation because of the "hedging
and cautious tone of Soviet statements." "In retrospect it is clear that
only if we posed specific tangible risks to important Soviet interests
would the Soviets have an incentive to exert pressure on their mono-
maniacal clients in Hanoi. Offering positive inducements would help,
but unless combined with risks posed by us, inducements would be
rejected as too embarrassing to Soviet standing in the Communist
world. When we finally did obtain Soviet help in 1972, it was through
just such a combination of pressures and incentives."[22]

In contemporary negotiations the United States still relies on pressures and incentives, juxtaposing risks against positive inducements.
An important new element driving the process is money and "practical
interest." The United States has the ability to provide a positive alternative to the policy it wants changed. Nunn-Lugar funds to destroy
missile silos and remove nuclear warheads is the most publicized example and has been the most dramatic success. At the same time, however, the United States can be outbid by other players: faced with the
choice between $1 billion from Iran for the sale of four nuclear reac-
tors and $250 million in U.S. aid, the Russian Federation has pro-
ceeded with the reactor deal (see chapter 2); U.S. attempts at the
Gore-Chernomyrdin meeting in Moscow in July 1996 to convince the
Russians that the Iranians would never pay for the reactors and the deal
should be canceled for nonproliferation reasons produced an equivo-
cal response from the Russians, who continue to deal with Iran.

PACKAGES

On the tactical level U.S. negotiators suggest "putting packages
together." "You can say, okay we could do this and this if you could do
that. If you start individually making concessions you will find that you
have made all the concessions and the Russians haven't made any.
Then you are going to have to make concessions on the big issues,
so try to create a package to make sure there is some balance," suggested an official of the Office of the U.S. Trade Representative who

negotiated during the Soviet period, and in 1997 was still negotiating with Russia. Packages are a way of avoiding the Russian aversion to compromise. The Russians see compromise as a form of weakness.

When negotiators can link issues, the overall shape of an agreement emerges and there is less emphasis on who made what concession. Packages are a good way to avoid the classic Soviet/Russian salami tactics of slicing off a concession from one part of the problem, then shifting to another area and attacking. Resolving smaller and peripheral issues to develop a negotiating momentum often makes it easier to settle the bigger issues. "Packages are a good way to make forward progress by allowing both sides to retain their pride and not make it appear that either one of them is making all the concessions. Both sides must retain a sense of dignity. If one feels beaten into submission the agreement will not last," said a senior American negotiator.[23]

DEALING WITH CULTURAL DIFFERENCES

Russian negotiators never let their American counterparts lose sight of the differences between their cultures. Western diplomats make attempts to bridge or narrow the cultural divide, but when it is too wide, they are forced to acknowledge the differences and adhere to their own agenda and style.

Americans and Russians have different attitudes toward time. "Time," noted Yale Richmond, "is not measured [in Russia] in minutes or hours but more likely in days, weeks and months. The venerated virtue in Russia is not punctuality but patience. . . . Such divergent views of time can create difficulties in cooperative efforts and joint ventures. Americans will want to negotiate an agreement quickly, schedule an early start on the venture, begin on time, complete the work as expeditiously as possible or show early results or profit. Russians will need more time to get organized, and there will be frequent delays and postponements. They will be less concerned with immediate results, and profit is a concept that they are only beginning to understand. . . . What to do? Not much, except to persist patiently and speak softly, but carry a big prod."[24]

The prod can be new data to convince the Russians of the need for an agreement or material incentives that provide jobs and economic development. Providing training and teaching for Russian officials in banking methods, tax policy, advanced management techniques, and the skills of the information revolution is becoming a part of the negotiating process. Beyond closing a deal is the need to make it self-enforcing. The incentives of continued economic growth and the ability to perform up to world standards are key to motivating Russian negotiators and business people. Americans have more to offer Russians than Russians have to offer Americans, but Russians bristle, bluster, and complain when reminded of their own internal problems and inadequacies. In diplomatic negotiations they may sulk or dissemble if too harshly attacked simply to indicate displeasure, but they are tough minded and readily return to the fray when they think it is to their advantage.

Russians tend to be less flexible than Americans and react badly to surprises. Russian diplomats cannot commit themselves to a new proposal or draft once a negotiation is under way without a strenuous renegotiation with their ministries. Therefore, Russians like to follow form and protocol. "From tsarist times, Russian diplomacy strictly followed French diplomatic protocol. Soviet diplomacy also held firmly and steadfastly to the same protocol and rules of procedure. Following this tradition will only enhance the negotiations," suggested Israelyan.[25]

Cultural disparities increase the chances of miscommunication. Jokes do not translate well and easily, and should be told only with great care. Miscommunication can also be deliberately exploited, for which reason Western negotiators should always bring their own translators to negotiations and never rely on the other side's translator, no matter how charming or effective he or she may appear to be.

In some instances, however, gift exchanges actually provide opportunities for improving the chances of a successful outcome to negotiations. Russians offer caviar and vodka and enjoy American gifts of scotch or bourbon. Russians collect souvenirs, especially lapel pins and badges, or *znachki*, and proudly offer them to their American counterparts. *Izvestia*'s chief editor presented his American joint-venture counterparts from the Hearst Corporation with pocket watches embossed with the newspaper's logo. The Hearst executives presented antique silver dollars to the Russians. Leonid Brezhnev received a Steuben glass sculpture of an American eagle from President Nixon as a summit present. Brezhnev offered it to Ambassador Dobrynin until Dobrynin told him it was worth several thousand dollars, at which point Brezhnev reclaimed it for himself.[26] Gifts can break the ice, establish a mood of conviviality, and open the way to friendship.

Gifts cannot be a substitute for what the Soviets used to call "a frank and comradely exchange of views," a code phrase to disguise difficult negotiations with sharp differences. George Kennan warned: "Do not be afraid of unpleasantness and public airing of differences." His advice given in 1946 is still pertinent and underscores the continuity of Russian negotiating style:

> The Russians don't mind scenes and scandals. If they discover that someone else does mind them and will go out of his way to avoid them, they will use this as a form of blackmail in the belief that they can profit from the other fellow's squeamishness . . . we need not fear that occasional hard words will have permanent bad effect on our relations. The Russian is never more agreeable than after his knuckles have been sharply rapped. He takes well to rough play and rarely holds grudges over it. Let us not forget Stalin's first reaction when he met Ribbentrop. It was to joke good-naturedly and cynically about the bitter propaganda war which had been waged for so many years between the two countries. The Russian governing class respects only the strong. To them, shyness is a form of weakness.[27]

Western efforts to engage the Russians in creating new structures for peacemaking and problem solving, from the level of president down through the desk officers of the Ministry of Foreign Affairs, require overcoming Russian suspicion of the outside world. Engagement requires a dramatic shift away from the winner-take-all outlook that is characteristic of Soviet mentality. The task for American negotiators is to educate Russians at every step along the way to begin treating negotiations as mutual problem solving rather than political battles to be won or lost.

■ ■ ■

Western negotiators must not underestimate the extent of the current Russian malaise and its effects on their Russian counterparts. Russia cannot yet meet international rules and standards posed by such organizations as the International Monetary Fund or the World Trade Organization. Russia faces serious inadequacies in its ability to finance its superpower ambitions. A collapsing army and an ailing Yeltsin fostered an internal power struggle. Open competition for power in the business community has led to the murders of six hundred Russians and several Americans. The growing presence of armed bodyguards accompanying business and banking executives on the streets has created a siege mentality. Law enforcement remains feeble and ineffective. Such an unstable environment undermines efforts to build institutions. Survivors cling to the old, familiar system with its predictable style and still-extant personal networks and power centers. Ideology-driven centralized control has given way to the demands of the market economy, but the old psychology of interpersonal relations remains. The Bolshevik Code endures.

Uncertainty permeates all areas of life, compounding a tendency among Russians to sacrifice long-term interests to short-term gains. For instance, the immediate need to sustain factories and shipyards in the former Soviet military industrial complex has led to arms sales that may threaten Russia's mid- and long-term strategic interests. Russia has become the People's Republic of China's largest arms supplier, directly contributing to China's military threat capacity in Asia. Clinton administration policies have been successful in reducing nuclear warheads within the former Soviet Union, but Russia's drive to sustain its military industrial complex and regain the Near Abroad has kept arms exports at a high level. Selling weapons offers short-term political or economic gain but holds a longer-term threat of destabilization.

Russia is, to be sure, readier to cooperate with the West, especially for material gain, than was the Soviet Union. Nonetheless, especially given Russia's current vulnerability, it is not surprising to find that the zero-sum expectations that Soviet negotiators brought to the negotiating table still persist. In a radio address to the Russian people after the Helsinki summit of March 1997, President Yeltsin defended the agreements he had reached with President Clinton: "Of course, we could have furrowed our brows and pounded the table with our shoes, as happened during the cold war years . . . but what would that have achieved? Another round of irreconcilable enmity, a new isolation for Russia."[28] Yeltsin's move to win-win negotiations was bitterly attacked by his rivals. Communist Party head Gennadi Zyuganov derided the summit as "the treaty of Versailles" and insisted that Yeltsin had "betrayed Russia's national interest."[29]

It will take time to establish a new era of negotiations in which the goal for both sides is to win. The legacy of seventy years of Soviet rule and centuries of suspicion, fear, and jealousy of the outside world will not fade swiftly. Even with a deepening and widening process of democratization, it will take at least a generation before the effects of Marxist-Leninist thinking and instruction diminish significantly. And it will take many generations before the influence of Russia's turbulent, bloody, and despotic history is transformed into a peaceful and cooperative foreign policy. In the meantime, Western negotiators will have to display strength, dignity, and constancy when they encounter in their Russian counterparts values and culture very different from their own.

▪ 5 ▪

Doing Business in Russia and Former Soviet Republics

The nature of doing business in Russia and the Near Abroad has changed from the days of the Soviet Union when all negotiations were controlled by the government. No longer is the Russian negotiator backed by a top-down economy run from the headquarters of the State Planning Commission in Moscow. Money has replaced ideology. Bankers, linked to government officials from the Kremlin on down to regional governors, play a critical role in negotiations. The negotiator must have ties to a bank and the bank has to have the backing of a government ministry. It is a vicious or convenient circle depending on whether you are inside, or outside looking for capital. The fragmentation of power at the top and the lack of formal enforceable banking laws have led to a Klondike-style gold rush where personal fortunes are made from the sale of state-owned factories and resources and then transferred abroad. Those who practice such a business style have derisively been tagged "the New Russians."

The future belongs to a new generation of Russian business people who come to the negotiating table unburdened by ideology. Now they are seeking material advantage, but they are using the same style and techniques that their mentors practiced in running Soviet state agencies trading for state-run corporations.

Neither the tsarist nor the Soviet past offers the tradition and institutional structure of a business culture; both the Russian Orthodox Church and the Communist Party reviled "profit," and those who bought and sold goods were labeled *spekulyanti* ("speculators"), an epithet of scorn and outrage. Seven decades of attacks on "the bourgeoisie" took their toll. Middle men and women were scorned as outcasts, although it was they who created a model for the future, bypassing the cumbersome government bureaucratic apparatus by doing things *na leva*—literally "on the left," but best translated as "under the table." Only when the Soviet Union came apart could women stand outside the entrances of Moscow Metro stations to sell parsley and dill from their gardens without fear of being harassed by the police.

Contemporary Russians are struggling to build a new business culture from scratch. Only slowly are they learning that Gromyko's rule for diplomatic negotiations—"Ask for something that does not belong to you, ask for more than they will want to give"—does not work in an arena in which profits must be measured against capital investment and operating costs. The concept of a return on invested capital is just beginning to be perceived and is barely comprehended. The Russians understand buying and selling; they operate from a trader's mentality of quick turnover, not within a settled legal framework that encourages long-term investment. The Russians' lack of comprehension of international business norms often leads to unrealistic demands or out-of-line, unacceptable pricing—a perspective driven by the short-term objectives of maximizing current income in an unstable political and institutional environment. With the safety net of the Communist Party eliminated, there is pervasive insecurity within the generation that came of age under socialism. They compensate by trying to go for a quick profit, because the instability of the government and the marketplace makes long-term payoffs of investments seem unlikely. Most Russian business negotiators believe that asking for more than one expects is an essential strategy, and they open with bids or demands that stalemate the proceedings or erode confidence before bargaining can begin.

"Today it depends on what you are negotiating. If you are negotiating with a government official, it is the same pattern as before. If you are dealing with a new entrepreneur, it is a contact with inexperience," said Simon Chilewich, head of the Chilewich Group, a resource developer and distributor of consumer goods, which has been doing business in Russia for the past thirty-five years.[1]

Foreign diplomats face Russian negotiators representing ministries whose responsibilities have been fragmented. Western business people in Russia must deal with contradictory or competing laws, when they exist. Political instability and confrontation among the presidency, the Duma, and regional and local power centers have created a maelstrom of conflicting legislation. The constitution of the Russian Federation includes more than one hundred amendments, all adopted between 1991 and 1993. "Russian legislation is like a cassette: You can remove one law and play another. In addition, each autonomous Russian republic has its own legislation, which sometimes differs from the Russian laws. Therefore, negotiators need to pay special attention to an agreement's legal aspects. It's very important to verify the validity of the laws the Russian partner is referring to," explained former Soviet negotiator Victor Israelyan.[2]

The nature of Russian business relationships is treacherous and uncertain. Today's promise can be tomorrow's betrayal. Even business people with long years of experience and a reputation in the former Soviet Union find that the power struggles within the ministries and between local and central governments make the establishment of a new business a bureaucratic and financial nightmare, thereby substantially reducing the incentives for business dealings. Stable channels and institutions for carrying on business have not yet been developed. In Moscow and other Russian cities the old communist leadership, the *nomenklatura*, still controls factory enterprises and demands a cut of any new joint venture.

Foreigners doing business in Russia have come to learn the hard way that the battle for privatization of state-controlled property is waged among the Russian bankers, business tycoons, and the state. "The real struggle is a war among clans over the division of the spoils of the Russian state and influence over its president, Boris Yeltsin. There will be winners and losers, but no heroes," wrote Paul Saunders, director of the Nixon Center for Peace and Freedom in Washington, D.C. "This has important implications for our evaluation of democracy and economic reform in Russia. First, of course, Russia is not as democratic and reform oriented as it may seem. Second, and much more important, victory for the 'reformers' is not equivalent to victory of democracy or the free market. There are important reasons for the U.S. to maintain, and even increase, its political and economic engagement with Russia. But for such engagement to be effective, it must be undertaken with open eyes."[3]

Many American business people, remarked Simon Chilewich, prefer to deal with one or other of the newly independent states. Kazakhstan has a small population, stable political leadership, and clear lines of decision making, all of which make for more predictable behavior and fewer surprises in the way of new taxes and restrictive legislation that change the terms of agreed-upon contracts. The corruption problem is more manageable because the lines of power are more clearly defined.

The situation in Russia is made worse by the presence of organized crime. The *mafiya* system has played a major role in retarding development of small business operations. Those who succeed are quickly devoured by the *mafiya*. "The only loyalty is to oneself and one's family. There is no such thing as somebody giving you their word. In the old days a Soviet contract was bullet proof, now there are defaults and no recourse. Is it possible for a decent person to survive?" rhetorically asked an American petroleum expert with wide experience in Russia, Kazakhstan, and Azerbaijan.[4] American and foreign business people were shocked when Paul Tatum, a U.S. entrepreneur embroiled in a battle for control of the Radisson Slavyanskaya hotel, was gunned down in an underpass near the hotel in November 1996.[5] His killing remains unsolved.

Despite the risks and horror stories of doing business in Russia and the newly independent states, for some Western business people the rewards are worth the trials. "Russia is a good place to invest and it can only get better," said Chilewich. "The risk:reward ratio is greater than on a normal deal; here it doesn't mean the risk is smaller, but the reward ratio is greater in anything from toothpicks to locomotives."

The biggest profits come from the sale abroad of natural resources for hard currency. Western companies in the oil service industry have made profits trading with Russian companies, selling equipment on a normal letter-of-credit basis. The inability to complete pipelines to bring the oil to market, however, remains a potential deal breaker.

Russian-made consumer products have difficulty in Western markets. An exception is optical goods such as binoculars, which have found a niche on the low end of the American market. American drug companies are not yet manufacturing in Russia on their own or in joint ventures; they are exporting to Russia primarily for barter. There have been some small foreign investments in manufacturing; cigarette factories have succeeded. Large-scale investment in manufacturing and process-ing awaits a commercial banking, tax, and distribution infrastructure.

THE PERVASIVE PROBLEM OF CORRUPTION

Before contracts are signed, officials and executives openly solicit bribes in the form of consultancy or management fees paid in advance. For independent American business people, the promising vision of long-term reward is too often obliterated by short-term demands for bribes and payoffs. All the business people interviewed for this book said there is no way to avoid the demands for payoffs. They can be re-jected outright, reconciled, or passed on to local Russian employees or associates to handle. Given the still tenuous and transitory nature of the shift from a command economy to a market-oriented economy, officials who grew up in the Soviet system are so wary of new business relation-ships that they seek immediate rewards, ignoring the concept of long-term—or even near-term—investment.

In April 1992 President Boris Yeltsin issued a decree, "On the Strug-gle against Corruption in Civil Service." The decree exhorts civil ser-vants to do their "utmost to strengthen the state apparatus and im-prove work to select, train, and place cadres," and precludes civil servants from engaging in "entrepreneurship" by relying on their "powers of office." The decree also precludes "paid work at spare-time jobs" or "being engaged in entrepreneurship via middlemen." Of par-ticular significance in the current Russian business climate is the pro-hibition against officials participating "in person or via an agent, in the management of joint stock companies, limited liability partnerships, or other business entities."

The *Russian and Commonwealth Business Law Report,* a journal that tracks the jungle of proposed legislation and regulation, noted: "West-ern firms conducting business in Russia, and particularly in the oil industry where the hard currency earning potential is the greatest, are invariably confronted with a variety of proposals whereby the Russian managers or officials stand to benefit personally. The blurred lines separating permissible from impermissible conduct have derailed more than one oil transaction, and enmeshed several exploration and development projects in controversy."[6]

The *Report* outlined some of the varied methods by which government officials participate in oil and gas projects:

- A deputy minister or a lower-ranking civil servant wishes to form a joint venture either in Russia, or, frequently, abroad. He and others with whom he is associated will hold stock in the venture in their private capacity, not as government officials.
- Russians in a newly privatized enterprise, with stock ownership in the hands of the former management, the former employees, or the ministry that supervised operations, will receive commissions or new stock ownership interests, or both, in connection with the transaction.
- Russians in a state enterprise wish to participate in the conversion of the enterprise into a new legal form, usually a joint stock company with or without foreign investment. The Russians will hold a small percentage of the newly privatized company. Consulting or commission fees will be paid, directly or indirectly, to Russian personnel.

Under the Yeltsin anticorruption decree the definition of a civil servant remains unclear, as does the relationship between "powers of office" and their use in contemplated transactions. The only specified penalty for violating the Yeltsin decree is "dismissal from the occupied position." At the same time the decree proposes "a safety net for civil servants" including the creation of "normal working conditions" and "rates of compensatory payments commensurate with the conditions of a free market and the regime of civil service."

The *Report* noted:

> Thus, the decree recognizes the inadequacy of civil service compensation, sanctioning by implication efforts by civil servants to supplement their abysmally low salaries through other mechanisms. In a broad sense, this precondition lays the foundation for either toughening the enforcement standards and concomitantly increasing civil service compensation or abandoning altogether the effort to introduce a meaningful ethical regime.
>
> While it will require considerable time for the Yeltsin administration, and the Russian parliament, to sort through complex issues associated with an ethical code of conduct, U.S. investors in the Russian market confront an immediate and more severe dilemma. Specifically, for U.S. firms and subsidiaries the U.S. Foreign Corrupt Practices Act (FCPA) is applicable.[7]

The FCPA was enacted in 1977 and amended by Congress in 1988. It prohibits payments and other gratuities to foreign persons made to influence business decisions. Section 103 specifically prohibits paying or offering to pay "any money . . . gift . . . or anything of value" to any foreign official, party officials, or party candidate in order to influence a business decision, or to "any person while knowing or having reason to know" that he or she will offer it to "such persons for such purposes."

Such practices, however, remain commonplace for Western companies doing business in Russia, Ukraine, and other members of the Commonwealth of Independent States. In discussing the implications of the FCPA and the Yeltsin anticorruption decree, the *Russian and Commonwealth Business Law Report* offered some practical suggestions for solving the problems raised:

- Agreements for agents or consultants that clearly set forth that payments prohibited by the FCPA will not be made. Agreements may include statements of compliance with the FCPA and may authorize the inspection of accounting books and records that might trace payments that violate the FCPA.
- Development of corporate policies in both the United States and Russia, and codes of conduct for individuals dealing with foreign businesses and officials.
- Establishment of procedures for securing legal advice regarding proposed transactions and payments or gifts under domestic and foreign law. The U.S. Justice Department has established procedures for securing advisory opinions with definitive guidance.

However, the *Report* concluded that "there is obviously a temptation to devise compensation mechanisms advancing the transaction with the hope that the details will never be investigated. For major U.S. oil industry players, however, the risks presented by the FCPA and the attendant adverse consequences of violating the act are simply too great to ignore. The April 4 (anticorruption) decree, the publicity that now surrounds many of the larger oil transactions, and the long-standing requirements of the FCPA mandate caution in this very sensitive area."[8]

The problems of business negotiations are directly related to economic survival and the lingering psychology of the Bolshevik culture. In most government agencies, salaries do not keep pace with inflation.

In his book *Autopsy of an Empire*, former U.S. ambassador to Moscow Jack F. Matlock, Jr., noted, "Sometimes during a spasm of budget austerity, civil servants were not paid for several months on end. Often given poor direction and unclear instructions, even normally honest bureaucrats could be tempted to make the most of whatever authority they had by selling their influence." Matlock, who served in Moscow from 1986 to 1991, observed that "corruption, furthermore, was not confined to the lower and middle reaches of the government. Evidence is necessarily anecdotal, but most Western businessmen looking for investment opportunities found that key ministries would usually demand that large fees be paid to shadowy 'consultants' before necessary approvals and licenses were issued."

Ambassador Matlock's account of the collapse of the Soviet Union cites the tale of a Russian friend who managed a medium-sized state firm in the provinces and was offered a ministerial portfolio in Moscow in 1992. He turned it down because he was privatizing the provincial company and wanted to complete the job. Six months later he was approached by the person who had been appointed to the ministerial position and who now wanted to invest $1 million in the newly privatized firm. Matlock's friend had known the minister in question for years. "Before he took that job in Moscow he didn't have a kopeck to invest. But in six months he had a million of hard American cash to throw around. And most are like that, though not, probably, Chernomyrdin and Yeltsin himself."[9]

Jack Grynberg, who heads Grynberg Resources in Denver, Colorado, an independent American oil, gas, and mineral developer, tried to establish projects in Russia. "How to make a million in the former Soviet Union?" asks Grynberg. "Bring two million and it will soon be down to one." Grynberg worked for two and a half years in Kyrgyzstan to structure a deal. When it finally came time to sign a contract, Grynberg was given a Swiss bank account number and told to deposit $4 million for the president of the country. He refused and the contract went to a Canadian company that paid the bribe.

"They laugh at the Foreign Corrupt Practices Act, we don't," said an American natural resources entrepreneur who refused to pay bribes of $200,000 in "closing costs" for operating a Siberian gold mine that had been idle for thirty-four years. The entrepreneur told the Russians he was prepared to invest $120 million over a three-year period and provide four hundred jobs. When he complained about the payoffs to the deputy chairman of the natural resources council in the area, the entrepreneur was told, "I don't care if the mine sits for another thirty-four years." The deputy chairman made it clear that he cared more about a payoff than reopening the mine.

THE HAZY LINE BETWEEN PUBLIC INTEREST AND PRIVATE INTEREST

Under the Soviet regime the deputy chairman might also not have cared, but for other reasons. Productivity was determined by ideology and controlled from the center. Once a quota was fulfilled there was no incentive to work harder. "They pretend they are paying us and we pretend we are working" was a prevalent attitude among Soviet workers. Today, workers go without wages for months at a time in government-controlled industries and factories. The socialist safety net has unraveled. Personal gain has replaced the socialist ethic of sharing and building a better tomorrow for one's children and the workers of the world. Environmental abuses by state-controlled corporations were a common practice because there was no concept of private property that could be protected by antipollution laws. One state organization did not file suit against another to protect the land or resources. The Communist Party, through the Central Committee, controlled construction and economic growth. Under the guise of building the state, the quality of life deteriorated. There were no restraints built in through the protests of environmental organizations or legal recourse with penalties.

What are considered gross conflicts of interest in American business practice are required forms of conducting business in Russia. Since Gorbachev's perestroika program began in 1985, the most common form of expediting approval of applications for joint ventures in Russia was to hire as consultants officials from the ministry providing the approvals. Paying officials from the ministries to speed the process was a practical solution to the problem of lengthy delays. The idea of a conflict of interest between public responsibility and private gain never occurred to the Russian officials involved; they thought it natural to be rewarded for their efforts.

With the breakup of the Soviet Union and the privatization of state factories and enterprises, the *nomenklatura* moved to maintain their control by establishing new free market structures with themselves still in charge. "These former communists want to hang onto power. They want a piece off the top. They want commissions paid on signing. They do not want to invest in an interest and work and wait for a return. If you have to pay commissions up front, that makes the whole project more expensive," explained J. Robinson West, president of Petroleum Finance Corporation, an independent Washington, D.C.–based adviser to oil companies and governments.[10]

Under Soviet-style socialism, all the natural resources of the Soviet Union theoretically belonged to the state and the people. There was no private ownership of property, and to this day the legal status of private ownership of land remains obscure, a no-man's-land of proposed legislation, decrees, and complex leaseholding. People take light bulbs and toilet seats from state offices because they cannot find such goods in the marketplace and believe, as "people," the goods are theirs by right.

The question of who owns the natural resources of Russia poses serious contradictions: economic development versus stagnation, foreign capital inflow versus continued Russian ownership and no growth. Leading communist and nationalist political leaders argue that oil, gas, and minerals are part of the national patrimony and must not be permitted to fall under foreign ownership. Soviet-era repudiation of "imperialist exploitation" has been replaced with a new nationalism that equates international business investment with an attempt to dominate and control Russia. Faced with communist resistance to proposals for attracting foreign investment, the Russian government has agreed to shorten the list of oil fields and other natural resources in which foreigners can take a stake. In July 1966 Aleksandr Shokin, deputy speaker of the Duma, told foreign oil executives that the government would submit to parliament a list of fewer than sixty priority areas where foreigners could seek concessions under a new production-sharing law. The government's original proposal, offering concessions in more than two hundred areas, was denounced by the communists, the largest bloc in the Duma, as a sellout of Russian interests.[11]

The continued debate and infighting over concessions for foreign investment in natural resources have led to a chaotic, unpredictable environment that has produced a series of wild cards such as new taxes, quotas, and customs regulations that can effectively cripple operations and exports. The shipment of supplies and secure transportation is still hazardous and expensive. Distribution systems, inadequate at best, collapsed with the Soviet Union and are still in a nascent stage of development. Veterans of the Afghan war with old army trucks are the new entrepreneurs trying to win hauling contracts and establish new distribution systems.

In the topsy-turvy world of building a market economy, Western investors face the uncertainty of government decrees like the one of April 1994, which imposed a 23 percent tax on foreign loans to Russian businesses. The Moscow office of the American Chamber of Commerce sent a letter to its 170 members urging them to stop all loans to Russian companies until the decree was reversed. It was.

MAFIYA RULES

Doing business in Russia requires fine-tuned antennae and the ability to ascertain what businesses are safe for foreigners to enter. *Wall Street Journal* correspondent Matthew Brzezinski offered a set of rules for avioding the perils of organized crime in Russia, the *mafiya*.[12]

- Pick a safe business. "The safest businesses include accountancies, law firms and other consulting agencies that keep low profiles, work out of unmarked buildings, deal mostly with corporate clients and get paid for their services through bank transfers, often abroad."

  Retail businesses where cash is collected are more risky. When the Philip Morris Companies set up kiosks in St. Petersburg in 1992 they were blown up night after night. Philip Morris decided to drop direct distribution to consumers. In June 1997 the wives of two Philip Morris employees in Moscow received kidnapping threats. The families were hastily evacuated from Moscow, but have since returned. Philip Morris says they are not in danger. A rival tobacco manufacturer says the incident coincided with now-aborted plans by Philip Morris to stop supplying a large distributor.

  Metals trading is a high-risk sector. In 1995, thirty-five people in the business died in mysterious circumstances, according to the Interior Ministry.

- Be aware of your "roof," or *krysha,* as it is known in Moscow. In the Russian intelligence service *krysha* is slang for a cover. In contemporary Moscow business it is the term for paying someone to shelter a business from criminal elements. Criminal gangs and security services offer the best *kryshas.* Gangs usually charge 25 percent of a retail business's gross sales for protection. Multinationals such as Reebok International Ltd., with a fancy retail store across the street from the American embassy, employs Most-Security, a private force of eleven hundred guards. Most-Security was formed by tycoon Vladimir Gusinsky to protect his banking, media, and real estate empire, and he now offers security services for hire.

- Pick a local partner carefully. The choice can mean success or failure. Western business people have supported a flourishing business for former Soviet intelligence officers who investigate and report on the background and financial resources of potential Russian business partners. Don't act without investigating first.

- There are established procedures for getting out of disputes with partners that rarely involve courts of law. Disagreements, Moscow veterans say, are best resolved quietly through the mediation of *kryshas.* The gangs themselves mediate and resolve disagreements either through the threat of force or payment of money.

- Resist any temptation to cheat on Russian taxes. It is not the tax police who will catch you but the *mafiya* who will blackmail you.

NEEDED: RULE OF LAW

Property laws, legal jurisdictions, a viable commercial court system, a predictable taxation system, and a reliable banking structure—the premises of a market economy—are all a glimmering hope far from fulfillment in Russia. The lack of these necessary support mechanisms contributes to a gold-rush mentality among Russian would-be entrepreneurs. "The main thing is that they are misinformed about how business is done in the West and that colors their attitude toward negotiating. They think that capitalism is Wild West–type capitalism and they have no appreciation of business or legal ethics. They don't have a sense, because it doesn't exist there, of the extent to which the law and the rule of law govern business relations," said Isaac Shapiro, a senior partner in Skadden, Arps, Slate, Meagher, and Flom, a New York–based law firm, who has done extensive business in Russia. "Too many people take Russian legislation at its face value without understanding that legislation is only as good as a functioning, mature court system."[13]

Shapiro and others have noted that before the Russian Revolution there was a court system with a Western-style civil code:

> Ironically under the tsars the legal profession and the judiciary were all quite exemplary. My father went to law school in Russia. I have his old textbooks and they could be French text books. The new civil code, the first part of which they have just adopted, has been written by the Dutch. It emanates from the Napoleonic Code, but they have improved on it, and throughout Europe people say it is the most advanced and modern. It is very much like the prerevolutionary code in the way it is structured.
>
> They can pass all kinds of legislation and Yeltsin can write decrees until he is blue in the face, but nothing is going to happen without a legal structure and people's confidence that if I go to court I am going to get a fair shake; the law is going to be applied; I am going to have an impartial, fair judge. That does not exist. If I pledge my assets to a bank, is the bank ever going to be able to realize on that? There are no bankruptcy judges. They don't know the first thing about bankruptcy. In the years to come if they are able to develop an honest, functioning judiciary—it is a very big if—they have to be paid enough not to take bribes and someone has to train them. Then they can succeed.

Shapiro sees signs for optimism, and believes that a business culture and infrastructure will develop:

> Things that I might have said a year or two ago to Russians, and they might have been incredulous about, time and experience teaches them. They are learning that we are not making this up. If someone says, "I cannot sign without the approval of my board," or "I cannot sign because it is not in the interests of my shareholders," it means just what it sounds like. They also are learning that money isn't everything, that there are legal and ethical considerations. Sometimes an American or European will not do something that would reward him or his company for these reasons. They are beginning to understand that the world in the West works that way.

Shapiro cited the case of the first Russian bank to be issued a license after four years of negotiations with the New York State Banking Commission and the Federal Reserve Board. "A bank thought just because it had money it could get a license tomorrow. We explained to them that the Federal Reserve and the New York State banking authority wanted to know who they were, what banking experience they had, and how they came by the money. Money alone doesn't get you everywhere, particularly with a system of laws and regulators who are not on the take, who are paid an ample wage, and who believe in what they are doing. This is an educational experience for them, to believe our stock exchange laws really work. A lot of it has to do with their total lack of understanding of the role of the judicial process and the enforcement mechanism," said Shapiro.

For the time being, Shapiro cautioned, it is not agreements and enforcement that one should look to but the self-interest of the parties. "They are only going to carry out the agreement and behave in a predictable way to the extent that, and for as long as, it is in their self-interest. It is self-defeating to try to strike a bargain that is not fair and not of mutual benefit because they will not live up to it."

THE CHANGING ROLE OF THE STATE

In Lenin's day and until the fall of the Soviet empire, the pattern for international trade negotiations was for the Communist Party leader or the Politburo to pick a businessman who would serve as an agent of influence. A favored foreign businessman could count on the government's word.

Armand Hammer, whose father was one of the founders of the American Communist Party, was Lenin's choice. Hammer carried funds from Russia to America to finance the American Communist Party and was rewarded with a franchise for an asbestos mine and a pencil factory. Later favorites were American steel tycoon Cyrus Eaton and Robert Maxwell, the Czech-born, British media magnate, who got his start as a publisher by translating Russian scientific journals into English. In his final years Maxwell became a publicist in the West for Gorbachev's policy of perestroika.

Leonid Brezhnev picked Richard Nixon's friend Don Kendall, the head of PepsiCo, and permitted a barter arrangement of Pepsi for Stolichnaya vodka. The experience of doing business in the Soviet Union has given PepsiCo an institutional memory and infrastructure that enabled it to win battles in its war with Coca-Cola for a share of the soft-drink market in Ukraine and other newly independent countries. Kendall's pioneering paid off with successful Pizza Hut franchises in Russia and Ukraine.

Dwayne Andreas, chairman and chief executive officer of Archer Daniels Midland (ADM), also benefited from introductions to Brezhnev and Gorbachev. ADM is a major supplier of grain to Russia, where an estimated 25 percent of the grain crop is lost through disease and rot, inadequate storage and transportation, and a lack of facilities to process agricultural products. Andreas's plan for building a collection, storage, processing, and distribution center for agricultural products depends not on Russian investment but on American government support or financing.

Paradoxically the scale of economic distress—industrial production dropped 9 percent in 1996 and the accumulated backlog of unpaid wages in the Russian economy was estimated at 50 trillion rubles (about $9 billion) in 1997—has accelerated U.S. government support for President Yeltsin. American concern with the economic and political transformation of Russia has grown to the point where the Clinton administration, fearing an economic collapse could bring chaos and new forms of dictatorship, made improving the Russian economy a top foreign policy priority. The U.S. Department of Energy and the Commerce Department have enhanced efforts to stimulate American investment in Russia. The Defense Department is leading a project to convert Soviet defense industries to peacetime uses, and the Commerce Department is actively encouraging U.S. investment in Russia.

Total foreign investment had risen only to $6.5 billion in 1996, with the figure for 1997 expected to be in the region of $9 billion. Foreign private direct investment (FDI) in 1996 was less than $2 billion, with over half of that being invested in Moscow. Russia's FDI per capita was $11, compared to $184 in Hungary and $117 in the Czech Republic. According to the International Monetary Fund, three-quarters of state-owned enterprises need radical restructuring, with one in three of these needing to declare bankruptcy. In 1996 over 40 percent of the 6,500 industrial enterprises in Russia finished the year with serious losses.[14]

Despite the corrupt environment and high risk of doing business in Russia, most American investors see long-term rewards in a market that is virgin territory for foreign investment, especially in oil, gas, raw materials, information technology, and mass communications.

As in other developing nations, corruption fills the void created by the absence of functioning government institutions. In developed societies, corruption is predictable—one knows who and how much to pay and in what ways to obtain predictable results. In undeveloped societies with no government structures, corruption is unpredictable, and no matter who or how much is paid there is no guarantee of results. Postcommunist Russia is wracked by unpredictable corruption. The Bolshevik Code, which looked after the Communist Party elite and maintained a closed and predictable system of corruption, has broken down. Its values still dominate the behavior of the ruling elite and are reflected in business negotiations, but the pattern of business negotiations is essentially dominated by power politics from the national to the local level. Lacking an effective system of rule of law, Russian society is in crisis.

The primary U.S. official in improving Russian-American economic ties is Vice President Al Gore, who has developed a close working relationship with Russian prime minister Viktor Chernomyrdin. The Gore-Chernomyrdin Commission, which meets twice a year, breaks major bureaucratic impasses obstructing U.S. investment in Russia. The commission is trying to lower tariffs in the aerospace field and on candy imports for Mars, the maker of Snickers (the most popular candy in Russia). Even when the Ministry of Foreign Economic Relations takes a free trade view, the Ministry of Finance and the Ministry of Economy may look at the impact on the budget and veto the proposal. The commission, however, can help break an impasse or forge a compromise. At the July 1996 meeting of the commission, major tax breaks for Western oil companies were agreed upon, along with promises to speed through approvals by early 1997 of two major oil production-sharing agreements involving Exxon, Texaco, and Amoco Corp.[15]

In the new democratic Russia, however, the government must deal with a communist-dominated parliament, which promptly voted down legislation for production-sharing agreements shortly after the Gore-Chernomyrdin meeting. According to Aleksei Y. Mikhailov, chairman of the Parliamentary Committee on Natural Resources, who supported the legislation, efforts by Vice President Gore on behalf of the legislation backfired. Gore's initiative prompted accusations by ultranationalist Vladimir V. Zhirinovsky that the West was pressuring the Duma to sell out the motherland. Yeltsin government officials promised to renew the fight and rally support from outlying regions seeking foreign investment and from Russian oil companies eager to join forces with Western partners ready to supply funds for capital investment in new oil fields.[16]

The promises have not been kept, and the expected oil bonanza that could produce an estimated $260 billion over the next fifty years and create, on average, four hundred thousand new jobs a year has suffered major setbacks. The combination of die-hard communist suspicions of the West, local government demands for a larger share of projects, and the calculation by Russian financiers that they should forgo foreign investment now for future gains has put major projects on hold.[17]

On a lower level, the system of Russian and American ombudsmen, established between the Commerce Department and the Ministry of Foreign Economic Relations, serves to resolve problems that emerge from the still uncoordinated Russian decision-making process.

"We cannot get representatives from all the ministries involved in the same room at the same time. Russian behavior is to let the phone ring forty times, nobody answers. When they do answer they are rude, and say nobody is available. Their telephone behavior has not changed except in the younger generation, and this is more in the private sector," explained a senior Commerce Department official.[18]

An ambitious plan for a Partnership for Economic Progress between Russia and America lies buried in a White House safe, a victim largely of the lack of advance coordination within the Russian government. The Ministry of Foreign Economic Relations approved the plan, which was then signed by President Clinton. The document was taken to Moscow in 1994 by the late commerce secretary Ron Brown to give to President Yeltsin for his signature. Before that could be accomplished, the Foreign Ministry saw a copy of the document and said it could not be approved. "They pulled the plug and insisted on changes which have never been approved. The deal has fallen apart. We were sandbagged a couple of times by this kind of behavior; now we know it is standard," said the Commerce Department official.

The lack of coordination within the Russian government is a major headache for both the U.S. government and private corporations. "We definitely have problems with the ministries," explained a senior White House official. "In the U.S., an interagency consensus is achieved first, then we enter a negotiation with the Russians. Just the opposite happens in Moscow: first they conduct a negotiation with us, then a consensus is sought by the Foreign Ministry with other ministries."

The process is plagued by independent actors such as Viktor Mikhailov, minister of Atomic Energy, who signed an agreement for the sale of plutonium and then blackmailed the United States with public threats and charges of noncompliance. The United States agreed to seek sources of funding to replace two plutonium-producing reactors by the year 2000. This turned into a public scandal; Mikhailov claimed the United States had backed down on its promise to pay and demanded the money be paid in advance before anything was done to replace the reactors.

After $75 million had been committed for other projects with the Ministry of Atomic Energy, Mikhailov tacked on another $1 million for design studies in the summer of 1994. Mikhailov apparently follows the rule that no good deed goes unpunished. At every occasion he turned on his American counterparts, demanding new funds and concessions.[19]

What is the significance of this recent history? The development of a workable, predictable business environment and associated institutions may come "from the top down," but the process is slow. The effort by the United States to help the Russians develop a business culture and institutions continues, while business people continue to invest despite the uncertainties, problems, and corruption. The distant light of a developed market economy glitters golden in the distance, and the payoff, if it comes, is on an order of magnitude surpassed only by the promise of developing markets in China, which has its own problems.

TIME ISN'T MONEY

Americans and Russians have different views of the importance of time and how to use it. Russians like to savor and reflect; Americans are concerned with immediate results, fast responses, future tasks, and preparing for them. "Americans will want to negotiate an agreement quickly, schedule an early start on the venture, begin on time, complete the work as expeditiously as possible, and show early results or profit. Russians will need more time to get organized, and there will be frequent delays and postponements. They will be less concerned with immediate results, and profit is a concept that they are only beginning to understand. The job may be completed but only after considerable prodding from the American side," explained former negotiator Yale Richmond.[20] Incentives such as access to funds, foreign travel, the promise of new technology, education, and training for staff, plus other material rewards, are expediting Russian entry into the market economy. These sweeteners have become essential elements of a contract negotiation.

OIL AND GAS FOR QUICK CASH

The problems and potentials of doing business in the former Soviet Union are well illustrated by the oil and gas industry, which is the major area of American investment in Russia and the Commonwealth of Independent States. Future projects could total as much as $100 billion over the next twenty years. In the grand design for turning the centrally planned Soviet socialist economy into a free market system, the centerpiece is development of oil and gas field reserves in the former Soviet Union. Oil and gas provide a hard currency flow, the quickest and most rewarding source of revenues to finance the reconstruction and economic development of Russia and the oil-rich but underdeveloped states of Central Asia and the Caspian region. However, large-scale investors such as Conoco and Chevron have found themselves hobbled by a plethora of add-on restrictions, from the central and local governments, which appeared after contracts had been agreed upon and approved.

The key to negotiating an oil and gas deal remains the same as in the Soviet era: the government must approve. In the new Russia, approval must come not only from the center in Moscow but also from regional governments and local officials, all of whom want to share in royalties from the concession. To approve deals and create an infrastructure that will make investments produce profits, negotiators face the challenge of generating a broad political momentum that will build support for foreign investment.

The gap between the conception and the reality of a functioning enterprise is vast; the huge cultural divide between U.S. and Russian negotiators can be spanned only by creating a new business culture. J. Robinson West of Petroleum Finance Corporation has studied the Russian market intensively. "The Russian word for revenues and profit is the same," West noted, "and that creates a serious problem. The Russians do not understand capitalism. The cost of capital and the cost of goods sold did not exist for Russian businessmen; that was something the government took care of through central planning. Time does not mean anything. The idea of return on invested capital is not part of the Russian experience."[21]

West cited Gazprom, the gas monopoly that controls about one-third of the world's proven gas reserves, Russia's biggest hard currency export earner. "Gazprom is a state within a state," explained West. The Soviet Union was not concerned about the cost of building the Gazprom infrastructure to ship gas from the Soviet Union to Western Europe because the system was financed internally by rubles and the gas was being sold for hard currency. The Soviet Union built a hard currency cash cow with rubles, which had nothing to do with the real cost of the system. "The idea of cost of goods sold and return on investment are only beginning to be comprehended," said West.

To maintain control over their oil and gas reserves, the Russian government continues to attempt to assert its influence over former vassal states of the Soviet Union. A study by Petroleum Finance Corporation noted a constant theme in Russia's behavior: "mounting Russian assertiveness to control Central Asia's access to Western markets."

The Tengiz field in Kazakhstan, in which Chevron has a 50 percent interest, has the potential for vast oil and gas production on a scale second only to Saudi Arabia or Kuwait. "Kazakhstan and Azerbaijan are seen by the Russians as their fields and they refer to the Azeris and Kazakhs as 'niggers,'" said West.

U.S. Deputy Energy Secretary William H. White believes that "the Tengiz field is a litmus test for major Western investment in Russia and the former Soviet Union. Tengiz is the dominant event affecting investor interest in that region. . . . We believe that all the states of the former Soviet Union that want to appear attractive to international investors have a stake in the success of Tengiz."[22]

The Tengiz field has estimated reserves of 6 to 9 billion barrels of oil with development costs estimated at more than $10 billion. Current output is 100,000 to 130,000 barrels per day (b/d), which could rise to a peak by 2010 of 700,000 to 750,000 b/d. Chevron has invested close to $1 billion since it targeted the Tengiz field in 1988, when Kazakhstan was still part of the Soviet Union. In April 1993 Chevron signed an agreement with the newly independent state of Kazakhstan for a 50 percent share of the Tengiz field and booked 1.1 billion barrels of oil reserves and 1.3 trillion cubic feet of gas reserves. In the four years since the first foreign-partnered production-sharing consortium in the former Soviet Union was launched, agreements to transport the oil to market remain unresolved.

Meanwhile, more partners have entered the consortium. Mobil paid $1.1 billion for 25 percent of Kazakhstan's 50 percent of the field. The Russians, with U.S. partners, own 5 percent of the field. The only existing pipeline route is to a Russian facility a hundred miles north of Tengiz at Samara. There it is received by the Russians into their pipeline system. Because there is no export pipeline from Samara, the Tengiz oil is credited to the foreign companies and exchanged for Russian crude oil at a number of export points from which Russian crude is delivered overseas. This is an unsatisfactory and economically inefficient system that must be replaced by a new pipeline if the field is to be exploited economically. The existing capacity of the line is 200,000 b/d.

The Russians have set out to regain a bigger share of the Tengiz field, which they once totally controlled. In January 1966, Lukoil paid $200 million for 10 percent of Chevron's 50 percent share, thus giving Lukoil 5 percent of the entire project and reducing Chevron's share to 45 percent. Lukoil is negotiating for another 5 to 10 percent share with its American partner, ARCO.

The oil must find its way to market, but the path has been obstructed by greed, the war in Chechnya, and internal bickering among Russian oil companies over control of the pipeline. Russian minister of fuel and energy Yuri K. Shafranik takes a patronizing attitude to his "little brothers" in the Kazakh ministry of energy, explained an American oil expert involved in the Tengiz field. "The Russians know how to control the play and take bribes," said the American familiar with the negotiations. "Huge payoffs are the order of the day. It all depends on the Russian will and intentions."[23]

The first consortium to export oil from Tengiz was formed in July 1992, but construction never got under way. A regrouped consortium, Caspian Pipeline Consortium (CPC), was created in April 1996 and finalized in December 1996, but it is being contested by Transneft, the powerful Russian state-owned pipeline company, which wants a share in the Tengiz project, not merely to operate the pipeline.

The proposed $2 billion pipeline with a 1.3 million b/d capacity would include two segments, but it is essentially being viewed as one pipeline in order to force the Russians' hand and ship oil not only to Russia but also for export. The first phase, purely Russian oil, will cost $400 to $500 million and will be financed by the oil companies. Completion is targeted for 1999. Phase two (CPC Kazakhstan) will cost $1.5 billion and is to be financed by loans from international banks and multilateral institutions; it is targeted for completion by 2001 or 2002. Some analysts believe that the announcement of the "phase one" pipeline was a ploy designed to pressure Chevron to improve its terms. Chevron, however, does not have to make a contractual payment of $400 million in bonus money to Kazakhstan until an export system is in place.

The numbers show that Chevron's plan will pay more in later years, but this does not seem to be the issue. The concept of risk versus reward is slow in taking hold; the rule for Russians is to maximize gains in the short term. This trading mentality reflects a pervasive fear of the future—a fear rooted in a national culture mindful of Russia's long history of invasions, wars, and political betrayal. The Russians, long used to exploiting Kazakhstan, continue to negotiate in a pattern that is based on their dominance in the region and a belief that time is on their side. The longer they hold back profits from Western investors the better deal they believe they can cut.

Essential to such negotiations are principles of geopolitical stability and the independence of states formerly part of the Soviet Union. American executives negotiating with heads of state or state oil companies must not only deal with basic economic issues of production-sharing breakdowns, taxes, and capital commitments, but also navigate through a fast-moving geopolitical transition that involves regional rivalries between Russia, Islam, and the West.

Oil and gas negotiations are the new "Great Game," played for high international political and economic stakes.[24] Azerbaijan's vast Caspian

Sea reserves, believed to be the world's biggest oil reserves outside the Persian Gulf and Russia itself, are being contested for by Russia and the world's major oil companies. Eight Western oil companies—Amoco Corp., British Petroleum, Exxon, McDermott International, Pennzoil, Ramco Energy PLC, Statoil, and Unocal Corp.—have joined to invest $7.5 billion in an international consortium to drill for oil and gas reserves estimated at 4 billion barrels. When the contract was first signed with Azerbaijan in September 1994, Russia said it would not recognize the agreement. In October 1995 Azerbaijan president Heydar Aliyev, after fierce lobbying by both the U.S. and the Russian governments, tried to reconcile conflicting proposals from Russia and Turkey by deciding that oil from the Caspian Sea would be shipped through two pipelines. One pipeline would run from Baku on the Caspian Sea, through Chechnya and the city of Grozny to the Russian Black Sea port of Novorossiysk. The other would flow from Baku through Georgia and Turkey to the Turkish port of Ceyhan on the Mediterranean Sea. Azerbaijan's early production from the new fields in 1997 is estimated at 80,000 barrels a day.

The Caspian fields are expected to produce 700,000 b/d by the end of the century. The United States favors the two-pipeline option because it would promote the economy of Turkey, a NATO member, and prevent Russian economic domination of the former Soviet republics. In the final negotiating session with the Russians in October 1995, President Clinton called President Aliyev to urge that the Russian route not be the only one used to export the oil. President Clinton asked former national security adviser Zbigniew Brzezinski to carry a personal letter to President Aliyev underscoring American support for Azerbaijan's independent status. In June 1997 agreement was reached among Azerbaijan, Russia, and Chechnya for oil to be shipped from the Caspian through the existing pipeline in Chechnya to the Black Sea port of Novorossiysk. The second pipeline to Turkey awaits financing from the consortium partners. Although Azerbaijan is friendly to Iran because of the large Azeri population in Iran, the American embargo of Iran, branded as a terrorist state, has halted any chance of a pipeline from Azerbaijan to Iran in the near term. However, the possibility for such a route to market for Caspian Sea oil would be considerable if the political situation changes in Iran.

The major oil companies are showing greater interest in Central Asia and the Caspian region as their projects in Russia stumble, are put on hold, or are deliberately delayed. As of September 1997, four major oil and gas projects were stalled, and American companies with existing projects protested that the Russian government has changed the terms of their deals by ending their privileged access to Russia's clogged oil pipeline and raising excise taxes.[25]

Major stalled projects are:

- Priobskoye. Amoco's projected $28 billion fifty-eight-year project with its Russian partner, Yukos, controlled by the powerful Menetep bank, is on hold. Amoco has invested $100 million but still lacks government approval for the project and a joint venture agreement with Yukos. Differences over how to evaluate the field and how investment costs will be shared have led to a stalemate. Menetep wants Amoco to finance all the investment costs in the project, which has estimated reserves of 4.7 billion barrels of oil.

- Sakhalin 3. Mobil, Exxon, and Texaco have projected $150 million in exploration costs.

- Northern Territories. Conoco's investment of $95 million in the field with estimated reserves of 500 million barrels, a thousand miles northeast of Moscow, has been stalled by problems with local officials demanding a larger share of the royalties and now insisting they do not need American capital.

- Timan Pechora. Texaco, Amoco, Exxon, and Norsk Hydro are planning a $50 million project with 2.4 billion barrels of oil in estimated reserves with two Russian partners, Rosneft and Arkhangelskgeolodbycha. They have been thwarted by the local government, which wants to retain a larger share of the natural resources.

Major projects still on track include:

- Sakhalin I, led by Exxon, with Japanese and Russian partners. A protocol has been signed and a production-sharing agreement approved. Estimated investment ranges between $200 million and $300 million.

- Sakhalin II, a projected $10 billion oil and gas development involving Marathon Oil, McDermott International, Mitsui, Mitsubishi, Royal Dutch Shell, and two Russian companies. National and local production-sharing agreements have been signed by the partners and the project is up and running. Estimated reserves are 1 billion barrels of oil and 14 trillion cubic feet of gas.

Existing joint ventures include:

- Chernogorskoye. Anderson/Smith has been producing oil since 1993. The venture is currently producing 14,000 b/d on an $86 million investment thus far.
- Polar Lights. Conoco's up-and-running project is producing 37,500 b/d on an investment of $400 million to date.
- White Lights. Phibro Energy's project is producing 12,500 b/d on an investment of $120 million. It is threatened by an excise tax dispute that extends investment recovery and reduces profits.[26]

Taxation on oil exports is a key test of how foreign investment will develop. A major impediment to investment has been the unpredictability of taxes on oil exports. By arbitrarily raising the level of export taxes on oil shipments, the Russian government created an atmosphere of uncertainty and concern about investments in oil and gas. Since it was introduced in January 1992, the tax on oil exports has destroyed the economics of investing in Russian oil projects because it has eliminated the profit margin on Russian oil, which can be sold for only about $15 a barrel on world markets. Production costs are in the vicinity of $10 a barrel. In October 1994 Prime Minister Viktor Chernomyrdin signed a decree granting exemption from a $5-a-barrel export tax on crude oil for six joint ventures.

The on-again, off-again negotiating environment has forced delays in investment and prevented increases in production. Legislation to rationalize taxes and standardize production-sharing agreements is still working its way through the Russian legislative system. The process received a boost from Chernomyrdin's July 1996 announcement that the Russian government would lower the excise tax on oil exports by six American companies, permitting the projects to become profitable. "This signals that the Russians are sensitive to foreign investment and recognize good projects," said one Western oil executive in Moscow.[27] But the latest developments in the fall of 1997 indicate a capricious, politically dominated shift in taxation of oil exports is still in play.

The Russian government has still to come to a unified position on foreign investment. "The structure of the Russian government makes it hard to solve the problem," said Lou Naumovski of the European Bank for Research and Development. "One agency is in charge of maximizing revenue and they're not necessarily interested in the investment picture. Another agency is interested in investment but they have little influence on tax policy. It will take time to work this out."[28] As the negotiations drag on, the cost to the Russians is higher than to the Western oil companies, but still it is a no-win situation for both sides. President Yeltsin's illness made it difficult to move forward. Until there is a law to be implemented and upheld, major oil investment will be stalled.

At a news conference in Moscow in July 1997 U.S. energy secretary Frederico Peña noted:

> The fact is that Russia has vast energy resources, and by many accounts international companies are ready to invest $60 billion in Russia's oil industry, but those investments are awaiting the development of a stable and transparent legal and regulatory framework to support them.
>
> A recent study by the Petroleum Advisory Foundation estimates that just six large projects will create more than 500,000 Russian jobs and generate more than $600 billion in wealth for Russia over the life of these investments. So it is in everyone's interest to see energy markets develop and open as quickly as possible here in Russia.[29]

To allow these multimillion-dollar projects to go forward, a new culture of negotiations is required, based on enforceable laws protecting foreign investment. Russia will need an independent judiciary to interpret the new laws and administrative agencies to enforce them. The bright light is that the younger generation of middle managers, those aged between thirty-five and forty-five, are willing to adapt to a new international business culture.

Russia's oil industry needs $60 billion in investments over the next ten years, according to estimates by Western analysts. Russian and foreign companies will have to operate on the same playing field under the same rules. American officials and Western oil companies are concerned about future access to the Russian pipeline system. Equal access to Russia's pipelines is one of the many guarantees Western investors need if they are to invest the billions of dollars required by Russia's deteriorating oil industry. The tension between incentives for encouraging new investment and reducing a rising Russian government deficit has produced a continuing series of anomalies.

Potential American investors in Russian oil and gas face a situation in which the Russian oil companies, although unable to provide the necessary capital investment to increase production, are resisting foreign investment. Domestic oil prices have been rising gradually in Russia, but they remain about 40 percent below world levels. Oil demand remains depressed because of Russia's continuing economic decline. Oil production dropped 11 percent in 1994, but exports increased. The gas industry has proved to be one of the most stable parts of the economy; production fell by less than 2 percent in 1994 to 606 billion cubic meters while gross domestic product fell by 12.4 percent.[30]

Most Russian companies appear to be more concerned with securing a position in their domestic industry than with developing international ties. The final shape of the rapidly evolving Russian oil industry has still be to decided. Igor Tsukanov, chairman of CentreInvest, a Russian consulting company, likens Russia's oil companies to players running around a Monopoly board. First they are desperate to seize every property they can. Then they try to rationalize their assets and swap properties with other players. Only when they have built up an attractive portfolio of assets do they start investing in houses and hotels.

BUILDING A WIN-WIN PROCESS

Until the structure of international business culture penetrates and is institutionalized in the former Soviet Union, Western business people are likely to find that negotiations will remain arcane, frustrating, and very often fruitless affairs. In the meantime, however, the intervention of high-level government officials can sometimes overcome the obstacles that stand in the way of reaching mutually profitable solutions.

A case in point is a $1.4 billion program for Russian purchase of American jet engines and avionics that became the center of controversy between Boeing and United Technologies Corporation. The U.S. administration's foreign policy goal, to help Russia build a viable market economy, clashed with domestic policy efforts to raise American production and increase jobs.

In November 1994 Clinton administration officials celebrated plans for a $1 billion U.S. government loan to help Russia build a new commercial airliner, the Alation-M96. At a ceremony at Andrews Air Force Base, Deputy Commerce Secretary David J. Barram praised the deal as "a historic partnership between Russian and U.S. aerospace companies." The agreement called for the U.S. Export-Import Bank to guarantee payment for twenty jet engines manufactured by the Pratt & Whitney division of United Technologies Corporation to be supplied to Aeroflot Russian International Airlines (ARIA) for the 300-seat Alation-M96s. Among the jet's most attractive features is its price of $68 to $75 million, 25 to 50 percent lower than the price of similar-size jets made by Boeing, McDonnell Douglas, and Europe's Airbus Industrie.

Boeing viewed American support for the Alation-M96 as setting a dangerous precedent, namely, assisting a foreign aircraft maker. Aeroflot is already subsidized by the Russian government. Boeing feared that the Russian-built jets would undercut Boeing's sales to countries such as India and China at prices that do not reflect the true development costs of the aircraft.

Boeing, against the deal, and United Technologies, for it, both lined up supporters within the U.S. government. Then U.S. trade representative Mickey Kantor and some Labor Department officials joined Boeing in raising questions about U.S. financing. Officials from the Commerce and State Departments sided with United Technologies, warning that to deny the loan now would discourage market reforms in Russia and anger its leaders.

While Boeing claimed the deal would cost the jobs of American workers, United Technologies (which said it had spent $50 million designing the engines) insisted that thousands of new employees would be needed to build the jet engines at Pratt & Whitney's Connecticut plants. The dispute was settled when the Gore-Chernomyrdin Commission forged a compromise: the Russians agreed to open their market to American aircraft sales, a move that pleased Boeing, in return for the loan going through, which satisfied United Technologies. Reaching this win-win solution depended on the intervention of high-level government officials and experts to press through issues with specific monetary and economic rewards for both sides. In a normal business culture, corporations can do that for themselves, but in the former Soviet Union the old bureaucracies in state industries are still defending their interests and their jobs.

The Boeing negotiations worked because the Russians need airplanes and want to revive their ailing aviation industry. The domestic politics in America were reconciled by the vice president in a skillful tradeoff. But few deals can be handled at that level. In the absence of such high-level assistance, most deals founder amid Russia's unpredictable, insecure, and unregulated business environment. In 1993 I visited a paper mill in Karelia that was seeking an infusion of foreign capital to purchase newsprint production machinery. An official from the Ministry of Economics sat in on the talks and demanded a ministry role and share in the deal. The project never got off the ground because there were no legal guarantees of ownership for the $30 million newsprint rolling mill the Russians wanted to import and pay for out of future production.

HOPE FOR THE FUTURE: A NEW GENERATION

The biggest change in Russia is generational. Lawyer Isaac Shapiro noted: "Enough time has gone by so that there are now enough young people who don't behave according to stereotypes. There are major differences now about how people think of themselves and their country. Ethnic differences are now able to be pronounced because there is no suppression. If you are talking to a Georgian or an Armenian they no longer think of themselves as a *sovietski chelovek* [a Soviet man]; there is no such thing as a *sovietski chelovek* anymore except in the minds of my generation. The generational difference is very important."

If they are not negotiating in a Russian context but are on their own home ground, non-Russians, particularly Central Asians, Georgians, and Armenians, are inclined to return to their own cultural traditions and style, moving away from the stiff top-down behavior of the Soviet era. Within their own cultural context there remains a lack of any institutional business framework. Family and regional group loyalties play a dominant role in power relations.

Shapiro has encountered a new breed of young, highly successful entrepreneurial people in their thirties. "Money is the name of the game. They care nothing about political orientation or ideology. Their mission in life is to make as much money as they can and they try to behave as they think Western businessmen behave, kind of acting," explained Shapiro.

The new Russian business people adapt quickest to trading; they do well with buying and selling:

> It does not require a lot of investment [said Shapiro], some brains, intu-ition, certainly not a lot of experience. The people whom I've observed who made money quickly are traders. They buy one thousand tons of oil and just sell it, so they know whom to pay off for the licenses. Those people have adapted very quickly to the notion of providing value and receiving money. When you say "risk:reward," that involves investment and that's slower in coming as an attitude because there is still a great fear on the part of many people I know that things may change tomor-row. If you invest in a hotel with a foreigner you are at great risk. Some-body may come and take your money away. It may be the *mafiya*. It may be the government. It could be Zhirinovsky. It could be Yeltsin. Things are too uncertain. . . .
>
> [Even so], they are beginning to develop a sense of a risk:reward ratio. Certainly, a number of the younger people I've met have practically no life experience before they started in business except that they may have had a job. I'm thinking of a young man written up in the *Wall Street Jour-nal* as the Russian Rockefeller. He came from Cita [in Siberia near the Mongolian border]. The attitude of someone who comes to Moscow from Cita is different from someone brought up in Moscow. He hasn't lived under the eye and weight of the oppression. One has to allow for the vastness of the country and allow for the fact that somebody from Cita is not the same as somebody from Chechnya. This fellow has a sense of risk versus reward and a sense of quid pro quo and value. I'll do this for you but you have to do this for me. He learned very quickly.

Doing business with those schooled in the Bolshevik Code remains an endless battle. Those companies that have fared well in Moscow have brought their own corporate culture to replace the Soviet way of doing business. McDonald's, which has its busiest restaurant in the world in Moscow, has invested for the long term. McDonald's employ-ees are trained to prize cleanliness, to respect personal and company property, and to make the customer feel welcome. Young people, with few preconceived notions, are the preferred applicants. They receive uniforms, meals, and pay above the Moscow norms. The McDonald's corporate culture extends to supporting local charities. It appears to be working. Muscovites go out to eat a Big Mac as a family outing, a break from the numbing routine of cramped apartment living and overpriced, bad service in Russian restaurants.

In the new Russia, making money has replaced ideological conformity as the key to success. Profit—a swear word both in the prerevolutionary and in the Marxist lexicons—still grates on the souls of those raised and trained to believe in the teachings of the Russian Orthodox Church or in the future of socialism. For the younger generation, ideology and the party line have been replaced by marketing tools and the basics of buying low and selling high. "Living a normal life" is the Muscovites' mantra of the 1990s, replacing "Workers of the World Unite," which no longer flashes from signs and billboards.

Western advertising and Western products flood Moscow; young people are the marketing target for consumer products. The big soft-drink and fast-food makers have found Russia a fertile market. Both Coke and Pepsi peg their advertising to rock concerts and television. They have set up factories that rely on local materials and labor, and they import the soft-drink syrup. McDonald's had to have long-term perspective and make accommodations to local government. It was necessary to innovate during the transition period by selling apple pies and catered meals to embassies for hard currency before the ruble was convertible.

Not all investment efforts have been successful. Western drug companies, hamstrung by government regulations and differences in standards, have found it difficult to manufacture in Russia. In 1995 Deputy Assistant Secretary of Commerce Mike Copps formed a committee with Minister of Public Health Major General Eduard A. Nechaev to develop a memorandum of understanding on standards. The Russian Ministry of Health has now promised to accept for sale on the Russian market medicines and pharmaceuticals approved by the Federal Drug Administration. A working group has been established to sign and implement the memorandum.

In the publishing field, the *New York Times'* translation of its articles into Russian, published in conjunction with *Moscow News,* was a commercial failure and was dropped after two years. The Hearst-*Izvestia* joint venture newspaper, *We/Mbl,* published in English in Washington, D.C., and in Russian in Moscow, was suspended in 1994 after two years of biweekly publication. Rising newsprint costs, lack of an effective distribution system, and inflation forced *Izvestia* to request an end to the joint venture. The contract called for a thirty-day notice by either partner wishing to cancel the contract, but the legal norm was meaningless in Moscow. *Izvestia* editor-in-chief Igor Golembiovsky simply canceled the contract with one week's notice. For the Hearst Corporation, the experience of working with *Izvestia* provided a successful entry into the Russian market for other Hearst products. *Cosmopolitan* and *Good Housekeeping* magazines now have successful Russian editions. The International Press Club, located in the Radisson Slavyanskaya hotel, proved to be an unsuccessful clone of the National Press Club in Washington, D.C., to fill the void of business news and public information while providing the opportunity for government officials and visiting leaders to meet with the foreign and local press. It has gone out of business. Supermarkets with foreign-made foods, boutiques with top-brand clothing, and automobile showrooms have proliferated. The conspicuous consumption of Moscow's new millionaires, who want to look like Westerners and flaunt their new wealth, has generated luxury markets and boosted demand and prices for French wines, Mercedes-Benzes and BMWs, leisure wear, and sports sneakers. However, the New Russians are not spending all the money they make; there is still a net flow of dollars overseas. Estimates vary regarding the scale of cumulative capital flight, with some reckoning that between $125 and $150 billion dollars have been stowed abroad since the fall of the Soviet Union,[31] while others put the figure lower, at between $40 and $60 billion.[32] John Hardt of the Congressional Research Service has remarked that "policy and legislative changes to improve the investment climate in Russia for foreign direct investment would also improve prospects for return of flight capital and increased domestic investment."[33] The government is using short-term loans from the International Monetary Fund to stabilize the ruble under a set of strict requirements, which are regularly violated by the Yeltsin government.

CAVEATS

In entering negotiations, those with no business experience in the Soviet Union or the new Russia must be prepared for the unexpected.

They need a long-term perspective, a willingness to assume high risk, and the ability to walk away from a deal if it does not meet their criteria for profitability. Unless a Western company has clear goals with phased investment, a Russian venture can drain its capital. Those companies with a solid base and support system, able to develop their own infrastructure, fare best. Rather than rely on Russian security, major oil companies weld shut their railroad cars and provide their own security guards. They build their own prefabricated housing shipped in from Europe and are prepared for a long-term but rich payoff.

Most Russians believe capitalism is a freewheeling and unrestrained dice game with no limits. They refer to Moscow as the Klondike and they expect the rewards of a gold rush. Russian traders in oil, gas, metals, and lumber have made fortunes by paying bribes to buy licenses to sell natural resources overseas for hard currency. In the transition to a market economy, the central government has continued to extract the resources; it provides them to traders at subsidized prices from which they can make a killing in world markets. The idea that privatized groups should bear the cost of production and assume the risks of price fluctuations in the international market is alien among those who still operate according to the Bolshevik Code.

The first task of Western business negotiators in Russia is to explain how a market economy works. Russian business people are only beginning to comprehend the importance of test marketing and properly introducing a product. In Soviet society, goods were made and sold under a state-planned system with no consumer input or choice. Whatever was made was sold because goods were in short supply and prices were subsidized by the state. Now, with supply meeting demand, price and quality are dominant criteria for both hard and soft consumer items.

Americans operating on a small scale in Russia have found difficulty in having contracts fulfilled on time and in collecting payments. On a larger scale, companies that have supplied machinery and then been faced with import duties and taxes have simply threatened to stop supplying their goods until contract terms are met. Without a strong central government to build a reliable tax and banking system, negotiations depend on payment in kind—oil, gas, diamonds, or metals. The foreign company must have the ability to cut off a contract without a major loss. Risk:reward ratios in Russia remain very high, and the length of time that must pass before an investment pays off is extremely unclear. Uncertainty prevails.

Conclusion

Continuity and Transition

Russian negotiating behavior is a litmus test for progress from a centrally planned and rigidly controlled Soviet-style society to that of a market economy governed by democratic institutions. Soviet negotiators operated according to the Bolshevik Code, a behavioral style that grew out of communist ideological indoctrination overlaid on centuries of authoritarian rule. Its essential elements were suspicion of the outside world, obsequiousness to authority, and an aggressive, mistrustful, and cynical approach toward negotiations. The Bolshevik Code required Soviet diplomats to be obdurate, didactic, often rude, and unpredictable in their behavior toward their counterparts. Soviet negotiators saw themselves as warriors in a life-and-death conflict with the capitalist West, waging class warfare in the interests of socialism and the construction of a Soviet state. As early as 1929 Stalin warned Molotov, "Remember, we are waging a struggle, negotiation with enemies is also a struggle . . . with the whole capitalist world."[1]

Contemporary Russia is trying to cope with two parallel and competing cultures, both in transition: the discredited Soviet system and Russia's new market economy. Inevitably, this cultural duality is creating confusion and uncertainty in all areas of Russian life, including contacts with the outside world. Senior American negotiators accustomed to the traits and tactics of their Soviet counterparts must now deal with Russians motivated not by Marxist-Leninist doctrine but by money and what is known as "practical interest," the promise of economic development, jobs, housing for servicemen, or funds to scrap nuclear weapons and leaking reactors.

Despite the official jettisoning of messianic ideology by Russia's contemporary leaders, however, much of the Soviet style of negotiating persists. The two cultures in contemporary Russia are in an intense struggle, but neither is likely to overcome the other any time soon. Instead, the presence of both is creating a confusing synthesis of negotiating styles that taxes the patience as well as the negotiating skills of Western diplomats, investors, and entrepreneurs.

■　■　■

The breakup of the Soviet Union lifted the veil of secrecy hiding the weaknesses of communism and the economic inefficiencies that drove it to ruin. Remnant supporters of the once dominant communist system, in which the party and the government took responsibility for all of society's basic needs and allowed no entrepreneurship or private initiative, are now struggling to justify the party's "historical" role and checkered past. Yet it no longer can claim to be the leading organ in building a society that will ensure the economic well-being of the Russian people. The badly frayed socialist safety net is about to break, but the majority of Russians, sustained by it, insist it is too soon to be cut loose from subsidized rent, bread, and milk, and from free health care.

The Russian leadership has had to grapple with the question of who owns the assets of the state, which in principle belong to the people. Efforts to redistribute state wealth equitably have proved fruitless. In an attempt to activate the economy, President Yeltsin "privatized" state assets by giving them to workers and factory managers. The result is a "new" class of entrepreneurs—the so-called *nomenklatura* capitalists who are largely the same managers, bureaucrats, and party officials who worked for and controlled the socialist state. These people bring to the nascent world of Russian business the behavioral styles and cultural outlook that was ingrained in them and that served them so well under Soviet power. The *nomenklatura* capitalists have adopted some Western business practices and consumer appetites, but they lack the flexibility and imaginative drive needed to create a new business culture. They are dominated by a small but powerful group of business tycoons who control banking, media, and real estate interests. This group has taken a dominant position in the transition from socialism to free markets, creating conglomerates that have stifled competition and failed to undertake needed industrial restructuring.[2] As long as the tycoons and *nomenklatura* capitalists retain their positions of power, the Bolshevik Code will continue to exert a strong influence on negotiating behavior.

Change toward a democratic political order and an efficient and healthy market economy is being obstructed by other hangovers from the Soviet past. Psychologically, the Bolshevik Code continues to exert a malign influence: Russians still perceive most economic transactions as zero-sum encounters, not as win-win opportunities for the development of lasting and mutually rewarding business relations.

In economic and structural terms the enduring Soviet legacy is impeding the process of transformation. The old military-industrial complex, the state within the Soviet state, which relies on the government for funding, has had a difficult time converting to postcommunist, post–Cold War economic realities. The old bureaucrats still cling to control of production. For Western businesspeople these vestiges of the past have proved formidable obstacles to joint ventures or new investment. As a result, the manufacturing sector has still to be reborn.

In the transition struggle, however, there is no doubt that the norms and values of the Soviet era are under attack from a new generation of political leaders and economic managers with new expectations and aspirations. A new generation of business tycoons has penetrated the system with bribes to obtain licenses to exploit the nation's resources at bargain prices and sell them at high profit to themselves. Others have manipulated their banking connections to buy state properties at bargain prices. These "New Russians" have clothed and housed themselves in luxury, lining the roads outside Moscow with red-brick country houses of exotic architectural designs. The New Russians dare not trust their wealth to the inadequate and often corrupt system of Russian banks; it has gone abroad to Swiss banks and offshore accounts, and to buy real estate in Spain, France, Malta, and America. A huge income gap marked by class antagonisms has formed between the New Russians and the old socialists.

The government's difficulties in reducing inflation and stimulating the manufacturing sector have been compounded by the state's inability to collect taxes. An estimated 20 to 40 percent of the gross domestic product is conducted off the books.[3] Huge, unregulated and untaxed open-air markets attempt to fill the demand for consumer goods. From Luzhniki stadium in Moscow to Khabarovsk near the Chinese border, individual small traders bring in bundles of cheap manufactured goods and clothing from South and East Asia for wholesale distribution. Men, women, and children arrive in buses that line the Moscow streets for a mile. They carry away their purchases in pushcarts, load them onto the buses, and ride back to their villages, tired but smiling, to resell the goods for a profit. The Russians call this their "black economy," which goes untaxed by the central government.

The very size of the black or "underground" economy indicates the weakness of the legal economy. It exacerbates the problems of the Russian government because it constitutes an enormous area of activity that goes untaxed. A leadership that cannot tax cannot govern. The Russian government runs at a distressing deficit and in its efforts to survive overtaxes visible production. The result is that some entrepreneurs lock the door and walk away, unable to pay the taxes of up to 130 percent demanded by the government. For foreign oil companies, capricious taxing of oil exports has led to a string of broken contracts and promises undercutting negotiating credibility at the highest levels of government.

At this stage of Russia's development, economic productivity tends to be limited to the area of trading; although reselling imports, depleting existing natural resources, and developing real estate can be lucrative endeavors, they do not create new products or generate long-term economic development and growth.

Dramatically expanded contacts with the rest of the world are propelling a generation of Russian business people, all aged under forty, into the global business arena. Since the end of the Soviet Union in 1991, a vast stream of human actors has moved back and forth between Russia and Europe and the United States; Russia and Israel; and Russia and China, Japan, and Korea. This volume of human exchange is generating a new cultural momentum that is forcing change.

For Russian business people, acquiring organizational ability, marketing skills, and financial resources to meet the demands of a competitive market freed from government subsidies remains a daunting challenge. They are only beginning to write the laws, establish the financial mechanisms, and train their college graduates to fulfill the obligations of the marketplace. Russians lack the capital for investment, development, and conversion of their best military high-tech advances to civilian products. Only when Russian investment statutes provide guarantees with financial recourse and independent courts of law will a self-sustaining market economy come into being. The Duma must draft production-sharing laws if the much heralded oil boom is to become a reality. In the meantime major investors wait in the wings or are beginning to move to Central Asia and the Caspian Sea.

Political reform and stability are other requisites for the development of a Russian state on which the West can rely for nuclear security and to negotiate business deals. Reforms are at the top of the national agenda and being openly discussed, yet not all Western-inspired reforms will solve the problems of the former Soviet Union. Every Russian knows that the country is struggling for its national and political identity. Sergei Kovalev, a member of the Duma and until 1996 chairman of the President's Human Rights Commission, believes that "Russian society has the opportunity to learn the truth about the country's condition and about proposed solutions to the crisis. True, the reformers are few; moreover they are divided and weak. Most of the talk centers around economic reform rather than serious legal reform, or, even more important, reform of the system of government." Kovalev acerbically notes that the old Bolshevik value system of forceful repression of all opposition was undermined in Chechnya when "the war was won by freedom of speech." Journalists, the organization Soldiers' Mothers, and Memorial (an organization of victims of Stalinist repression) raised their voices against the war and made an impression on the Russian "silent majority." The new element in Russian life, argues Kovalev, is that the war in Chechnya was ended by "democracy at work: society has mechanisms with which it can force the authorities to what it demands, and not what the authorities themselves would like to do."[4]

Democracy in Russia is fragile and can easily be undermined. Negotiating behavior by the U.S. government has taken that into consideration, sometimes to a fault. Diplomatic concerns for Yeltsin's survival tempered official American criticism of the war in Chechnya. Continued progress in Russia toward a Western-style democratic system is likely, but not certain—no more certain than continued movement toward an open, transparent Western-style market economy. The Soviet era continues to cast a long shadow, but there is little chance of a resurrection of the Soviet system and empire. However, old Bolsheviks persist in greeting visitors in their living rooms with the admonition: "Come in, it's safe. Here you are back in the Soviet Union." There is still no certainty in predicting how the two cultures currently competing for predominance in Russia will evolve.

RULES OF THUMB FOR WESTERN NEGOTIATORS

In the current unsettled transitional society, how should Western negotiators, whether diplomats or entrepreneurs, deal with their Russian counterparts? The following rules of thumb offer some general guidance.

- *Be sensitive, but not oversensitive, to Russia's problems and circumstances.* Conscious of Russian problems, negotiators can begin to discern the bottom line of what their counterparts need in a negotiation, unclouded by ideology or bluff. They can get to the core of problems to be solved a lot faster than in the days of superpower rivalry with deliberately orchestrated delays. No longer do Russian negotiators need to intimidate and destroy their negotiating counterparts. Another significant change is that American negotiators, while retaining a clear vision of their instructions and the U.S. national interest, now resolve problems by thinking through what the Americans and Russians both need to meet their interests in a deal. However, negotiators should not fall prey to Russian guilt techniques, intended to make Americans feel sorry for their Russian counterparts. Playing for sympathy was a ploy often used by Soviet negotiators in the past. Americans should not make concessions in response to appeals for commiseration with the Russian negotiators' political problems. Pressures by nationalist factions in the Duma will not be reduced by U.S. concessions. We must not allow our understanding of contemporary Russia's problems—the centrifugal forces of separatism, ethnic violence, and the rapidly growing gap between rich and poor—to be manipulated for unequal concessions. The pressures generated by such internal disorder can be excruciating;

American negotiators must demonstrate strong will and consistency. "All we need is another twenty years for a new generation to come to power," said a senior American official after a particularly trying negotiating session with his counterpart trained in the Bolshevik Code.[5]

- *Treat one's Russian counterpart with respect.* Although Russia poses a vastly diminished military threat to the West, making it a vulnerable negotiating partner, it is wise to maintain a relationship of civility and respect. Russia's potential for losing control of its nuclear arsenal and destabilizing its former empire remains the focus of Western concern. To sustain its defense industries, Russia has intensified efforts to sell advanced weapons, which threaten the stability of Southeast Asia. In the international marketplace, Russia has the advantage over the United States of producing advanced military equipment more cheaply and of selling it with little or no regard for the human rights or terrorist records of its customers.[6]

The historical myth of encirclement dies hard. Russia still feels surrounded by NATO and threatened by Islamic fanatics in Central Asia. Yet in an increasingly interconnected world, risk is rarely localized: what is dangerous to Russia also threatens the United States. There is mutual self-interest in reducing and controlling nuclear weapons. The big change from the days of the Soviet Union is that the United States now finds it in its own interest to enhance Russia's international status to achieve common goals. It is in both nations' interest for the United States to pay for and encourage the transformation of Russia's advanced military high-tech capabilities to civilian use.

- *Stand tall and hang tough with dignity.* Ignore aggressiveness, but do not tolerate rudeness. Maintain consistency in your position. Never insist you cannot deviate from a position if indeed you have flexibility. If you give ground after you have said there is none to give you lose credibility. Do not fear to speak critically about their stalling tactics. Be prepared to withdraw support or adjourn if necessary. Create problem-solving mechanisms to break impasses. Wariness is necessary. Keep your back to the wall and judge each proposal for its long-term commitments and implications. To minimize downside risk, project what can go wrong as well as right for the period of any agreement. Identify the relevant decision-making source of power for direct negotiations and touch all necessary bases. If possible, find a counterpart in the other camp with mutual interests who will protect you in the negotiating process.

• *Insist on agreed-upon rules and procedures, spelled out in detail with an ongoing verification process as part of the contract terms.* The negotiating process, in business or diplomacy, requires not only mutual respect but also constant verification and definition. Ronald Reagan expressed it in Russian: *doberai no proverai,* trust, but verify. Specificity is essential; nothing should be left to goodwill or unwritten agreement. Unless the Russian side meets its obligations, Western negotiators should be prepared to walk away from the deal.

Russian diplomatic negotiators are proud and will promise the world, but too often they cannot deliver. Like Russian business people, they lack resources and an adequate administrative support system. In business, uniform accounting systems that meet international criteria are being slowly introduced by multinational companies; provisions must be made for verification of funds and auditing. Verification, whether it is of missile dismantlement or shipments of raw materials, is the key to trust.

• *Make use of the new incentives for Russian cooperation.* The greatest change in dealing with the Russians is the end of ideology. Negotiations can now be conducted on the basis of financial incentives, "practical interest," and access to technology. Soviet negotiators were rarely tempted to make concessions in consideration for any of these inducements. Contemporary Russian negotiators, however, both business people and government officials, share the vision of industrial development, jobs, access to new energy sources, and the opening of improved communications through satellites and mobile phones. Stripped of ideology, they are eager to partake as equals in this new wealth. U.S. negotiators must reassure partners to agreements that the terms will be fulfilled according to contract and that there are no loopholes that will leave them vulnerable to failure.

• *Establish problem-solving mechanisms to be implemented at an early stage.* Russia is still uncertain of its internal unity and fears that its resources will be robbed and plundered. Russia's new capitalists accept money for project development and then renege, leaving Western partners stranded. There must be penalty provisions for nonperformance and a detailed schedule for obtaining all necessary permissions before work commences.

■ ■ ■

Despite its diminished international and military status, Russia remains a key negotiating partner for the West. The Russian national psyche, crushed by the loss of the Soviet empire, is angered at losing the rich oil resources of Central Asia and the Caspian Sea. The Russian Federation and its leaders are fearful of being plundered by rich foreign capitalists. To negotiate with people who harbor such a sense of vulnerability requires firmness and new skills in balancing self-assurance with reassurance. We have to negotiate our aid to Russia in a way that does not undercut and destroy Russia's own fragile markets. Our goals are nuclear disarmament and a restructuring of the Russian economy so that Russian arms sales will not destabilize Asia and the Middle East. Russian sales of nuclear reactors to Iran and advanced aircraft and submarines to China present serious proliferation problems that need to be integrated into a comprehensive negotiating strategy for dealing with Russia.

Our other goals are to help replace the communist system with democratic institutions that will support a market economy; tap the rich human potential of Russia, especially its scientific talents; participate in the exploitation of Russia's vast natural resources; and secure a share of the potentially enormous Russian market for Western expertise and technology.

All these goals are good reasons to maintain and expand contacts and relationships with Russia. The commitment is high risk, but the reward will be Russia becoming a market economy based on democratic institutions and international legal norms. American negotiators have become keenly attuned to daily shifts in Russian business and diplomatic culture that reflect the competition between the values of the old Soviet system and the new market economy. The key question is: To what extent and at what pace will the cultural norms and expectations that predominated during the Soviet era decay and disappear?

Culture is not something that is organized by governments; it is built from experience, from repeated negotiating encounters and trade deals. Sitting across the green baize-covered tables Russians still swagger, smile, and pretend they are as rich as their Western counterparts. Russians are no less talented or astute than their American counterparts, but they are playing on a new field with limited strength, and the rules have changed. Only negotiators who understand the cultural and emotional baggage their Russian counterparts are carrying can hope to be effective and achieve their goals.

Notes

INTRODUCTION

1. Paul Nitze, foreword to *The Big Five: Arms Control Decision-Making in the Soviet Union,* by Aleksandr G. Savel'yev, Nikolai N. Detinov, and Gregory Vartall (Westport, Conn.: Praeger, 1995).

2. Better studies on Soviet negotiating behavior between 1945 and 1991 include U.S. Congress House Committee on Foreign Relations, Special Studies Series on Foreign Affairs Issues, vol. 2, *Soviet Diplomacy and Negotiating Behavior—1979–1988: New Tests for U.S. Diplomacy* (Washington, D.C.: Government Printing Office, 1988); George F. Kennan, *Memoirs 1925–1950* (Boston: Little, Brown, 1967); Fred C. Iklé, *How Nations Negotiate* (New York: Praeger, 1964); and Raymond F. Smith, *Negotiating with the Soviets* (Bloomington: Indiana University Press, 1989).

3. Iklé, *How Nations Negotiate*, 56.

4. Speaking to the cabinet after Yalta, President Roosevelt characterized Stalin as "having something else in him besides this revolutionist Bolshevik thing." He ascribed that special quality to Stalin's early education for the priesthood: "I think that something entered into his nature of the way in which a Christian gentleman should behave." See Henry A. Kissinger, *Diplomacy* (New York: Simon & Schuster, 1994), 417; quoting Robert Dallek, *Franklin D. Roosevelt and American Foreign Policy, 1932–1945* (New York: Oxford University Press, 1979), 521.

When President Truman met Stalin for the first time at Potsdam in 1945 he commented that Stalin "was as near like Tom Pendergast as any man I know." Pendergast was the corrupt Kansas City political boss who supported Truman for election to the U.S. Senate in 1934. See Charles L. Mee, Jr., *Meeting at Potsdam* (New York: M. Evans, 1975), 11–12.

5. Kissinger, *Diplomacy*, 416–417.

6. Another people and another nation, Stalin said, would have asked the government to end the war sooner by concluding a peace treaty with the Germans, but the Russian people had displayed confidence and patience in their government's policy of fighting Germany until it was defeated, and he thanked the Russian nation for that confidence. See Pavel and Anatoli Sudoplatov with Jerrold L. and Leona P. Schecter, *Special Tasks: The Memoirs of An Unwanted Witness—A Soviet Spymaster* (Boston: Little, Brown, 1994), 170–171.

7. Nathan Constantin Leites, *The Operational Code of the Politburo* (New York: McGraw-Hill, 1951).

1. INHERITANCE

1. Yale Richmond, *From Nyet to Da: Understanding the Russians* (Yarmouth, Maine: Intercultural Press, 1992), 52.

2. Johanna Hubbs, *Mother Russia: The Feminine Myth in Russian Culture* (Bloomington: Indiana University Press, 1993), 231.

3. "Zhirinovsky Savors Russian Kingmaker Role," *New York Times*, June 14, 1996, 1.

4. Henry V. Dicks, "Observations on Contemporary Russian Behavior," *Human Relations* 5, no. 2 (1952): 111–175; quoted by Daniel Bell in *World Politics*, no. 10 (April 1958): 329.

5. Quoted in Ronald Hingley, *The Russian Mind* (New York: Charles Scribner's Sons, 1977), 197.

6. Richmond, *From Nyet to Da*, 57.

7. Ibid., 9.

8. Hingley, *The Russian Mind*, 197.

9. Richard Pipes, "Russia's Past, Russia's Future," *Commentary* (June 1996): 31.

10. See Smith, *Negotiating with the Soviets*, 8–11.

11. Leon Sloss and M. Scott Davis, "The Soviet Union, the Pursuit of Power and Influence through Negotiation," in *National Negotiating Styles*, ed. Hans Binnendijk (Washington, D.C.: Foreign Service Institute, U.S. Department of State, 1987), 18–19.

12. Quoted in ibid., 19.

13. Richmond, *From Nyet to Da*, 81.

14. Ibid., 84.

15. Roberto Calasso, *The Ruin of Kasch* (Cambridge, Mass.: Harvard University Press, 1994), 252.

16. Richmond, *From Nyet to Da*, 69.

17. George F. Kennan, "Long Telegram" from Moscow, February 22, in *Foreign Relations of the United States*, vol. 6, *1946* (Washington, D.C.: U.S. Government Printing Office, 1969), 666–709.

18. The theory that cultural influences (such as swaddling) are reflected in normative behavior patterns was first developed by the British anthropologist Geoffrey Gorer. See Geoffrey Gorer and John Rickman, *The People of Great Russia* (London: Cresset Press, 1949), 152–153.

19. Ibid., 154–155.

20. Smith, *Negotiating with the Soviets,* 5–6.

21. Hedrick Smith, *The Russians* (New York: Quadrangle, 1976), 259, 264, 265.

22. Pipes, "Russia's Past, Russia's Future," 30.

23. Ibid.

24. Leites, *Operational Code of the Politburo;* and *A Study of Bolshevism* (Glencoe, Ill.: Free Press, 1953).

25. Leites, *Operational Code of the Politburo,* xv.

26. See Leites, *A Study of Bolshevism,* especially p. 427.

27. Elizabeth Wirth Marvick, ed., *Psychopolitical Analysis: Selected Writings of Nathan Leites* (New York: John Wiley and Sons, 1977), 13.

28. Ibid., 15.

29. Ibid., 309.

30. Ibid.

31. Leites, *Operational Code of the Politburo,* 51.

32. Marvick, *Psychopolitical Analysis,* 309.

33. Iklé, *How Nations Negotiate,* 40.

34. Quoted in William Taubman, *Stalin's American Policy* (New York: W. W. Norton, 1982), 40.

35. Kalevi J. Holsti, *International Politics: A Framework for Analysis* (Englewood Cliffs, N.J.: Prentice Hall, 1988), 139.

36. Victor Israelyan, interview by author, Boalsburg, Pa., June 1995.

37. Holsti, *International Politics,* 136–137. Holsti's observations are echoed by former secretary of state Henry Kissinger: "The conflict between the forces of revolution and counterrevolution is irreconcilable. To the industrial democracies peace appears as a naturally attainable condition; it is the composition of differences, the absence of struggle. To the Soviet leaders, by contrast, struggle is ended not by compromise but by the victory of one side. Permanent peace, according to communist theory, can be achieved only by abolishing the class struggle and the class struggle can be ended only by a communist victory. Hence, any Soviet move, no matter how belligerent, advances the cause of peace, while any capitalist policy, no matter how conciliatory, serves the ends of war." Henry Kissinger, *White House Years* (New York: Little, Brown, 1979), 116.

38. Margaret Mead, *Soviet Attitudes toward Authority* (New York: McGraw-Hill, 1951), 37–38.

39. Gerhardt Niemeyer and John S. Rehstar, *An Inquiry into Soviet Mentality* (New York: Frederick A. Praeger, 1956), 69.

40. Edward L. Rowny, *It Takes One to Tango* (Washington, D.C.: Brassey's [U.S.], 1992), 107.

41. Leites, *Operational Code of the Politburo,* 10.

42. Mead, *Soviet Attitudes toward Authority,* 44–45.

43. Smith, *The Russians,* 17.

44. Quoted in *Soviet Behavior in World Affairs,* comp. and ed. Devere E. Petony (San Francisco: Chandler, 1962), 78.

45. Ibid., 81.

46. Lenin declared that "Marxism doesn't altogether reject compromises. Marxism considers it necessary to make use of them, but that does not in the least prevent Marxism . . . from fighting energetically against compromises. Not to understand this seeming contradiction is not to know the rudiments of Marxism." Vladimir I. Lenin, "Against Boycott: Notes of a Social-Democratic Publicist," in *Collected Works,* vol. 13, trans. from the Russian, 4th ed. (London: Lawrence and Wishart, 1962), 23.

47. Smith, *Negotiating with the Soviets,* 24–25.

48. Philip E. Mosley, "Some Soviet Techniques of Negotiation," in *Negotiating with the Russians,* ed. Raymond Dennett and Joseph E. Johnson (Boston: World Peace Foundation, 1951), 295.

49. Quoted in Smith, *Negotiating with the Soviets,* 26.

50. Mead, *Soviet Attitudes toward Authority,* 15.

51. Hingley, *The Russian Mind,* 147.

52. Ibid., 146.

53. Kissinger, *White House Years,* 525.

54. James A. Baker III, with Thomas M. DeFrank, *The Politics of Diplomacy: Revolution, War, and Peace, 1989–1992* (New York: G. P. Putnam's Sons, 1995), 81. Baker noted that Gorbachev was asked if the United States could announce that Soviet arms shipments to Central America had ceased. Gorbachev parried by asking whether we might announce a "moratorium on arms transfers to the region from all sources. It was a double dose of trying to get something for nothing. He knew that Congress had effectively ended our military assistance to the contras anyway. . . . Moreover, it turned out that while Soviet arms shipments to Nicaragua had stopped, shipments to Cuba had not, and Cuban transshipments to Managua continued."

55. Holsti, *International Politics,* 138–139.

56. Ibid., 140.

57. Richard Nixon, *The Memoirs of Richard Nixon* (New York: Grosset and Dunlop, 1978), 618.

58. Holsti, *International Politics.* The significance of the Soviet pullout from Afghanistan goes beyond the military abandonment of a fraternal party. It was the first time in history that the Soviet Union had been a party to a UN mediation effort. Although the United Nations was used as an avenue for retreat, the acceptance of UN intermediaries to help terminate an unsuccessful military effort was unique for the Soviet Union. The United States has never been a party in a UN mediation effort.

59. Gorbachev pleads ignorance of the scope of the disaster and blames just about everybody but himself and the Kremlin leadership. Gorbachev attacks the "closed nature and the secrecy of the nuclear power industry . . . [which] had a bad effect. The Cold War and the mutual secrecy of the two military alliances had also been a factor." Mikhail Gorbachev, *Memoirs* (New York: Doubleday, 1995), 189–193.

60. Eduard Shevardnadze, *The Future Belongs to Freedom* (New York: Free Press, 1991), 174–177.

61. Shevardnadze was succeeded by Aleksandr Bessmertnykh as foreign minister from January 15, 1991, to August 1991, and by Boris Pankin from August to November 1991. Shevardnadze agreed to return as foreign minister in November 1991, but he was forced to resign when the Soviet Union ceased to exist in December.

62. David Hoffman, "Yeltsin Vows to 'Restore Order,' Pledges Government Shakeup," *Washington Post,* March 7, 1997, A1, A26.

63. Sergei Kovalev, "Russia after Chechnya," *New York Review of Books,* July 17, 1997, 30.

2. THE DURABILITY OF THE INHERITANCE

1. Anatoli Dobrynin, *In Confidence: Moscow's Ambassador to America's Six Cold War Presidents, 1962–1986* (New York: Times Books, Random House, 1995), 627–628.

2. Senior U.S. official, interview by author, Washington, D.C., May 1996.

3. Israelyan, interview, June 1996.

4. Senior American diplomat, interview by author, Washington, D.C., June 1995.

5. John J. Maresca, interview by author, Washington, D.C., September 27, 1994. Richard Burt, a defense intellectual who was a *New York Times* national security affairs correspondent, was named head of the Bureau of Political and Military Affairs by Secretary of State Alexander Haig during the Reagan administration. Richard Perle, a longtime aide to Democratic senator

Henry Jackson of Washington, was named assistant secretary of defense for international security policy in the Reagan administration. The two competed furiously for dominance of their viewpoints in the bureaucracy, with their principals, and with the president.

6. *International Herald Tribune,* September 8, 1995, 5.

7. John Le Carré, "My New Friends in the New Russia," *New York Times Book Review,* February 19, 1995, 32–33.

8. Victor Israelyan, interview by author, Washington, D.C., May 1996.

9. Maresca, interview.

10. Julia Preston, "Russian Shows Testy New Assertiveness at U.N.," *Washington Post,* December 20, 1994, A20.

11. *Financial Times,* September 9, 1995.

12. Members of the Partnership for Peace can modernize their military forces and make them interoperable with NATO, and participate in formal decision-making bodies at NATO and in NATO military exercises and operations, working toward common doctrine and training standards in preparation for full membership. See Council on Foreign Relations, *Should NATO Expand?* (New York: Council on Foreign Relations, 1995), 15–16.

13. *Washington Post,* June 9, 1994, A22.

14. *Financial Times,* November 27, 1994.

15. Michael Dobbs, "For Clinton, Sticking with Yeltsin Sealed Agreement on NATO," *Washington Post,* May 27, 1997, A11.

16. *Washington Post,* December 6, 1994.

17. *New York Times,* October 21, 1995, 5.

18. Michael R. Gordon, "Russia Accepts Eastward Growth of NATO, But Only Inch by Inch," *New York Times,* March 4, 1997, 1.

19. Jim Hoagland, "Russia's 'Red-Line' Limits," *Washington Post,* March 9, 1997, C7.

20. Henry Kissinger, "The Dilution of NATO," *Washington Post,* June 8, 1997, C9.

21. Robert E. Hunter, "Fear Not for NATO," *Washington Post,* June 27, 1997, A25.

22. Quoted in Stephen S. Rosenfeld, "The New Balance of Power," *Washington Post,* May 30, 1997, A25.

23. Rowny, *It Takes One To Tango,* 61. Rowny says he "knew the story was false—if Gromyko sat on a cake of ice it would never melt; I was convinced he had ice water in his veins."

24. During the period from 1969 to the spring of 1985 when he was the party boss in Sverdlovsk, Yeltsin ordered the destruction of the building in which the tsar and his family were executed so that it could not become a memorial and encourage monarchist tendencies. At the time Yeltsin followed the Bolshevik Code to rise within the system. Only when he became critical of the system and his career failed did he embrace democratic reforms. Sverdlovsk has now been renamed Ekaterinberg, its name when Tsar Nicholas II and his family were executed there in 1917.

25. Quoted in Marvick, *Psychopolitical Analysis,* 15.

26. David Hoffman, "Chechen War Escalates Once More," *Washington Post,* July 12, 1996, A26.

27. Serving East European diplomat, interview by author, Washington, D.C. Churkin has been a vice foreign minister since 1995.

28. See Alessandra Stanley, "Spendthrift Candidate Yeltsin: Miles to Go; Promises to Keep?" *New York Times,* May 4, 1996, 1.

3. THE NEGOTIATING PROCESS

1. James Goodby, interview by author, Washington, D.C., September 1995.

2. See chapter 1 for a fuller discussion of the Soviet mind-set.

3. Quoted in Smith, *Negotiating with the Soviets,* 59.

4. See chapter 2.

5. Kissinger, *White House Years,* 1055–1056.

6. Russian diplomat, interview by author, March 1994.

7. John R. Deane, *The Strange Alliance* (New York: Viking Press, 1947), 33.

8. Smith, *Negotiating Behavior,* 15.

9. "House Panel Approves Intelligence Reforms," *Washington Post,* May 10, 1996, A25.

10. Sudoplatov, with Schecter, *Special Tasks,* 222–226.

11. John J. Maresca, *To Helsinki: The Conference on Security and Cooperation in Europe, 1973–1975* (Durham, N.C.: Duke University Press, 1987), 56.

12. Ibid., 56–57.

13. Kissinger, *White House Years,* 113–114.

14. Former Russian and American negotiators, meeting on February 25–27, 1993, at a Princeton University conference, "Witnesses to the End of the Cold War: Decision Makers' Testimony on the End of the U.S.-Soviet Antagonism," agreed that the promotion of "human values" over ideology and the emphasis on reduction of nuclear weapons instead of international class warfare were the dramatic changes initiated by Gorbachev during the 1986–89 period. The participants included U.S. secretaries of state George Shultz and James Baker, and Soviet foreign minister Aleksandr Bessmertnykh. The conference proceedings were published in book form by the Johns Hopkins University Press in 1996.

15. In March 1993 former President Richard Nixon urged Clinton to support Yeltsin. In a telephone conversation Clinton asked Nixon, who had just returned from a trip to Russia, if Yeltsin would last. "I told him it would be a very tough thing and he won't survive unless he has U.S. support. He is the best politician in Russian, the most popular—and elected. We cannot leave any distance between the United States and him," replied Nixon. See Monica Crowley, "Presidential Chronicles, Nixon Unplugged: How Richard Nixon Saw His Surprising Relationship with Bill Clinton," *New Yorker,* July 29, 1996, 47.

16. Rosenfeld, "The New Balance of Power."

17. Kissinger, "The Dilution of NATO."

18. Maresca, *To Helsinki,* 56–63.

19. Ibid., 58.

20. See Michael R. Beschloss, *Mayday: Eisenhower, Khrushchev, and the U-2 Affair* (New York: Harper & Row, 1986), 273–304; and Beschloss, *The Crisis Years: Kennedy and Khrushchev, 1960–1963* (New York: HarperCollins, 1991), 211–236.

21. Brent Scowcroft, interview by author, Washington, D.C., March 22, 1995.

22. Rowny, *It Takes One to Tango,* 53.

23. See Savel'yev, Detinov, and Vartall, *The Big Five.*

24. Israelyan, interview, June 1995. Unless otherwise indicated, subsequent quotations from Israelyan are taken from this interview.

25. American experts found shifts in the Soviet policy line or evidence of conflicts within the Soviet leadership by comparing the placement of names and adjectives in official documents, and by interpreting veiled messages in historical references. Techniques of content analysis developed by Harold Lasswell and later by Alexander George were carried over into the Soviet field. Harold Inkeles pioneered Kremlinology through content analysis in his work *Public Opinion in Soviet Russia* (Cambridge, Mass.: Harvard University Press, 1950). Kremlinology, while often derided as talmudic for its arcane exegesis, was a major tool in penetrating Soviet intentions, especially during the Sino-Soviet conflict between Khrushchev and Mao Zedong (Donald S. Zagoria, *The Sino-Soviet Conflict, 1956–1961* [Princeton, N.J.: Princeton University Press, 1962]) and in periods of crisis during the Cold War. By comparing written texts with unofficial statements, Kremlinologists found it possible to penetrate Soviet policy intentions. As Czeslaw Milosz wrote in *The Captive Mind* (New York: Alfred A. Knopf, 1953): "What is important is not what someone said, but what he wanted to say, disguising his thought by removing a comma, placing an 'and,' establishing this rather than another sequence in the problems discussed. Unless one has lived there one cannot know how many battles are being fought . . . what this warfare is being waged over."

26. Max Kampelman, interview by author, Washington, D.C., July 1995.

27. Kissinger, *White House Years,* 1132.

28. Ibid., 1152–1153.

29. Victor Israelyan, interview by author, Boalsburg, Pa., July 1995.

30. Maresca, *To Helsinki,* 56.

31. Smith, *Negotiating with the Soviets,* 57.

32. Igor Khripunov, interview by author, Athens, Georgia, July 24, 1996.

33. Rowny, *It Takes One to Tango,* 54–55.

34. Senior American diplomat, interview by author, Washington, D.C., June 1996.

35. Savel'yev, Detinov, and Vartall, *The Big Five,* 39.

36. Dobrynin, *In Confidence,* 475.

37. Serving American negotiator, interview by author, Washington, D.C., November 1996.

38. Taubman, *Stalin's America Policy,* 117.

39. Kissinger, *White House Years,* 554–555.

40. Rowny, *It Takes One to Tango,* ix.

41. Max Kampelman warns against such meetings: "I have always despised, mistrusted, and avoided all-night meetings, with their tensions, exhaustion, and potential for unclear thinking." Kampelman, interview.

42. Rudy Abramson, *Spanning the Century: The Life of W. Averell Harriman, 1891–1986* (New York: William Morrow, 1992), 292.

43. Ibid., 293.

44. Joseph Whelan, House Committee on Foreign Affairs, Special Studies Series on Foreign Affairs Issues, vol. 1, *Soviet Diplomacy and Negotiating Behavior: Emerging New Context for U.S. Diplomacy* (Washington, D.C.: Government Printing Office, 1979), 101.

45. Maresca, *To Helsinki,* 56–62.

46. Ibid., 103.

47. Rowny, *It Takes One to Tango,* 78.

48. Maresca, *To Helsinki,* 61.

49. Dobrynin, *In Confidence,* 350.

50. Smith, *Negotiating with the Soviets,* 55–57.

51. Ibid., 33. See chapter 2 for a discussion of Russian attitudes on compromise.

52. Ibid.

53. Warren Zimmermann, interview by author, Washington, D.C., November 2, 1994.

54. Bryant Wedge and Cyril Muromcew, "Psychological Factors in Soviet Disarmament Negotiations," *Journal of Conflict Resolution* 9, no. 1 (March 1965): 33.

55. Maresca, *To Helsinki,* 59–60.

56. Quoted in Petony, *Soviet Behavior in World Affairs,* 64.

57. Quoted in Smith, *Negotiating with the Soviets,* 59.

58. Jonathan Dean, interview by author, Washington, D.C., October 2, 1994.

59. Maresca, *To Helsinki,* 59.

60. Ibid.

61. Richmond, *From Nyet to Da,* 135.

62. Rowny, *It Takes One to Tango,* 52.

63. Paul H. Nitze, *From Hiroshima to Glasnost: At the Center of Decision—A Memoir* (New York: Grove, Widenfeld, 1989), 276–389.

64. Dobrynin, *In Confidence,* 635.

65. Strobe Talbott, *Deadly Gambits* (New York: Alfred A. Knopf, 1984), 96.

66. Marquis de Custine, *Empire of the Czar* (New York: Doubleday, 1989), 437.

67. Rowny, *It Takes One to Tango,* 51.

68. Max M. Kampelman, *Entering New Worlds: The Memoirs of a Private Man in Public Life* (New York: HarperCollins, 1991), 239.

69. Michael R. Beschloss and Strobe Talbott, *At the Highest Levels: The Inside Story of the Cold War* (Boston: Little, Brown, 1993), 413.

70. Kampelman, *Entering New Worlds,* 321.

71. Kissinger, *White House Years,* 112.

72. Dobrynin, *In Confidence,* 587.

73. Kampelman, *Entering New Worlds,* 335.

74. For a detailed argument on how the Reykjavík summit influenced future negotiations, see George P. Shultz, *Turmoil and Triumph: My Years as Secretary of State* (New York: Charles Scribner's Sons, 1993), 751–780.

75. Kampelman, *Entering New Worlds,* 301.

76. Beschloss and Talbott, *At the Highest Levels,* 413.

77. For the story of Washington *rezident* Alexander Feklisov, alias Fomin, and ABC journalist John Scali, see Christopher Andrew and Oleg Gordievesky, *KGB: The Inside Story* (New York: HarperCollins, 1990), 473.

78. Andrew and Gordievsky, *KGB,* 472.

79. James G. Blight and David A. Welch, eds., *On the Brink: Americans and Soviets Reassess the Cuban Missile Crisis* (New York: Hill & Wang, 1989), 248.

80. Dobrynin, *In Confidence,* 54.

81. Ibid., 53.

82. For details of the incident, see Kissinger, *White House Years,* 632–653.

83. Ibid., 650.

84. Dobrynin, *In Confidence,* 235.

85. Kissinger favors the latter explanation (see Kissinger, *White House Years,* 819), whereas Dobrynin opts for the former (see Dobrynin, *In Confidence,* 214–215).

86. Dobrynin, *In Confidence,* 214–215.

87. Kampelman, interview; and Kampelman, *Entering New Worlds,* 269–273.

88. Zbigniew Brzezinski, *Power and Principle* (New York: Farrar, Straus & Giroux, 1983), 339–340.

89. Shultz, *Turmoil and Triumph,* 728–750.

90. Ibid., 750.

91. Kissinger, *White House Years,* 1148.

92. Jonathan Dean, "East-West Arms Control Negotiations: The Multilateral Dimension," in *A Game for High Stakes,* ed. Leon Sloss and M. Scott Davis (Cambridge, Mass.: Bollinger, 1986), 86.

93. Quoted in Smith, *Negotiating with the Soviets,* 55.

94. Shultz, *Turmoil and Triumph,* 464.

95. Ibid., 464–465.

96. Ibid., 522.

97. Aleksandr Bessmertnykh, interview by author, Moscow, March 1996.

98. See Baker, *The Politics of Diplomacy,* 473–474, for details.

99. "Statements by Clinton and Yeltsin at Summit," *Washington Post,* March 22, 1997, A22.

100. Michael Dobbs, "For Clinton, Sticking with Yeltsin Sealed Agreement on NATO," *Washington Post,* May 27, 1997, A11.

101. David Hoffman, "A New Yeltsin Flies to Summit," *Washington Post,* June 20, 1997, A1.

102. Steve Erlanger, "Clinton's Loyalty Pays Dividends," *New York Times,* March 23, 1997, 16.

4. COUNTERSTRATEGIES AND COUNTERTACTICS

1. Richard H. Solomon, *Chinese Political Negotiating Behavior, 1967–1984* (Santa Monica, Calif.: RAND Corporation, 1995), 145.

2. Kennan, *Memoirs 1925–1950,* 562–563.

3. Strobe Talbott, interview by author, Washington, D.C., June 19, 1996. All subsequent quotations from Talbott are taken from this interview.

4. Victor Israelyan, "Death of 'Nyet Negotiators,'" *Foreign Service Journal* 73, no. 6 (June 1996): 46.

5. Even in the past American negotiators noticed cracks in the Kremlin wall. In analyzing Soviet diplomatic behavior, Henry Kissinger rejected the proposition that Soviet policy necessarily followed a master plan. At the end of 1969 Kissinger wrote: "It is always tempting to arrange diverse Soviet moves into a grand design. The more esoteric brands of Kremlinology often purport to see each and every move as part of the carefully orchestrated score in which events inexorably move to the grand finale.

"Experience has shown that this has rarely if ever been the case. From the Cuban missile crisis, through the Arab-Israeli war, to the invasion of Czechoslovakia, there has been a large element of improvisation in Soviet policy. . . . In sum, there does not seem to be any single unifying thread to Soviet policy." Kissinger, *White House Years,* 161–162.

6. Kampelman, *Entering New Worlds,* 322.

7. In his memoirs Baker notes, "Shevardnadze visibly brightened as soon as I mentioned the idea. Without a word, his body language signaled his approval: that was our first step together." Baker, *Politics of Diplomacy,* 137.

8. U.S. government official, interview by author, Washington, D.C., June 1996.

9. Israelyan, "Death of 'Nyet Negotiators,'" 46.

10. Ibid.

11. Serving official, Office of the U.S. Trade Representative, interview by author, Washington, D.C., March 17, 1997.

12. Ibid.

13. Henry Kissinger, *Years of Upheaval* (Boston: Little, Brown, 1982), 245.

14. Ibid., 1162–1163.

15. Kennan, *Memoirs 1925–1950,* 561–562.

16. Ibid., 563.

17. Don Oberdorfer, *The Turn: From the Cold War to a New Era* (New York: Poseidon Press, 1991), 115–118.

18. Dobrynin, *In Confidence,* 387.

19. Brzezinski, *Power and Principle,* 189.

20. Dobrynin, *In Confidence,* 402–407.

21. Kennan, *Memoirs 1925–1950,* 562.

22. Kissinger, *White House Years,* 161–162.

23. Serving official, Office of the U.S. Trade Representative, interview by author.

24. Richmond, *From Nyet to Da,* 123–124.

25. Israelyan, "Death of 'Nyet Negotiators,'" 46.

26. Former Soviet diplomat, interview by author, Moscow, March 1996.

27. Kennan, *Memoirs, 1925–1950,* 563–564.

28. Alessandra Stanley, "Yeltsin Tells Russians That Bending on the NATO Issue Paid Off," *New York Times,* March 27, 1997, A5.

29. Ibid.

5. DOING BUSINESS IN RUSSIA AND FORMER SOVIET REPUBLICS

1. Simon Chilewich, interview by author, New York City, March 15, 1995. All subsequent quotations from Chilewich are taken from this interview.

2. Israelyan,"Death of 'Nyet Negotiators,'" 46.

3. Paul Saunders, "Russia's 'Clan' Wars," *Wall Street Journal,* November 13, 1997, A23.

4. Interview by author, Washington, D.C., October 1996.

5. Nick Allen, "Tatum Shot Dead by 11 Bullets," *Moscow News,* November 5, 1996, 1.

6. *Russian and Commonwealth Business Law Report* (Moscow), September 21, 1992.

7. Ibid.

8. Ibid.

9. Jack F. Matlock, Jr., *Autopsy of an Empire* (New York: Random House, 1995), 691.

10. J. Robinson West, interview by author, Washington, D.C., July 14, 1995.

11. "Russia Tightens Foreign Access," *Financial Times,* July 30, 1996, 2.

12. Matthew Brzezinski, "Foreigners Learn to Play by Russia's Rules," *Wall Street Journal,* August 14, 1997.

13. Isaac Shapiro, interview by author, New York City, April 3, 1995. All subsequent quotations from Shapiro are taken from this interview.

14. Figures from Russian Federation's presentation to the European Bank for Reconstruction and Development meeting, April 1987; John P. Hardt, *Russia's Opportunity to Enter a New Stage in Transition: Update,* CRS Report for Congress (Washington, D.C.: Congressional Research Service, Library of Congress, October 29, 1997), 4, 6–7.

15. Neela Banerjee, "Russia Offers Key Tax Breaks for U.S. Firms," *Wall Street Journal,* July 17, 1996, A10.

16. Michael R. Gordon, "Yeltsin Is Loser in Plan to Lure Oil Investment," *New York Times,* July 25, 1996, A1, A7.

17. Michael R. Gordon, "The Gusher That Wasn't in Russia," *New York Times,* September 5, 1997, C1.

18. Senior official in the Commerce Department, interview by author, March 1995, Washington, D.C.

19. Ivan Selin (former head of the U.S. Nuclear Regulatory Commission), interview by author, Rockville, Md., July 1995.

20. Richmond, *From Nyet to Da*, 124.

21. West, interview by author.

22. *Washington Post*, March 12, 1995, H5.

23. Oil company executive, interview by author, Washington, D.C., October 1996.

24. The Great Game is a term said to be have been coined by British army officer Arthur Conolly, who in 1840 used it to describe the Central Asian power struggles between the British and their rivals. These struggles continued into the late nineteenth century, with Russia, Japan, and China vying with Britain for influence in the region. U.S. policy toward Caspian oil in Central Asia and the Caucasus was defined by Deputy Secretary of State Strobe Talbott as a "positive sum game." Talbott outlined U.S. policy in this area in a speech at the Johns Hopkins School of Advanced International Studies in Washington, D.C., on July 21, 1997.

25. Gordon, "The Gusher That Wasn't in Russia," C1, C3.

26. Ibid.

27. Banerjee, "Russia Offers Key Tax Breaks for U.S. Firms."

28. *Boston Globe*, April 25, 1994.

29. As quoted in Hardt, *Russia's Opportunity to Enter a New Stage in Transition*, 7.

30. Zbigniew Brzezinski and Paige Sullivan, eds., *Russia and the Commonwealth of Independent States: Documents, Data, and Analysis* (Armonk, N.Y.: M. E. Sharpe, 1997), 811.

31. Fedor Burlatsky (a member of a Russian Federation commission investigating the flow of capital abroad), interview by author, Washington, D.C., July 1997.

32. Hardt, *Russia's Opportunity to Enter a New Stage in Transition*, 38.

33. Ibid., 39.

CONCLUSION

1. Quoted in J. L. Gaddis, *We Now Know* (New York: Oxford University Press, 1997), 21.

2. David Hoffman, "Yeltsin Seeks Halt in Attacks on Reforms, 6 Tycoons Called In to Hear Kremlin Plea," *Washington Post*, September 16, 1997, 1.

3. See Hardt, *Russia's Opportunity to Enter a New Stage in Transition*, 8.

4. Sergei Kovalev, "Russia after Chechnya," *New York Review of Books,* July 17, 1997, 30–31.

5. Serving senior American diplomat, interview by author, Washington, D.C., June 1997.

6. Michael Richardson, "Slap at U.S. as Russia Gets Jakarta Fighter Deal," *International Herald Tribune,* August 3, 1997, 1.

List of Interviewees

The following individuals kindly consented to be interviewed for this book. This list does not include those diplomats, government officials, and business people who generously gave of their time but who requested anonymity.

Aleksandr Bessmertnykh
Vadim Biryukov
Marshall Brement
Zbigniew Brzezinski
Ashton Carter
Simon Chilewich
Jonathan Dean
Gloria Duffy
Daniel J. Gallington
James Goodby
Tom Graham
Jack Grynberg
Laura Holgate
Victor Israelyan
Jan Kalicki
Max Kampelman
Igor Khripunov
Susan Koch
James Levinnas
Yuri Luik
Robert MacFarlane
Charles McPherson
John J. Maresca

Katerina Mathernova
Spencer Oliver
William Odom
Richard Perle
Pavel Palazchenko
Thomas Pickering
Rozanne L. Ridgway
Pierre Salinger
Ivan Selin
Brent Scowcroft
Thomas Simmons
Robert Strauss
Anatoli P. Sudoplatov
Viktor Sukhodrev
Sergei Tarasenko
Strobe Talbott
Dmitri Trenin
Elizabeth Verville
J. Robinson West
Aleksandr Yakovlev
Andrei I. Zobov
Warren Zimmermann

Bibliography

Abramson, Rudy. *Spanning the Century: The Life of W. Averell Harriman: 1891–1986*. New York: William Morrow, 1992.

Andrew, Christopher, and Gordievsky, Oleg. *KGB: The Inside Story*. New York: HarperCollins, 1990.

Arbatov, Alexei; Chayes, Abram; Chayes, Antonia Handler; and Olson, Laura, eds. *Managing Conflict in the Former Soviet Union*. Cambridge, Mass.: MIT Press, 1997.

Aslund, Anders. *Gorbachev's Struggle for Economic Reform*. Ithaca, N.Y.: Cornell University Press, 1991.

———. *How Russia Became a Market Economy*. Washington, D.C.: Brookings Institution, 1995.

Anand, R. P. *Cultural Factors in International Relations*. New Delhi: Abbinay Publications, 1981.

Bailey, Thomas A. *America Faces Russia: Russian-American Relations from Early Times to Our Day*. Ithaca, N.Y.: Cornell University Press, 1950.

Baker, James A. III, with DeFrank, Thomas M. *The Politics of Diplomacy: Revolution, War, and Peace, 1989–1992*. New York: G. P. Putnam's Sons, 1995.

Bangert, David Charles. *Culture and Negotiation*. Honolulu, Hawaii: University of Hawaii Press, 1991.

Beschloss, Michael R. *Mayday: Eisenhower, Khrushchev, and the U-2 Affair*. New York: Harper & Row, 1986.

———. *The Crisis Years: Kennedy and Khrushchev, 1960–1963*. New York: Harper-Collins, 1991.

Beschloss, Michael R., and Talbott, Strobe. *At the Highest Levels: The Inside Story of the Cold War*. New York: Little, Brown, 1993.

Bialer, Seweryn, ed. *The Domestic Context of Soviet Foreign Policy*. Boulder, Colo.: Westview Press, 1981.

Binnendijk, Hans, ed. *National Negotiating Styles*. Washington, D.C.: Foreign Service Institute, Center for the Study of Foreign Affairs, U.S. Department of State, 1987.

Birnbaum, Henrik, and Flier, Michael S. *Medieval Russian Culture.* Berkeley: University of California Press, 1984.

Blight, James G., and Welch, David A., eds. *On the Brink: Americans and Soviets Reassess the Cuban Missile Crisis.* New York: Hill & Wang, 1989.

Bohlen, Charles. *Witness to History: 1929–1969.* New York: W. W. Norton, 1973.

Brzezinski, Zbigniew. *Power and Principle.* New York: Farrar, Straus & Giroux, 1983.

Brzezinski, Zbigniew, and Sullivan, Paige, eds. *Russia and the Commonwealth of Independent States: Documents, Data, and Analysis.* Armonk, N.Y.: M. E. Sharpe, 1997.

Bullock, Alan. *Hitler and Stalin: Parallel Lives.* New York: Alfred Knopf, 1992.

Burlatsky, Fedor. *Khrushchev and the First Russian Spring: The Era of Khrushchev through the Eyes of His Advisor.* New York: Charles Scribner's Sons, 1988.

Calasso, Roberto. *The Ruin of Kasch.* Cambridge, Mass.: Harvard University Press, 1994.

Callahan, David. *Dangerous Capabilities: Paul Nitze and the Cold War.* New York: HarperCollins, 1990.

Channon, John, and Hudson, Rob. *The Penguin Historical Atlas of Russia.* London: Penguin Books,1995.

Cohen, Raymond. *Theatre of Power.* London, New York: Longman, 1987

Crowley, Monica. *Nixon off the Record.* New York: Random House, 1996.

de Custine, Marquis. *Empire of the Czar.* New York: Doubleday, 1989.

Daniels, Robert V. "The Revenge of Russian Political Culture." *Dissent* 41, no. 1 (winter 1994): 32–34.

Dean, Jonathan. "East-West Arms Control Negotiations: The Multilateral Dimension." In *A Game for High Stakes,* ed. Leon Sloss and M. Scott Davis. Cambridge, Mass.: Bollinger, 1986.

Deane, John R. *The Strange Alliance.* New York: Viking Press, 1947.

DeJonge, Alex. *Stalin and the Shaping of the Soviet Union.* New York: William Morrow, 1986.

Dicks, Henry V. "Observations on Contemporary Russian Behavior." *Human Relations* 5, no. 2 (1952): 111–175; quoted by Daniel Bell in *World Politics,* no. 10 (April 1958): 329.

Dobrynin, Anatoli. *In Confidence: Moscow's Ambassador to America's Six Cold War Presidents, 1962–1986.* New York: Times Books, Random House, 1995.

Dobrynin, Anatoli; Kennan, George F.; and Billington, James. *Fifty Years of Diplomatic Relations between the United States and the Union of Soviet Socialist Republics.* Washington, D.C.: Kennan Institute for Advanced Russian Studies, Woodrow Wilson Center for International Scholars, 1983.

Druckman, Daniel, ed. *Negotiations: Social-Psychological Perspectives.* Newbury Park, Calif.: Sage, 1977.

Ekedahl, Carolyn M., and Goodman, Melvin A. *The Wars of Eduard Shevardnadze.* University Park: Pennsylvania State University Press, 1997.

Fisher, Glen. *International Negotiation : A Cross-Cultural Perspective.* Yarmouth, Maine: Intercultural Press, 1980.

Garthoff, Raymond L. *Détente and Confrontation: Soviet American Relations from Nixon to Reagan.* Washington, D.C.: Brookings Institution, 1985.

George, Alexander; Farley, Philip J.; and Dallin, Alexander, eds. *U.S.-Soviet Security Cooperation.* New York: Oxford University Press, 1988.

Gorbachev, Mikhail. *Memoirs.* New York: Doubleday, 1995.

Gorer, Geoffrey. *The People of Great Russia: A Psychological Study.* London: Cresset Press, 1949.

Gromyko, Andrei. *Memoirs.* New York: Doubleday, 1989.

Gromyko, Andrei, and Ponomarev, B. N. *Soviet Foreign Policy*, vols. 1 and 2. Moscow: Progress Publishers, 1980; English translation, 1981.

Hahn, Jeffrey W. "Continuity and Change in Russian Political Culture." *British Journal of Political Science* 21, pt. 4 (October 1991): 393–421.

Harriman, Averell W. *America and Russia in a Changing World: A Half Century of Personal Observation,* New York: Doubleday, 1971.

Harriman, Averell, and Abel, Ellie. *Special Envoy to Churchill and Stalin: 1941–1946.* New York: Random House, 1975.

Haviland, William A. *Cultural Anthropology*, 3d ed. New York: Holt, Rinehart and Winston, 1990.

Hecht, James L. *Rubles and Dollars: Strategies for Doing Business in the Soviet Union.* New York: HarperCollins, 1991.

Hingley, Ronald, *The Russian Mind.* New York: Charles Scribner's Sons, 1977.

Holsti, Kalevi J. *International Politics: A Framework for Analysis.* Englewood Cliffs, N.J.: Prentice Hall, 1988.

Hubbs, Johanna. *Mother Russia: The Feminine Myth in Russian Culture.* Bloomington: University of Indiana Press, 1993.

Iklé, Fred C. *How Nations Negotiate.* New York: Praeger, 1964.

Inkeles, Alex. *Social Change in Soviet Russia.* Cambridge, Mass.: Harvard University Press, 1968.

Isaacson, Walter. *Kissinger Biography.* New York: Simon and Schuster, 1992.

Israelyan, Victor. *Inside the Kremlin during the Yom Kippur War.* University Park: Pennsylvania State University Press, 1995.

Jensen, Kenneth M., ed. *Origins of the Cold War: The Novikov, Kennan, and Roberts 'Long Telegrams' of 1946,* rev. ed. Washington, D.C.: United States Institute of Peace Press, 1993.

Johnson, U. Alexis. *The Right Hand of Power: The Memoirs of an American Diplomat.* Englewood Cliffs, N.J.: Prentice Hall, 1984.

Kampelman, Max M. *Entering New Worlds: The Memoirs of a Private Man in Public Life.* New York: HarperCollins, A Cornelia and Michael Bessie Book, 1991.

Kennan, George F. *Memoirs 1925–1950.* Boston: Little, Brown, 1967.

———. "Long Telegram" from Moscow, February 22, in *Foreign Relations of the United States*, vol. 6, *1946*. Washington, D.C.: U.S. Government Printing Office, 1969.

———. *Memoirs 1950–1963.* New York: Pantheon Books, 1972.

———. *The Nuclear Delusion: Soviet-American Relations in the Atomic Age.* New York: Pantheon Books, 1983.

Khrushchev, Nikita S. *The Crimes of the Stalin Era: Special Report to the Twentieth Congress of the Communist Party of the Soviet Union.* New York: New Leader Press, 1962.

Kissinger, Henry. *White House Years.* Boston: Little, Brown, 1979.

———. *Years of Upheaval.* Boston: Little, Brown, 1982.

———. *Diplomacy.* New York: Simon & Schuster, 1994.

Lahusen, Thomas, and Kuperman, Gene. *Late Soviet Culture: From Perestroika to Novostroika.* Durham, N.C.: Duke University Press, 1993.

Lebow, Richard Ned, and Stein, Janice Gross. *We All Lost the Cold War.* Princeton, N.J.: Princeton University Press, 1994.

Le Carré, John, "My New Friends in the New Russia." *New York Times Book Review*, February 19, 1995.

Leffler, Melvyn. *A Preponderance of Power: National Security, the Truman Administration, and the Cold War.* Stanford, Calif.: Stanford University Press, 1992.

Leites, Nathan Constantine. *The Operational Code of the Politburo.* New York: McGraw-Hill, 1951.

———. *A Study of Bolshevism.* Glencoe, Ill.: Free Press, 1953.

———. *Psychopolitical Analysis: Selected Writings of Nathan Leites.* New York: Sage Publications, 1977.

———. *Soviet Style in War.* New York: Crane Russak, 1982.

———. *Soviet Style in Management.* New York: Crane Russak Press, 1985.

Lempert, David. "Changing Political Culture in the 1990's: Parasites, Paradigms, and Perestroika." *Comparative Studies in Society and History* 35, no. 3 (July 1993): 628–646.

Lenin, Vladimir I. "Against Boycott: Notes of a Social Democratic Publicist." In *Collected Works*, vol .13, trans. from the Russian, 4th ed. London: Lawrence and Wishart, 1962.

Lotman, Yuri; Ginzburg, Lydia; Uspenski, Boris; et al. *The Semiotics of Russian Cultural History: Essays.* Ithaca, N.Y.: Cornell University Press, 1985.

Maisky, Ivan. *Memoirs of a Soviet Ambassador: The War: 1939–43.* New York: Charles Scribner's Sons, 1967.

Mandelbaum, Michael, and Talbott, Strobe. *Reagan and Gorbachev: The Chances for a Breakthrough in U.S.-Soviet Relations.* New York: Council on Foreign Relations, 1987.

Maresca, John J. *To Helsinki: The Conference on Security and Cooperation in Europe, 1973–1975.* Durham, N.C.: Duke University Press, 1987.

Marvick, Elizabeth Wirth, ed. *Psychopolitical Analysis: Selected Writings of Nathan Leites.* New York: John Wiley and Sons, 1977.

Matlock, Jack F., Jr. *Autopsy of an Empire.* New York: Random House, 1995.

Mead, Margaret. *Soviet Attitudes toward Authority: An Interdisciplinary Approach to Problems of Soviet Character.* RAND Corporation, 1st ed. New York: McGraw-Hill, 1951.

Millar, James R., ed. *Politics, Work, and Daily Life in the USSR: A Survey of Former Soviet Citizens.* New York: Cambridge University Press, 1987.

Milosz, Czeslaw. *The Captive Mind.* New York: Alfred A. Knopf, 1953.

Moore, Barrington. *Soviet Politics: Dilemma of Power: The Role of Ideas in Social Change.* Cambridge, Mass.: Harvard University Press, 1950.

———. *Terror and Progress in the U.S.S.R.: Some Sources of Change and Stability in the Soviet Dictatorship.* Cambridge, Mass.: Harvard University Press, 1954.

Morrison, John. *Boris Yeltsin: From Bolshevik to Democrat.* New York: Dutton, 1991.

Mosley, Philip E. "Some Soviet Techniques of Negotiation." In *Negotiating with the Russians,* ed. Raymond Dennett and Joseph E. Johnson. Boston: World Peace Foundation, 1951.

Niemeyer, Gerhardt, and Rehstar, John S. *An Inquiry into Soviet Mentality.* New York: Frederick A. Praeger, 1956.

Nitze, Paul H. *From Hiroshima to Glasnost: At the Center of Decision—A Memoir.* New York: Grove, Widenfeld, 1989.

Nixon, Richard. *The Memoirs of Richard Nixon.* New York: Grosset & Dunlop, 1978.

Nogee, Joseph, and Donaldson, Robert H. *Soviet Foreign Policy since World War II,* 2d ed. New York: Pergamon Press, 1984.

Nye, Joseph S., ed. *The Making of America's Soviet Policy.* New Haven, Conn.: Yale University Press, 1984.

Oberdorfer, Dan. *The Turn: From the Cold War to a New Era.* New York: Poseidon Press, 1991.

O'Connor, Timothy Edward. *The Politics of Soviet Culture: Anatolii Lunacharskii.* Ann Arbor, Mich.: UMI Research Press, 1983.

Palazchenko, Pavel. *My Years with Gorbachev and Shevardnadze.* University Park: Pennsylvania State University Press, 1997.

Petony, Devere E., ed. *Soviet Behavior in World Affairs.* San Francisco: Chandler, 1962.

Pipes, Richard. *Survival Is Not Enough.* New York: Simon & Schuster, 1984.

———. "Russia's Past, Russia's Future." *Commentary* (June 1996).

Pobedonostov, Konstantin P. *Reflections of a Russian Statesman.* Ann Arbor: University of Michigan Press, 1965.

Ponomarev, B. N.; Gromyko, A. A.; and Khvostov, V. *History of Soviet Foreign Policy.* Moscow: Progress Publishers, 1974.

Proffer, Carl, and Proffer, Ellendea. *The Silver Age of Russian Culture: An Anthology.* Ann Arbor: University of Michigan Press, 1975

Pryce-Jones, David. *The Strange Death of the Soviet Empire.* New York: Henry Holt, 1995.

Raeff, Marc. "The People, the Intelligentsia, and Russian Political Culture." *Political Studies* 41 (1993): 93–106.

Resis, Albert, ed. *Molotov Remembers: Inside Kremlin Politics—Conversations with Felix Chuev.* Chicago: Ivan R. Dee, 1993.

Richmond, Yale. *From Nyet to Da: Understanding the Russians.* Yarmouth, Maine: Intercultural Press, 1992.

Rowny, Edward L. *It Takes One to Tango.* New York: Brassey's, 1992.

Sakwa, Richard. *Russian Politics and Society.* London: Routledge Press, 1993.

Sayel'yov, Aleksandr G.; Detinov, Nikolai N.; and Vartall, Gregory. *The Big Five: Arms Control Decision-Making in the Soviet Union.* Westport, Conn.: Praeger, 1995.

Schecter, Jerrold, and Luchkov, Vyacheslav V., eds. *Khrushchev Remembers: The Glasnost Tapes.* Boston: Little, Brown, 1990.

Sestanovich, Stephen, ed. *Rethinking Russia's National Interests.* Washington, D.C.: Center for Strategic and International Studies, 1994.

Shevardnadze, Eduard. *The Future Belongs to Freedom.* New York: Free Press, 1991.

Shields, John M., and Potter, William C. *Dismantling the Cold War.* Cambridge, Mass.: MIT Press, 1997.

Shultz, George P. *Turmoil and Triumph: My Years as Secretary of State.* New York: Charles Scribner's Sons, 1993.

Smith, Hedrick. *The Russians.* New York: Quadrangle, 1976.

Smith, Raymond F. *Negotiating with the Soviets.* Bloomington: Indiana University Press, 1989.

Solomon, Richard H. *Chinese Political Negotiating Behavior, 1967–1984.* Santa Monica, Calif.: RAND Corporation, 1995.

Solovyov, Vladimir, and Klepikova, Elena. *Boris Yeltsin: A Political Biography.* New York: G. P. Putnam's Sons, 1992.

Steibel, Gerald Lee. *Can We Negotiate with the Communists?* New York: National Strategy Information Center, 1972.

Sudoplatov, Pavel and Anatoli, with Schecter, Jerrold L. and Leona P. *Special Tasks: The Memoirs of an Unwanted Witness—A Soviet Spymaster.* Boston: Little, Brown, 1994.

Talbott, Strobe. *Deadly Gambits.* New York: Vintage Books, Random House, 1984.

Talbott, Strobe, ed. *Khrushchev Remembers.* New York: Little, Brown, 1970.

———. *Khrushchev Remembers: The Last Testament.* New York: Little, Brown, 1974.

Taubman, William. *Stalin's American Policy.* New York: W. W. Norton, 1982.

Ulam, Adam. *International Negotiation: Communist Doctrine and Soviet Diplomacy.* Washington, D.C.: Government Printing Office, 1970.

U.S. Congress, House Committee on Foreign Affairs. *Soviet Diplomacy and Negotiating Behavior: Emerging New Context for U.S. Diplomacy,* vol. 1. 96th Cong., 1st sess., 1979. Washington, D.C.: Government Printing Office, 1979.

U.S. Congress, House Committee on Foreign Relations. Special Studies Series on Foreign Affairs Issues, vol. 2, *Soviet Diplomacy and Negotiating Behavior: 1979–1988: New Tests for U.S. Diplomacy.* Washington, D.C.: Government Printing Office, 1988.

Wedge, Bryant, and Muromcew, Cyril. "Psychological Factors in Soviet Disarmament Negotiations." *Journal of Conflict Resolution* 9, no. 1 (March 1965).

Weisberger, Bernard A. *Cold War, Cold Peace: The United States and Russia since 1945.* New York: American Heritage Publishing, 1984.

Whelan, Joseph G. *Soviet Diplomacy and Negotiating Behavior: The Emerging New Context for U.S. Diplomacy.* Boulder, Colo.: Westview Press, 1983.

———. *Soviet Diplomacy and Negotiating Behavior, 1988–1990: Gorbachev-Reagan-Bush Meetings at the Summit.* Washington, D.C.: Library of Congress, Congressional Research Service, 1991.

White, Stephen; Pravda, Alex; and Gitelman, Zvi, eds. *Developments in Soviet and Post-Soviet Politics.* Durham, N.C.: Duke University Press, 1992.

White, Stephen; Gardner, John; Schopflin, George; and Saich, Tony. *Communist and Post-Communist Political Systems,* 3d ed. New York: St. Martin's Press, 1990.

Wolfe, Bertram David. *Khrushchev and Stalin's Ghost: Text, Background, and Meaning of Khrushchev's Secret Report to the Twentieth Party Congress on February 24–25.* New York: Praeger, 1956.

Wortman, Richard S. *Scenarios of Power: Myth and Ceremony in Russian Monarchy,* vol. 1. Princeton, N.J.: Princeton University Press, 1995.

Yeltsin, Boris. *An Autobiography: Against the Grain.* New York: Summit Books, 1990.

Zagoria, Donald S. *The Sino-Soviet Conflict 1956–1961.* Princeton, N.J.: Princeton University Press,1962.

Zoshchenko, Mikhail. *Scenes from the Bathhouse, and Other Stories of Communist Russia,* trans. Sidney Monas. Ann Arbor: University of Michigan Press, 1973.

Index

Jerrold Schecter is an author and a journalist with extensive firsthand experience in Russia, Japan, China, and Southeast Asia. He began his career with the *Wall Street Journal,* and then spent eighteen years with *Time* magazine, serving as a foreign correspondent, bureau chief in both Tokyo (1964–68) and Moscow (1968–70), and White House correspondent and diplomatic editor (1973–77). While based in Moscow, he traveled extensively in the Soviet Union and Eastern Europe; he was instrumental in the acquisition of Nikita Khrushchev's memoirs and oversaw their preparation for publication. In 1977 Schecter was invited to join President Jimmy Carter's White House Staff by National Security Adviser Zbigniew Brzezinski. He served as associate White House press secretary and spokesman for the National Security Council until 1980. During the 1980s, Schecter was a corporate officer with Occidental Petroleum Corporation, served as Washington editor for *Esquire* magazine, and returned with his family to Moscow in 1987 to report on glasnost and perestroika (an experience that was the subject of a book and a PBS television documentary, both titled *Back in the USSR*). From 1990 to 1994 he was a founding editor of *We/Mbl,* an independent Russian-American weekly newspaper, started by the Hearst Corporation and *Isvestia.* Schecter's many books include *Khrushchev Remembers: The Glasnost Tapes* (co-translator and editor, 1990); an award-winning biography of Soviet colonel Oleg Penkovsky, *The Spy Who Saved the World* (1992); and *Special Tasks* (1994), written in collaboration with former Soviet spymaster Pavel Sudoplatov.

United States Institute of Peace

The United States Institute of Peace is an independent, nonpartisan federal institution created by Congress to promote research, education, and training on the peaceful resolution of international conflicts. Established in 1984, the Institute meets its congressional mandate through an array of programs, including research grants, fellowships, professional training programs, conferences and workshops, library services, publications, and other educational activities. The Institute's Board of Directors is appointed by the President of the United States and confirmed by the Senate.

Chairman of the Board: Chester A. Crocker
Vice Chairman: Max M. Kampelman
President: Richard H. Solomon
Executive Vice President: Harriet Hentges

Jennings Randolph Program for International Peace

This book is a fine example of the work produced by senior fellows in the Jennings Randolph fellowship program of the United States Institute of Peace. As part of the statute establishing the Institute, Congress envisioned a program that would appoint "scholars and leaders of peace from the United States and abroad to pursue scholarly inquiry and other appropriate forms of communication on international peace and conflict resolution." The program was named after Senator Jennings Randolph of West Virginia, whose efforts over four decades helped to establish the Institute.

Since 1987, the Jennings Randolph Program has played a key role in the Institute's effort to build a national center of research, dialogue, and education on critical problems of conflict and peace. More than a hundred senior fellows from some thirty nations have carried out projects on the sources and nature of violent international conflict and the ways such conflict can be peacefully managed or resolved. Fellows come from a wide variety of academic and other professional backgrounds. They conduct research at the Institute and participate in the Institute's outreach activities to policymakers, the academic community, and the American public.

Each year approximately fifteen senior fellows are in residence at the Institute. Fellowship recipients are selected by the Institute's board of directors in a competitive process. For further information on the program, or to receive an application form, please contact the program staff at (202) 457-1700.

Joseph Klaits
Director

Russian Negotiating Behavior

This book is set in New Baskerville; the display type is Twentieth Century. Hasten Design Studio designed the book's cover, and Joan Engelhardt and Day Dosch designed the interior. Pages were made up by Helene Y. Redmond. David Sweet copyedited the text, which was proofread by Catherine Cambron. The index was prepared by Susan Nedrow. The book's editor was Nigel Quinney.